Welcome to...

Macintosh Multimedia

Nilson Neuschotz

MIS:
PRESS

A Subsidiary of
Henry Holt and Co., Inc.

First Edition—1994

Neuschotz, Nilson.
    Welcome to--Macintosh multimedia / by Nilson Neuschotz
        p. cm.
    Includes index.
    ISBN 1-55828-339-0 : $27.95
    1. Multimedia systems. 2. Macintosh (Computer) I. Title.
    QA76.575.N47 1994
    006.6--dc20   94-25873
                                                       CIP

Printed in the United States of America.

10 9 8 7 6 5 4 3 2 1

MIS:Press books are available at special discounts for bulk purchases for sales promotions, premiums, fund-raising, or educational use. Special editions or book excerpts can also be created to specification.

For details contact: Special Sales Director
                                MIS:Press
                                a subsidiary of Henry Holt and Company, Inc.
                                115 West 18th Street
                                New York, New York 10011

Trademarks

Publisher: Steve Berkowitz

Development Editor: Laura Lewin

Production/Design: Stephanie Doyle

To Lita, Carmen Maria Tirado,
and to my grandmother, Lillian Gonzalez Kowalski

Contents

Part II:
Building the Multimedia System.......... 39

Chapter 5: The Multimedia Macintosh 45

Chapter 6: Hard Drives and Other Storage Methods 61

Part IV:
Starting with Graphics........................ 181

Chapter 13: Drawing Software 185

Chapter 14: Paint and Image-Editing Software 197

Chapter 15: Three-Dimensional Graphics Programs 211

Acknowledgments

Many people have influenced and have played a role in the completion of this work. I would like to take a moment to acknowledge them here. Carmen Kowalski Neuschotz, Lillian Gonzalez Kowalski, Carmen Maria Tirado, Ruth Neuschotz, Eva Kowalski, Emily Neuschotz, Liz & Izzy Gomez, Sondra K. Newman, Laurence & Lauri Hitchens, Rustam Schoenholt, Gary Hoste, Ken Burkard, Amy Schulman, Jules Gilder, Brenda McLaughlin, Steve Berkowitz, Laura Lewin, Stephanie Doyle, Bob Whitney, Andy Moore, Kenneth Burkard, Macromedia, Inc., Adobe, Inc., Strata, Inc., Fractal Design, Inc.

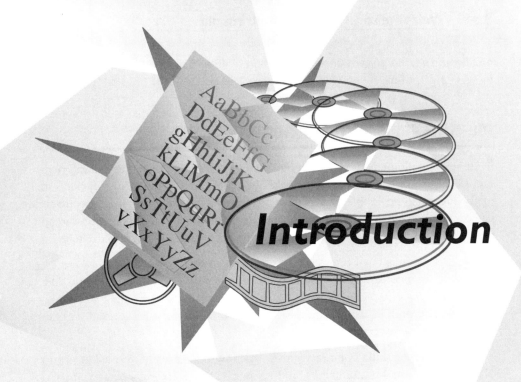

Introduction

One Day This Book Will Be on CD

Multimedia is a powerful form of media project development that brings together any combination of video, sound, graphics, photography, and animation within a computer and uses them to create everything from business presentations and point-of-sale kiosks to CD-ROM interactive games, and graphics for television. With the growing number of low-cost, accessible multimedia development programs available today, entry costs are low, and the techniques are fairly easy to learn. This translates to a tremendous number of opportunities for those with skills in the area. And multimedia's rapid growth ensures that there will be many more opportunities in the very near future.

Multimedia is a Phenomenon

Evidence of multimedia is everywhere! We see it in the computer-animated openings of television news and sports broadcasts. We see it in interactive displays in malls and building lobbies. We see it in schools, and we see it in electronic games and interactive encyclopedias. Creative professionals are beginning to reap the benefits! Moreover, working in the multimedia industry is fun and exciting.

Multimedia has been referred to as *the information highway, virtual reality,* and *electronic publishing.* You have heard about media wars among giants like Paramount, Viacom, and QVC, and plans for "new media" branches in companies like Sony and Panasonic. Interestingly enough, multimedia is usually at the center of the controversy.

Though multimedia is more widespread now than ever, if you ask a group of people to describe multimedia, the answer varies with each person. This is probably because a simple definition is hard to come by.

What Is Multimedia?

You've just read that multimedia combines video, sound, graphics, photography, and animation into one digital form. Once these elements are put together in the computer, you can manipulate them in effective ways. Generally, multimedia projects are highly dynamic in that they frequently combine motion and sound in some manner. If you scan a photograph into a computer, add a computer graphic to it, and print it out, you have not created multimedia, you have created an example of print media. On the other hand, if you set that new image to music and put it onto video tape, you've created multimedia. In the latter example, the project combines the dynamic media of video with the digital media of computer software to create a final product that includes motion and sound.

Once a multimedia project is completed, you can view it and interact with it in the computer. It could take the form of a game, a software program, or a presentation. A multimedia project can also be output to video tape, film, or CD-ROM.

Multimedia and the Mac

The Mac has made learning how to use a computer extremely easy. Its intuitive graphical user interface presents computing in a straightforward, visual manner that is easy to understand and learn. Not only have Macs had an impact on the growth and popularity of computers in general, they have also had a great impact on multimedia.

Most of the early adopters of multimedia were video artists, musicians, graphic artists, or animators. The art world was used to the Mac. Therefore the transition to a computerized method of developing artwork made sense.

Current improvements in the speed and processing capability of the Mac, along with new low costs, have opened up the Mac market tremendously. Businesses have introduced multimedia to the workplace so that they can generate computer presentations. The Mac made it possible to produce professional results quickly, and with little training.

Macs are capable of producing high-quality graphics, digital video, and audio, and they have a great deal of support from the most talented and accomplished software developers in the industry. Such support makes the Mac the perfect platform for multimedia development. The comfortable interface, increasing power, and decreasing cost of the Mac makes it the multimedia development computer of choice for accomplished multimedia artists and beginners alike.

What Can Multimedia Do for You?

Traditional businesses, such as book publishers, television production studios, and film companies are now entering the electronic publishing arena. Electronic publishing involves producing books on CD-ROM so that people can have a full media experience (sound and video) as they read. Electronic publishing houses need multimedia developers. Also, television studios hire multimedia developers to create those terrific news and sports broadcast graphics that you see. Advertising agencies also hire multimedia developers to create graphics for commercials.

These are just a few of the opportunities available to multimedia talent. But multimedia can do much more for you. You can start a business with tremendous growth potential at extremely low expense, because most of the equipment necessary for multimedia development is available at the consumer level. In other words, you can set up a multimedia production studio at home for under $10,000. You can spend much less (under $5,000) to obtain a Macintosh multimedia development system that will run most of the software that you need to produce multimedia. Also, money may not be the driving force in your interest in multimedia, as it is after all a new art form.

How This Book Can Help You

This book contains information on how to select and purchase a Macintosh multimedia system. You will learn about the software used in multimedia, and you will even get the opportunity to use it! The CD-ROM included with this book offers save-disabled versions of Adobe Photoshop, Adobe Dimensions, Adobe Illustrator, Adobe Premiere, Macromedia Director, Strata StudioPro and Fractal Design Painter. This wonderful collection of software gives you the opportunity to experiment with the most powerful software available for Macintosh multimedia today. The CD also provides tutorials to help you along in using the software. This book will give you a thorough understanding of Macintosh multimedia as an industry, and an art.

Part I offers information about multimedia as an industry and presents some of the opportunities that are available for multimedia developers. **Part II** offers information on the Macintosh computer so that you can set up a multimedia-capable computer system. **Part III** discusses in detail the peripherals that turn a Macintosh computer system into a multimedia system. **Part IV** is an introduction to basic multimedia software programs while **Part V** introduces you to multimedia composition and interactive authoring software, which are the tools used to create projects for video and CD-ROM. Part V also supplies information about how to get your multimedia presentations out of the computer and onto CD-ROM and video tape. There is also a glossary of multimedia terminology and five appendices that offer information about the many manufacturers of multimedia software and hardware. The CD-ROM gives you the opportunity to try some of the most popular multimedia software available for the Macintosh today!

Part I

Understanding the Nature of Multimedia

If you're new to multimedia, then you may not know exactly what it is. This uncertainty is not unusual, because multimedia is a fairly new technology and involves some technical knowledge. Multimedia is also extremely diverse in its applications. This section clarifies the subject for you.

Multimedia Is a Technology

Multimedia combines video, audio, graphics, and animation in the computer, possibly alters them, and finally returns them to video or encodes them onto CD-ROM so that they can function as a computer program.

The digital nature of multimedia allows you to treat multimedia projects like any other computer data. Therefore, ordinary video can be manipulated within the computer to become interactive media. This means that the viewer can perform actions, such as pressing buttons, to make things happen in the video. They might be able to move objects around in the scene, which could not happen if the media were simply in a video form. *Chapter 1* goes into greater detail about multimedia as a technology.

Multimedia Is an Industry, a Skill, and an Opportunity

Multimedia is now easier to use, cheaper, and more dynamic than it has ever been. Therefore, it is now being used more readily in business presentations, video production, computer entertainment, and educational programming. The industry presents new challenges to anyone who is interested in entering a visual media industry such as video or business presentations. Media developers who understand multimedia will have a clear advantage from the start. *Chapters 2* and *3* provide information about how you can clearly benefit from learning more about multimedia and its current applications.

Multimedia Is a Creative Process

The process of creating a multimedia project is very similar to the video or film production process, but it adds a few new steps. Like a video production, a multimedia project is planned, scripted, and storyboarded. The multimedia production process can also involve some computer programming to incorporate the viewer control that turns the project into a game or educational computer program. The multimedia project can then be distributed to the audience on CD-ROM, video, or some other distribution method. *Chapter 4* provides more on what is involved in the multimedia production process.

Chapter

1

The Marriage of Art and Technology

The rapid development of computers and supporting software in areas such as graphic arts, photo-retouching, and animation has made the computer a powerful artistic tool. The new hardware and software, along with the integration of other artistic elements such as video and audio in computers has generated a new platform, which in turn has facilitated a new career—*the multimedia developer.* Just as stereo equipment makes record companies possible and record companies make recording artists possible, so have computers been responsible for the rise of the multimedia developer. This profession is so new and fresh that anyone can become involved. It is the next great chapter in the story of the computer industry and the art world.

Increased power and lower expense of computer equipment has made it possible for almost anyone to have a multimedia studio at home. With the ever-increasing popularity of CD-ROM and interactive programming and hardware players such as CD-ROM drives and systems like the Philips CD-I, the stage is set for a new genre of creative production. Plenty of people are waiting for good CD-ROM and other multimedia content; all that's missing are the people to create it.

What This Book Offers You

This book is designed to give you much of the information necessary to start creating multimedia and interactive projects on the Macintosh computer. It also discusses how to get your projects onto professional media such as CD-ROM and professional-grade video tape for distribution and broadcast playback. A concise glossary keeps you up to date with the terms presented in the book.

By the end of the book, you will know a great deal about the terminology and technology involved with multimedia for the Macintosh computer. This book gives you plenty of information on the technology that makes multimedia possible. This knowledge—along with the provided tips and recommenda-tions—helps you to choose and care for the components that will make up your multimedia system. Multimedia equipment alone is not enough, though. So this book also provides a wealth of information about the various categories of mul-timedia software and their common elements—thereby making your software selection an easier process.

Included with this book is a CD-ROM with demo software from all of the major software developers for the Macintosh platform: Adobe, Macromedia, Fractal Design, and Strata. The demo software is *save-disabled*, which means that the software is complete in every way except in the ability to save your files. An interactive tutorial helps you to become familiar with the software in the CD so that you can get to work immediately learning how to create multi-media. If you decide that you like the software on the CD, *Chapter 20* describes the operation of the CD-ROM with information on how to get a copy of the complete versions of the software.

Multimedia Composition and Interactive Multimedia

Multimedia composition is the integration of animation, sound, graphics, and video with computers. The ability to control all of these elements in one machine on a desktop means that you can have many of the same capabilities of a professional video or recording studio at your fingertips in your home. The only prerequisite you need to work with multimedia on the Macintosh computer is conceptual skill—that is, the ability to imagine and plan creative ideas.

Interactive multimedia is similar to multimedia composition in the sense that it incorporates all of the same elements. The difference is that the viewer controls the presentation. For example, Compton's Interactive Encyclopedia is an interactive program that allows viewers to choose categories by selecting buttons on screen with the mouse. A video game is another example of an interactive program, but the interactivity is based upon the user's skill at the game, as opposed to simply making category selections.

Programs made with a multimedia authoring tool, such as Macromedia Director, can be just as detailed as software written with programming languages such as Fortran and C++. The advantage to using an authoring tool is that you do not need to be a programmer to produce an effective multimedia program. All of the graphics, sound, and animation can be created in other programs designed specifically for those purposes—programs such as SuperPaint, MacDraw, and QuickTime movie recorders. These individual elements can then be imported into the program that will be used to create the interactivity. The authoring program provides all of the tools to combine the separate multimedia elements into one program that can be encoded on CD-ROM, written to diskettes, or otherwise distributed on digital media. The end result of your work with an authoring tool is a multimedia program—an interactive one, if you desire. Interactive programs can be as simple as kiosk presentations, which can be similar in design to Automated Teller Machines or as complex as popular CD-ROM games with sophisticated graphics and sound.

Now Is the Time for the Multimedia Developer

The first opportunities in the computer industry came to people who understood the hardware. These people now run the companies that sell you their computers and are viewed as icons within the industry. For many people, and for most industries, owning a computer is simply a necessity.

The next great opportunities came to those who understood programming languages and were capable of creating operating systems and other software for computers. Many of these original software developers have also become icons in the industry. Software such as Microsoft Word and Excel, and Adobe Illustrator and Photoshop are just a few of the software products that helped general industry to accept computers as serious work tools.

Hardware and software development has been a phenomenon both financially and historically. No other industry boom has moved faster, generated more money, and created more fortunes than the computer industry. In 1976, Apple was just a tiny company that literally operated out of a garage. Over the next 10 years, it would become one of the largest computer companies in the world. Today, Apple is IBM's chief competition for the computer buyer's dollar. Apple's rapid growth has contributed to the many successes of software and hardware developers who support the Mac platform.

Until today, however, the opportunities have only been available to computer programmers. Presently, the opportunities exist for those who can use the software and hardware to a successful end. What is important currently is the ability to combine different media towards educating and entertaining viewers. These are the goals of the multimedia developer.

The Macintosh Has Opened Doors

The advent of the Apple Macintosh computer opened new doors to computer opportunities. Now individuals could be effective with a computer without being a programmer. Quickly, industries such as computer graphic arts and desktop publishing emerged. At first, general industries were skeptical, but desktop publishing, for example, went from a publishing alternative to a publishing definition. The world of computer power had become available to artists and designers. And computer art had become comparable to art created with traditional methods. Edges and lines on computers became smooth, and software was now capable of simulating the natural media effect of tools like air brushes and spray cans. The Macintosh computer allows people with no prior computer experience to operate a computer with ease.

What Gives the Macintosh This Power?

The Macintosh operating system is a *graphical user interface.* For example, all programs have an icon that you can see and move around on the screen. All files also have icons of their own on screen. This allows you to discern differences among files just by looking at them. If you want to open one, it is as easy as locating the file's icon on the computer screen and selecting it with the mouse. Other operating systems such as DOS for IBM compatibles require that you type information into a text entry area. For these computers, you need to know exactly what to type in order to complete simple tasks, such as opening or duplicating a file. It takes time to learn the syntax and procedure of getting around a system like DOS. The graphical user interface of the Macintosh greatly reduces the learning curve and allows people to use the computer immediately.

The Macintosh operating system also uses *pull-down menus,* which are listings of functions that are contained in window-shade-style graphics that are selected from the top of the screen. By clicking on the name of a menu at the top of the screen, you produce a listing of items from which you can select. By selecting an item on the menu, you execute a command. You need no typing, code, or other complexity; you simply select with the mouse what you want, and the computer does it.

The final and probably most important element of the Macintosh computer is its *point-and-click* feature, which involves the mouse. By moving the mouse around a flat plane such as a desktop, you cause a cursor to move around on the screen. The combination of positioning the cursor over objects and menus on the screen and pressing the button on the mouse allows you to select objects and execute commands. This feature makes opening, navigating, and organizing your Mac and its software a simple matter.

All software for the Mac conforms to certain standards, such as universal commands, the pull-down menus, graphic icons, and the point-and-click interface. In fact, Apple insists programmers follow these conformities, which makes learning new software on the Mac simple because users are familiar with many features if they have already learned one program on the platform. *Chapter 5* offers more information on the Macintosh operating system and how to choose the best Mac for multimedia.

Digital Conversion Makes It Possible

Technology has made possible converting different forms of media into computer information. The ability to scan images into computers has been possible for a long time; creating computer-generated or synthesized sounds has also been possible for some time. All that had to be done to clear the path for true multimedia was to extend the capability of the software that is used with those audio and graphic elements.

First, animation was developed in graphics programs. Initially the animation was quite simple and could not compete with conventional methods of animation such as cell animation, in which each frame of the animation is hand-drawn separately. This process changed as computer graphics improved. The process of conversion from the computer to video or film was quite costly in the early stages, but the process had begun.

The next step towards developing multimedia involved adding control over sound. Previously computers were only used to control external sound producing devices, such as MIDI synthesizers. Software development had made it possible to record sounds directly to the computer's hard drive and edit them there. It also became possible to combine sound and animation on the hard drive. Now, true digital multimedia development was a reality.

Prior to this feat, we could create multimedia productions, but not within the computer. The elements of the multimedia production were created separately and then combined by some method such as editing with conventional video postproduction equipment. Creating a complex multimedia production entirely within the computer is now possible for everything from professional video broadcast to interactive CD-ROM.

Chapter 2

Multimedia—A Booming Industry

We are privileged to be around during the introduction of a whole new industry. Many people don't see multimedia as being truly separate from video, computers, and the other industries that multimedia brings together, but it is. Multimedia is to video and computers as film is to television. The result is similar, but a whole new method is used. Multimedia is an industry with a technology and opportunities unique to itself.

Ask any independent film producer what it's like to compete against a major film studio, and the response will invariably be a tale of small studio David meeting the Goliath of Hollywood. Or, consider the millions, no, billions that it would take to create a new television network, and you will know that the best time to have gotten involved with the television industry was when it was new.

Multimedia opportunities are here, now, and they are waiting for enterprising and creative people to take advantage of them. This technological breakthrough in an industry is very rare and is certainly appealing at such a low entry expense. Few things appeal so thoroughly to both the entrepreneurial and creative spirits alike.

Those Knowledgeable Are in Demand

As more companies discover the benefits of multimedia for their presentations and other projects that require different media, they are noticing a shortage of people who are trained in multimedia techniques. Plenty of people are trained in different areas within multimedia, but the need now is for people who can manipulate all areas within one environment—a digital environment. The phenomenon is similar to what occurred as businesses realized that integrating desktop publishing into their art departments was a better alternative than giving the work to professional print shops.

Many businesses are already equipped with much of the equipment needed for multimedia development, so they are very open to the idea of introducing it to their work. Multimedia is the answer for many companies that have been wanting to improve their presentations. Desktop publishing has become a norm in most industries, and as a result has lost much of its competitive edge.

Formal training programs in multimedia have only recently emerged in art schools. They are evolving because to design a curriculum around a brand new trade is virtually impossible. As a result, businesses can't simply recruit many qualified people for multimedia positions the way they can for other positions. Their only alternative is the independent multimedia developer, whose resumes consist of the projects that they can show to their credit.

Currently the market for multimedia belongs to the multimedia developer. It is one of the most creative positions that exists within a company, and since it is new, the developer can help shape the definition of the position. It is also possible to remain a freelance developer serving many companies at once.

Becoming as Much a Part of Everyday Life as TV

Plans for interactive television are well known. The programming that will be produced for this promising endeavor has yet to be determined; nonetheless, the development of television that will allow viewers to interact with the programs is the subject of a great deal of attention. Skill with multimedia and interactive programming will almost certainly be a requirement for any job related to this new method of delivering information. At the very least, workers must have an understanding of multimedia.

Multimedia doesn't replace video and audio technology, it simply makes working with them easier by expediting and enhancing the results. More immediately, multimedia is a part of virtually everything that you see on television. Many of the graphics that are used in the opening and closing of news and sports programs, as well as the graphics in commercials, were developed using the same tools that you will read about in this book. The production companies responsible for creating those television clips are not as much concerned with the expense of the systems that the graphics are created on as they are with the quality of the graphics. Since it is possible to create the same quality graphics at your desktop as those that you see on television, developing a relationship with one or many production companies that create graphics for them is entirely possible. You could potentially even produce commercials.

Inexpensive, Accessible, Easy to Learn and Use

Multimedia equipment is available through the same channels that computer equipment and software are available. Now there is enough of a market to make this possible. Improved market also means that new software and hardware development companies will emerge. As a result, prices will drop with the competitive environment.

Computers are also less expensive than they have ever been, and the power of these computers has increased dramatically. The first Macs that were made available in the early 1980s provided about 5 percent of the power available in computers today. Early Macs also lacked color, hard drives, and had less than 1M of RAM. They also had small screens, and lacked properties such as NuBus expansion slots that would have allowed for multimedia or multimedia upgrades. Consider that you can now buy a powerful, multimedia-capable

Macintosh for the same amount as that early Mac, and you will realize that the cost of computer equipment is lower now than it has ever been.

A testament to this was the introduction of the PowerPC line of Macs in early 1994. These computers, which are designed to run IBM software as well as Macintosh software, were very aggressively priced to compete with the enormous market for IBM/compatible computers. The cost of IBM/compatible systems was driven low by a very competitive environment, and now Apple has entered that arena. These new Macs were also more powerful than any other Macs released up until that point. You can be certain that the situation will only get better for you as the consumer with so many companies vying for your buck.

Brings Corporate Applications In-House for Greater Control

Most companies want to accomplish every aspect of their work in-house. This means that they want to have all of their work created by people on the company payroll. What determines when a company chooses to bring a particular service in-house is when it becomes less expensive than paying an outside house to do the same work.

Before desktop publishing was integrated into virtually every art department in the corporate world, businesses sent their concepts to an outside desktop publishing house for support. This arrangement continued until the cost of computers and other equipment dropped, and there was more of a general understanding of the process involved in desktop publishing. Once buying the equipment and training, or hiring an already trained, computer layout and graphics artist was a better move than sending the work out, companies made the transition to in-house production.

This same transition will almost certainly occur in multimedia development. Control of such a dynamic media for presentations, training, and other corporate applications is the sort of thing that businesses look for to stand above the competition. This means three things to the multimedia developer:

1. The multimedia developer is a hot commodity today.

2. There will be a massive job market available to the multimedia developer in the future.

3. This is a great time to start a business with tremendous growth potential.

The transition to in-house development did not put desktop publishing service bureaus out of business; it simply redefined the type of work that service bureaus do for businesses. Generally, in-house desktop publishing does the production work, and service bureaus do the finishing work and output. Professional grade printers are still too expensive to be justified in corporate budgeting.

The Visual Appeal

Multimedia appeals to the senses of sight and hearing, creating a powerful method of delivering information that demands the attention of a viewer. Interactive multimedia also incorporates involvement on the part of the viewer, making the presentation even more engrossing. It is up to the multimedia developer to program a presentation that appeals to the viewer.

"A picture paints a thousands words" is more than just an old adage, it's a truth. A single printed advertisement can have more influence on the decisions made by an audience than any number of radio spots. The element of image accomplishes most of the work and keeps the attention of the viewer.

The introduction of motion to image added a whole new dimension to the effectiveness of media to influence decision making. It's a fact that the sense of sight responds to motion. There is a simple explanation in our genetic ancestry; if something is moving, it can possibly be one of two objects of interest—something you can eat or something that can eat you. Quick response to motion meant survival.

Today we're less concerned with the perils of nature, but motion still attracts our attention, and there is little we can do about it. If "A picture paints a thousand words," then there is no saying what moving pictures can accomplish. A single 30-second commercial can have more influence on the decisions made by an audience than any other method known. Couple this with the fact that the multimedia nature of television permits the integration of sound, and you can see part of the reason why television demands the attention it has generated.

Multimedia gives you a great deal of power, and there are numerous techniques to bring your production to an audience. The ability to educate, influence, and entertain is the target of all media. Multimedia accomplishes these goals easily and gives you the power to appeal to an audience using both voluntary and involuntary attention-attracting elements. It gives you this power from a computer.

Chapter 3

What You Can Do with Multimedia

Advertising

Advertising was one of the first places where multimedia was professionally used. With the digital control of images that multimedia provides, production companies can create situations entirely within a computer. Not only does this have a money-saving effect, but it also transcends limitations in the real world. Do you need a car on a mountain top? You may not need to hire a photographer. Do you need to change the color of the car? All it takes is another 15 minutes at the computer.

Composite imaging, where two different images are combined seamlessly with one another, is by no means limited to still images. Some of the most sophisticated commercials are created with digitally based multimedia tools. Of course, the machines used, such as Silicon Graphics workstations, are usually more sophisticated (and expensive) than Macintosh computers, but that is only because production companies frequently require a tremendous amount of speed in order to meet production deadlines. Production companies are also usually not as restricted by budget as most private users are.

Given the time, the appropriate system configuration, and the proper software, the Macintosh multimedia developer can create commercial programming competitive with almost anything produced by more expensive machines. The result can easily be equal; the difference will be in the amount of time invested. The process involved in creating multimedia will remain the same regardless of the system that you ultimately choose to work with.

An immediate market for the beginning multimedia developer in advertising is generating simple graphics for production companies. Many production companies staff their production and postproduction teams on a hire-as-needed basis; as a result, they don't have staff multimedia graphic artists. You could create a sample tape with your animated graphics work and distribute it to advertising agencies and production companies as your portfolio. Use simple animation, like animated logos, a price flying across the screen, or animated squares with photographs of faces applied to them as surfaces. It's a great start and can easily lead to more detailed multimedia work from your desktop.

Presentation and Sales

Businesses are constantly looking for new ways to present their products. The more exciting the technique, the better. Because the competition is offering similar products and services, businesses want their offerings to stand out. Frequently, the presentation is what distinguishes one from the other.

Presentations can take the form of a simple slideshow where information is presented to the viewer in an interesting manner. This presentation can be enhanced with transition effects between product information and narration or background music. They can also take on an interactive form, where the information is presented to the viewer in a fashion similar to a slideshow, but viewers can choose the progression of the presentation by using buttons and other selection methods, such as entering data that you incorporate into your presentation. Presentations do not need to remain in a digital format either; you can transfer them to video tape to accommodate people who want to see your presentation but do not own a computer.

Multimedia development for sales is very similar in form to presentation: both are designed to provide information about products and services in a manner that is favorable to the offering. The clear distinction is multimedia offers a benefit to sales because it can be used to help qualify potential customers.

For example, a point-of-sale kiosk in a retail establishment can provide information about products. This type of information does not need to change and is best given with a high level of energy each time it is spoken about. Using a kiosk can help to free salespeople so that they are no longer functioning as information dispatches. Many salespeople can easily give you the first ten questions they are asked by a new customer, so that you can incorporate that information into an interesting and dynamic interactive presentation.

This method of presenting information is especially useful for businesses that offer many products that are similar to one another. Customers can narrow their selection and speak to a salesperson from a more informed position. This suggestion is not meant to further "dehumanize" customer relations. A salesperson can always be available in the event a customer prefers to not use the machine. You may find, however, that if a presentation is done well, people will enjoy using it. The key is to never lose sight of the entertainment origin of multimedia.

Whatever the method of creation or distribution that you choose, multimedia gives you a great deal of control over how information is presented. The possibilities for creating your work in an interesting and dynamic fashion are endless, and the results are effective. It will benefit you either in presenting your own product and services or in offering your expertise in generating presentations for others.

Entertainment

One of the first functions of multimedia is entertainment. As a central environment for the control of audio, video, and computer elements, it is the perfect platform for entertainment programming. Much of what once required a great deal of expensive equipment and personnel can now be accomplished by one person, at a desk, at home.

Many of the multimedia tools described in this book are used to produce television commercials and graphics, as well as best-selling computer games. These games are the most immediate entertainment applications because they use the technology in the same way that the separate media elements did alone. There are many unexplored areas for entertainment development in multimedia, and as mentioned in *Chapter 2*, multimedia is the basis of the developing technology of interactive television.

Education

Information can now be presented to students in a fashion that is interesting and exciting. Since the information is computer based, it can also serve such functions as gathering data and calculating student performance.

Using different media has long been a practice of many schools. Digitally based multimedia allows teachers to create detailed and entertaining programs easily and at little expense. It also leaves a wide-open market for multimedia developers who can help to convert educational agendas into multimedia programs.

Multimedia can especially help in educating young children where there is the likelihood of attention span issues. By presenting information in the form of an interactive game or another interactive program, educators can use methods that are known to be effective in retaining a child's attention: television, video games, and the like.

Training and Demonstrations

Multimedia is an excellent tool for training, not just because of its entertainment quality but because images and materials can be updated easily as needed. Interactive training sessions can track performance and store any data for later review. Interactive multimedia training can also be designed to proceed at the current viewer's discretion.

All other benefits of multimedia apply here as well. It can be used to create dynamic training material to be presented on some current training media such as video tape, but the ability to convert multimedia projects into interactive media is the bonus. Interactive authoring in training allows nonprogrammers to generate truly effective feedback methods of training.

Currently many companies distribute training tapes with their products. They can do this because they are relatively certain that their customers own a VCR. The rapid growth in the popularity of interactive CD players for television, such as the Philips CD-I, will eventually eliminate the need for a computer to use interactive CD programming. This progress presents a tremendous opportunity for multimedia developers who are prepared to offer their services for the development of training materials.

Customized Applications

Interactive multimedia can be used to create simple software that is designed to fit specific needs. For example, a company may want to design an electronic sales order form. The sales order form would allow for the input of names, addresses, specific orders, financial information, and any other information that the company requires in a sales order. The order form could then be linked to a network that passes the data on to other areas of the company that use the information.

Another alternative is to use interactive programming as a *front-end* to another program. A front-end is the portion of a program that the user actually interacts with. If you find that you need a database program, but don't want all of the features of the database program to be available to the end user, you can create a front-end that allows access only to certain aspects of the database program.

For example, you could make a front-end in Macromedia Director that is connected to a shared database made with FileMaker Pro. The connection would be made with an XObject which will allow the two to communicate and pass information between them (XObjects are covered in *Chapter 17*). You can give different departments different versions of the front-end to allow access to different portions of the database. The sales department will have access to the parts of the database that pertain to sales, the accounting department will have access to the portions of the database that pertain to accounting. You could also program in the ability to view the other portions of the database, but not change them. This system will allow a company to use a single database that is shared among all of the departments, but will also provide security against unauthorized or inadvertent changes. You could think of the front-end as a filter. You could also design the front-end to your specifications, so that each screen includes the corporate logo, and even video and sound.

Small Business

Aside from businesses that are based upon multimedia development alone, multimedia can be used to add new dimension to other media businesses and services. For example, wedding videos have been a largely successful small media business for years, but they have leveled off in growth potential because there are already so many companies. Bringing multimedia in can provide a competitive edge that will help these companies to grow again and to create new opportunities for new small businesses.

There are also opportunities for businesses that provide services to other multimedia businesses. New multimedia companies will need properly equipped service bureaus to encode CD-ROMs, print to video tape, and provide other services that require equipment and expertise that may be too time- and money-consuming for a new company to consider. Acting as a service bureau can also help new multimedia companies to generate money with their equipment until their own projects pay off.

Title Authoring and Publishing

The process of developing electronic titles is similar to producing a book or a movie. The early stages are like a movie: an idea is developed, outlined, and then scripted. Next a storyboard is made to give form to the visual elements. Then, the elements are created: video is taken, sound is recorded, and graphics are created. Elements that are not in the computer—such as video recorded with a camcorder—are then digitized so that they can be compiled in multimedia composition software. Finally, all of the elements are edited together and interactivity is added with a program like Macromedia Director. The process then becomes similar to book publishing. Once the project has been completed, it is encoded onto a CD-ROM and mass produced. The CD-ROM is then marketed and sold in the same manner as are software and books. The entertainment or educational factor is more important than the media that the information is distributed on. This means that the same people who have ideas that they can express through book, film, or other media, should also consider multimedia.

You must understand that you do not need to be a technical or computer expert to author a multimedia title, just as you do not need to be a cinematographer to direct a movie. Of course, it helps to be technically inclined, so that you can understand the media. Any good film director usually has some technical background in other areas of film making. However, like film, multimedia is an entertainment media. Technical knowledge is necessary, but a successful multimedia title relies upon more than simply clean programming; it involves creativity. Multimedia developers and artists are starting to be recognized for their work just as recording and film artists are recognized for theirs. One day we will watch the Multimedia Developers and Artist's Awards (MeDiA Awards) on interactive television, where we will decide who should win the award for Title Of The Year from our living rooms.

The Multimedia Process

Concept

Concept is the development of any creative idea you have for a multimedia project. This is where you determine the content of your project, the audience that it is intended for, and the method by which the project will be brought to the audience. The process is the same as any creative first step.

As an example we will go through the process for creating an animated corporate logo in a three-dimensional graphics program. The completed logo can be used for video tape, in on-screen presentations, or as part of an interactive project on CD-ROM.

Scripting, Storyboard, and Logic Flow

The next part of the multimedia production process involves a progressive mapping, in which you flesh out the project with written description and drawings. Using these techniques to develop the project is helpful because they help to schedule the progression of the work. These techniques also make the project clearer to you and everyone else involved.

While planning your project, pretend that there are no limitations, even if you think your ideas are impossible. In this way, you can come from a vantage point of having the technology work for your ideas as opposed to tailoring your ideas to fit the technology. Frequently "impossible" ideas in multimedia are really only methods and combinations of tools that haven't been tried yet or documented.

Scripting

Scripting is a written description of the multimedia project. The goal is to describe the action of the project in as clear detail as possible, creating images through the words. This will help clarify the idea in your mind and guide any following steps.

Here is a script for the animated logo to be created in a three-dimensional graphics program:

Opening Logo

Graphics: Fade in from black to the word *Motion* in three-dimensional letters. "Motion" is positioned over a bar that separates it from an abstract clock with a single hand, also extruded in a three-dimensional program. This is a symbolic representation of the company name Motion Over Time.

The viewer's point of view is above and to the right of the word *Motion*. The animation begins with the viewer's point of view swinging in an arc down and to the left, stopping directly in front of "Motion" and the clock. The movement of the point of view takes approximately 3 seconds.

While the point of view is animating, the objects in the scene are animating as well. Each of the letters in the word "Motion" rotate once around an axis. The *M* and *N* rotate around an axis set from front to center (*z* axis), the *O*s rotate in opposite directions around an axis set from the top of the letters to the bottom (*y* axis), the *T* and *I* rotate in opposite directions on an axis through their sides (*x* axis). The rotations are completed in the same 3 seconds in which the movement of the point of view takes place.

The bar that "Motion" is positioned over morphs into the word *Over* during the same 3 seconds of the other animations. Also, the hand of the clock rotates once around the face from 12 o'clock to 12 o'clock. This rotation takes 2 seconds. In the last second the clock and hand morph into the word *Time*. By the end of the animation, the symbolic representation of Motion Over Time has become the words.

Audio: During the 3 seconds of the animation above, there is the sound of an alarm clock ticking. The sound grows steadily louder until the animation stops, then there is a loud alarm clock ring that lasts approximately 2 seconds. Then, a voice shouts, "Yo! Wake Up!"

Storyboarding

A *storyboard* is a series of drawings that represents the scenes in your project. The drawings are simply sketches that are meant to give the project graphic form and begin the process of visual composition. These drawings also serve as a map by which you can keep track of what has been completed and what still must be done.

The storyboard is an extension of the script in the sense that it describes the action of the project in graphic detail. Each image in the storyboard includes the time in which it takes place in the composition, measured in Hours:Minutes:Seconds:Frames. Each image also includes any dialog, description of sound effects, music and any other detail in the scene, including camera movements.

Figure 4.1*a–d* shows a storyboard for the animated logo Motion Over Time.

Logic Flow

If your project includes any interactivity, you need to plan how to integrate it in the design. This plan takes the form of a flowchart that shows all of the possible branches that a single decision point can lead to. For example, if you have a menu with three category choices, your flowchart will begin with three boxes, each leading to whatever other choices are available if that category is selected. (See Figure 4.2.)

Figure 4.1a *Video: The camera is positioned above and to the right of the symbolic three dimensional representation of the Motion Over Time logo: the word "Motion" separated by a bar from an abstract clock that has a single hand.* **Audio:** *A monotone hum.*

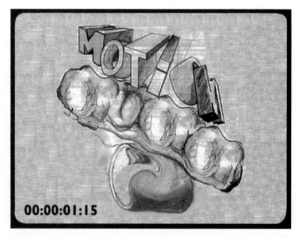

Figure 4.1b *Video: The camera swings from its starting position to a position directly in front of the logo. As it moves the logo distorts in the following manner: each letter of the word motion rotates once around an axis, the bar morphs into the word "Over", and the hand of the clock rotates around the face three times before the clock morphs into the word "Time".* **Audio:** *A ticking clock that grows steadily louder.*

Figure 4.1c *Video: The camera stops directly in front and slightly below the logo which has transformed into the words "Motion Over Time". **Audio:** A loud alarm clock ring. **V.O.:** "Yo! Wake up!"*

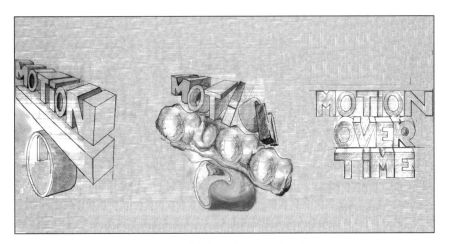

Figure 4.1d *Motion Story Board*

If your interactive program contains more complex logic, then you can describe the possible results that can occur with different actions from within a decision point. A game is an example of a multimedia project that would contain this type of complexity because you must have some of the logic based upon *combinations* of decisions made by the viewer. The logic flowchart works with storyboards and scripting because it doesn't describe images or sounds, only possible *decision paths* that link different portions of a presentation. Later it is replaced with actual program scripts.

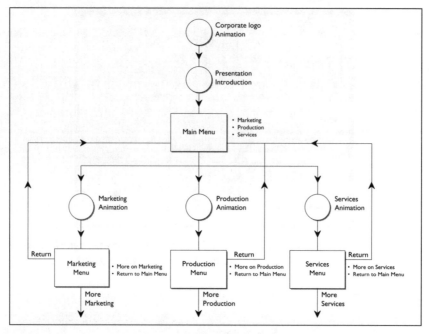

Figure 4.2 *A logic flowchart*

Creation of Different Elements

The creation of different elements is the process of producing graphics, shooting video, recording audio, and any other process involved in generating the separate elements of your multimedia project. Each element is treated as its own project with a script and storyboard if necessary (still graphics need only a sketch). These different elements are combined in the computer within a multimedia composition program like Adobe Premiere or an interactive authoring program like Macromedia Director. (See Figure 4.3.)

When you create the different elements of your multimedia project, keep track of any common criteria that everything must follow. For example, a project for NTSC video (United States standard) requires graphic images that are 640×480 pixels in dimension. You must make sure that any images you create are exactly that size or they will be either too large or too small for a television screen. *Chapter 19* provides more information about the different criteria you should be aware of when generating your multimedia elements.

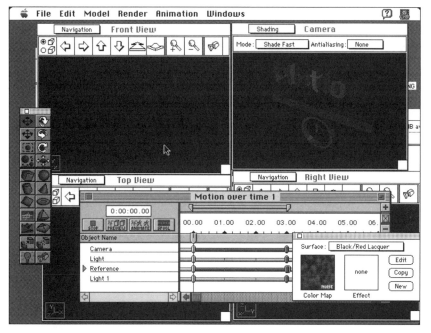

Figure 4.3 *Three-dimensional animation created in Specular International's Infini-D*

Digitizing Components That Are Not Already in the Computer

Anything created outside of the computer must be digitized so that it can be used in the computer. This means that the photograph, video, or sound is converted into a form that the computer can understand. This is called *digitizing* because the new form the material is converted to are the 0s and 1s of binary code, the fundamental computer language that all computers understand. Since binary code is digital in nature, the process of transferring material from outside into a computer is called digitizing. *Chapters 10 and 11* provide more information on how scanners and analog-to-digital transfer cards digitize photographs, video, and sound into the computer.

When all of your video, sounds, and photographs have been digitized, you can combine them with your computer graphics and with each other. Since they are all digital information now, the computer can recognize them all as data and manipulate them with software. Now you can mold all of your elements into a multimedia composition that can be presented from within the computer, output to video tape, or encoded onto CD-ROM.

The three-dimensional animation that we started does not use video, but it does use sound effects and a voice-over. For this step the sound effects and voice recording were done through Macromedia's MacRecorder and saved as sound files in SoundEdit Pro. When all of the needed elements were created, we collect them and bring them to the next step of production—composition. (See Figure 4.4.)

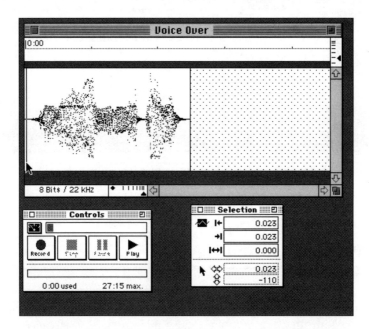

Figure 4.4 *Voice-over recorded in Macromedia's SoundEdit Pro*

Composition

During *composition* you bring all of your separate elements together into a software program where you combine them into a multimedia project. This consists of collecting all of the different elements into the same place, much the way that you would gather all of the ingredients for a recipe together. Then you edit, organize, and remix the elements with one another into your project.

If your project is interactive, then after the aesthetic composition is complete you incorporate the buttons and other controls that the viewer uses to control the presentation. Interactivity allows your presentation to be more like a software program than a commercial. To bring it all together, use composition programs like Macromedia Director that are designed with interactive capability to incorporate interactive user control with your project.

During composition you actually work with multimedia because this is where the different media are finally brought together. It is important, but not more important than all of the preceding steps. Compared to desktop publishing, composition is the layout of the page, but the planning and creation of the elements is the content of the articles. Bad elements and planing will make for inferior composition, no matter how skillfully you arrange them. (See Figure 4.5.)

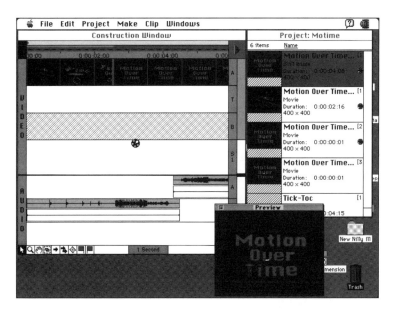

Figure 4.5 *The logo and sound effects arranged in Adobe's Premiere*

Finishing the Project

Once your composition is completed, you must save it in a form that is best for the method that you plan to use to deliver your project to your audience. If your project is intended for video, then you must either save your files as individual images for output one at a time or save them as a QuickTime movie or other digital video form such as a Macromedia Director movie. Interactive projects are packaged as stand-alone programs that can be distributed just like any other software program, without the necessity for the original development software you used. In short, this is where you end the development stage and prepare your project for output to another media or for distribution.

The finishing stage is actually quite simple; it just involves making the appropriate selections in a save dialog box. When your project is in the composition program it is usually in a form that can be understood only by that program. When you save your project you will have the opportunity to convert it into a file format that can be used in other programs. For example, the corporate logo used in this chapter was created in Adobe Premiere and then saved as a QuickTime movie. This was accomplished by selecting **Save** from the File menu, selecting **QuickTime** as the destination format, naming the file, and then pressing a button to confirm all of the settings. *Chapter 16* provides more information about the different digital file formats in which you can save your projects. (See Figure 4.6.)

Figure 4.6 *Logo saved as a QuickTime movie*

Output

The output step is used for projects that you want on video tape or CD-ROM. For video you must transfer the file through an analog-to-digital transfer card into a video recorder. For CD-ROM, you need to first make sure that your files will play properly on a CD-ROM by using a CD-ROM playback emulation utility, which causes the file to play from your hard drive as if it were playing from the slower CD-ROM player.

You can use equipment that you have available at your desktop system, such as an analog-to-digital transfer card and video recorder or a rewritable CD-ROM drive, or you can send your files out to a service bureau for output to your media of choice. Many multimedia developers use a combination of both. They use output hardware at their desktop system to preview their files and then use a service bureau to output to professional grade video tape or to encode onto a CD-ROM master that will be used for mass production. Our logo project will be used for computer on-screen presentations, so it does not need any additional processing after the QuickTime stage. However, we could always go back to the original files in Infini-D and Premiere if, for example, we want to output to video or CD-ROM later.

All of the steps in multimedia production are quite simple and straightforward. The most demanding elements involve coming up with the idea and spending the hours on the computer developing the project.

Part II

Building the Multimedia System

Buying your multimedia system is similar to buying a car, only worse. With so many models, makes, and extras, getting lost in the options and jargon is so easy that you could wind up wasting cash. The best thing, the *only* thing, for you to do is to be as educated as possible.

Multimedia is demanding. You can take few shortcuts without some level of compromise. You need speed where speed is a factor, you need a lot of capacity where capacity is a factor. As a general rule, more of everything is better. Fortunately, however, multimedia equipment is upgradeable and modular; you can start with the minimum and let the system grow with time.

Consider the following simple steps to narrow down the information that you need to buy your system.

Prepare A Budget

What people expect to spend and what things cost are often two very different figures. Get a feel for the market through advertised prices and magazine reviews, and be sure you understand exactly what is being advertised. Does that great price for the Macintosh include a hard drive? How much RAM does it have? Also, be sure that you account for everything else including monitor and keyboard which are not usually included in the computers price. These things add up, especially when you get around to buying multimedia software.

Know What You Want to Accomplish

Do you want to create animation? Interactive presentations? Do you intend to distribute your work? By video tape? By CD-ROM? On disk? Do you intend to use your work in presentations? Will you give these presentations from your computer or another computer? Will you be using video or sound in your work?

All of these factors play a vital role in determining what hardware and software you will need.

Know the Software You Plan to Use

You do not need to know everything about operating the software, but you do need to know its hardware requirements. How much RAM does it require? How large can files become? If you expect to work with video or animation, your files are going to be large.

As a rule, expect full-resolution video and animation (what you would use for television) to be at least one megabyte (or 1M) per frame. At 30 frames per second (video standard), that's 30M per second. That's not including the space required for the program and system or other programs and their files.

Consider that you will frequently be creating files in one program and then importing them into another program for changes. For example, you may create an animation in a three-dimensional graphics program and later want to add titles to the animation in a QuickTime movie-making program. You need to account for the amount of RAM that both programs require to run effectively as well as the amount of storage space needed for both the animation and the QuickTime movie.

Buy Only What You Will Need and Use

If you are just starting to learn about multimedia, then all you probably need right now is the basic computer along with the software that you plan to use. You can work with the software, learn how to use it, and buy the other components when you feel comfortable with what you've been working with. For starters, you will need a Macintosh with at least 8M of RAM, a 230M hard drive, and at least 8-bit color (256 colors). You will probably need more RAM and hard disk space soon enough, but this is enough to get started.

Buying the least amount you will need is good advice for everyone, including advanced users. Maintaining this policy will help you in three major ways.

* It can reduce the amount of cash you need to get started.

* It will allow your system to grow with your ability. It doesn't make much sense to buy equipment that you don't use or don't know how to use.

* It will allow you to benefit from technological advancements. Prices change quickly in multimedia. If you can wait, you may be able to get a better deal.

Buying only what you need and will use simply means taking advantage of how this industry changes. Money may not be an issue, and you may be a multimedia expert looking to bring something new to your work so it isn't an issue of knowing how to use what you will buy. If this is true for you, then it means that it will suit you best to keep as current as possible. The simple rule is this: If you can hold off on buying any part of your system, do so. In six months it will be cheaper or obsolete or something better will be available for the same money.

Keep the Future in Mind

You should know if your equipment can be upgraded. The cash value of computer equipment tends to drop dramatically and quickly; upgrading is usually the only way to keep up with the most sophisticated technology available. When Apple improves a computer line, it sometimes offers motherboard trade-ups, which usually cost the difference in suggested retail value. In addition, many other companies offer products that enhance the performance of Macs; find out if there's a product like that for your model. You should also know whether your computer will support software and hardware that you eventually want to bring into your system.

Be Certain That You Are Getting the Best Possible Deal

Consider all channels: dealerships, mail order, used equipment. Shop around. Systems are modular and can be bought that way. You may find that you can get a much better deal purchasing your hard drive, RAM, and monitor separately from your computer.

An excellent strategy is to shop for the components of the system separately and then to go to a good dealership with the combined price. Large dealerships can often offer better deals if they are selling a complete package because a small profit over a lot of equipment is still better than no profit at all. Even if they don't beat your price, buying from one place means that you need to go to only one place if any issues come up.

Mail order is also an excellent channel. Service turnaround is usually better than at dealerships. Just keep accurate records of when and where you bought all of your components if you buy them from different sources.

Also consider buying a used computer. There are very few moving parts in a computer and the people who own them really don't have too many ways that they can abuse them. Besides, people who use Macs usually love them and wouldn't do anything to hurt them.

You may want to buy a new hard drive because they can be abused inadvertently and can crash (break down) without warning. You may also want to consider starting out with a new monitor because the picture tube can blow just like a television's. Other than that, you can buy almost anything else used: sound cards, RAM, video capture cards, accelerator cards. If they work and there isn't any corrosion or other type of damage, then they will probably continue to work for a very long time and will cost you much less then anything new. Remember that you are paying for technology and its demand more than equipment, so price almost never reflects the equipment's condition.

Guidelines for Building a Macintosh Multimedia System

Selecting a complete Mac multimedia system involves research—that's why the next several chapters exist. Before digging in, a quick overview will familiarize you with some of the terminology and will serve as a guide to the steps involved in building your own Macintosh multimedia system.

The Computer

The computer is the main part of your system. It contains the central processing unit (CPU) which determines the type of software and peripherals that you can run with it. You need a Macintosh with a 68030 or later model CPU with at least 8M of RAM and the ability to further increase RAM capacity. It is also helpful to have NuBus expansion slots where system accelerators can be installed.

RAM and System Accelerators

Random Access Memory (RAM) is storage area in your computer that allows the CPU to retrieve information for software operation. It is only a temporary storage area in that it stores information in the form of electricity, rather than magnetic patterns. As a result, RAM only works while the computer is running. As soon as the computer is shut down, the storage in RAM is lost. The important function of RAM is that what it stores can be retrieved very quickly. Therefore, RAM is crucial to the fast operation of your computer. Most multimedia programs require large amounts of RAM in order to operate properly, so that the more RAM you have installed in your computer, the wider the range of software you can use, and the smoother your work flow will be.

Accelerators are optional cards that can speed the performance level of your computer. They are available as cards to be installed in the computer's NuBus slots or, in some instances, the cache slot. Using an accelerator can often allow you to use an earlier model Macintosh and still work at current performance standards. RAM and system accelerators are covered in greater detail in *Chapter 5.*

Hard Drives and other Storage

Chapter 6 covers hard drives, which are the storage-medium for your multimedia files and all software. There are two types of hard drives: fixed internal drives and removable drives. Fixed drives are your primary storage, and you will store your system software here. Removable drives are optional and are good for storing files to keep your fixed drive's storage free and for transporting files to other computers and service bureaus which will print or transfer your projects to video tape or CD-ROM.

Monitors

Chapter 7 covers monitors, which allow you to view your software operations. You judge a monitor by its quality of image based upon sharpness and color accuracy. You will want plenty of both.

Alternative Input Devices

The standard input devices are the keyboard and the mouse. All Macs come with a mouse from Apple, but the higher-end models do not come with a keyboard and have to be purchased separately. The keyboard allows you to enter text, numbers, and commands through key combinations. The mouse allows you to take advantage of the Macintosh system's point-and-click interface. You can work effectively with just these two devices, but you may prefer some of the alternatives, such as a Wacom Tablet or a Trackball. These and other input alternatives are detailed in *Chapter 8.*

Chapter 5

The Multimedia Macintosh

You want to work with multimedia, and you want to do so on a Macintosh. But *which* Mac? This chapter will help you make that decision.

Choosing the Right Mac

To start a Macintosh multimedia development system, you need a Macintosh computer, and not just any Macintosh. You need to be certain that it has the capability to run your multimedia software and other equipment. Ideally, you want the latest Macintosh designed for multimedia, but since this may not be feasible financially, you may want to consider an earlier model. (See Figures 5.1 and 5.2.) The Quadra 840 was designed with multmedia specifically in mind. The power and features necessary for multimedia are built in to this Macintosh. The IIci is the earliest Mac that can be used for multimedia. Its built-in speed and features are adequate for getting started, and its open-ended design is easy to upgrade for higher performance.

Figure 5.1 *The Macintosh Quadra 840 AV*

Figure 5.2 *The Macintosh IIci*

The Power Mac and the PowerPC Microprocessor

The Power Macintosh is a new addition to Apple's computer line that promises to bridge the gap between Macintosh and IBM computers. The very unique thing about the Power Mac is that it is capable of running Macintosh and IBM software (both DOS and Windows). It does so in emulation mode, which means that a software program that is built into the Macintosh translates the Mac or PC software into code that the PowerPC microprocessor can read. And in development for the Power Mac line are native applications designed to work directly with the new microprocessor. Every major Macintosh software developer has already developed, or will soon release, versions of their software for the Power Mac. Remember that the Power Mac is not an upgraded Macintosh, nor is it some hybrid between the Macintosh and an IBM computer. It is a new computer that will most certainly influence the direction of hardware and software development for multimedia, and computers in general. The influence involves the Power Mac's ability to run applications much faster than Mac's or IBM's run applications native to their systems, and the Power Mac does it a very low price. Power Macs start at under $2,000.

The PowerPC microprocessor is a joint venture between Apple, IBM, and Motorola. Both Apple and IBM now have the freedom to manufacture computers that use the PowerPC chip. Apple has already done so, and the result is the Power Macintosh line. The basic design of the Power Mac was taken from the Quadra 610, 650, and 800. In fact, Apple is offering an upgrade to PowerPC motherboards for their computers that share the design. This group also includes the 840AV. DayStar Digital also offers a NuBus expansion card, and upgrades for their 040 accelerator cards, which bring PowerPC capability to earlier Macs, such as the IIci. The Power Mac, itself, can be upgraded for AV capabilities as well. A NuBus card available from Apple gives the Power Mac the ability to play video in a floating window on screen, and output full motion video and audio.

The Power Mac has a different architecture than other computers and a new processor. It also sends information in groups of 64 bits as opposed to 32 bits of current Quadras and PCs. All of these differences result in a computer that can run as much as 2 to 5 times faster than the Quadra 840AV (MacUser bench tests May, 1994) when it operates native applications.

It is still too early to recommend the Power Mac for multimedia, simply because native software is not yet available. However, the Power Mac is very promising, in that it will offer tremendous power at prices that make sense for entry-level computer users. Until the Power Mac software is fully unleashed and debugged the best Macs for multimedia remain the high-end Quadras, such as the 840AV.

Power and Speed are Musts

Two criteria that a Macintosh will need if you are to use it in multimedia development are processing power and speed. A third criterion that is equally important is *upgradeability*. Upgradeability is the computer's built-in capability to be enhanced to meet more demanding specifications. Another issue of upgradeability deals with the expense and availability of products to enhance your computer.

Remember that multimedia software and applications for the Macintosh are still fairly new. Therefore, the only machines designed specifically for this purpose are all fairly new. In 1991 desktop publishing was the most popular professional use for Macs. Therefore, the ability to run desktop publishing software and hardware was the standard on which Macintosh computers were rated. A fast Mac was one that could quickly complete desktop publishing tasks, such as page scrolls. Multimedia places a far greater demand on a computer, so that a fast desktop publishing Mac can rate as only entry-level for multimedia work.

You boost the performance of a Macintosh by upgrading its RAM, installing a processing accelerator device, or replacing the motherboard with a newer model, all of which are detailed later in this chapter. There are upgrade options available for all Macintosh computers, but not all Macs can be upgraded to the performance level required for multimedia. You may also find that upgrading your Mac can cost as much as buying a new Macintosh with multimedia capability built-in. Some of the multimedia-ready Macintosh computers are: Quadras, Quadra AVs, and the Power Mac line. Appendix A lists all of the multimedia-ready Macs, as well as the older Macs that can be upgraded for multimedia.

WARNING

The Macintosh IIci is the earliest Macintosh that you can consider for multimedia, but there are Macs that were introduced after the IIci and are not multimedia-capable. The IIsi, LC line, some of the Performas, and some of the Powerbooks are not multimedia-capable.

These Macintosh computers lack appropriate upgrade paths. They were designed to offer the user friendly Mac interface at lower expense and, in the case of the Powerbooks, portability. They're excellent for running office management, educational, desktop publishing, and graphics applications, but for multimedia and the software associated with it, they basically run CD-ROMs or show simple presentations. The IIfx is capable of running multimedia applications. However, since Apple discontinued the model, the number of third-party companies developing products for this computer have dwindled, so upgrading can be difficult.

Look for the important upgradeability factors outlined throughout this chapter, as well as processor model and speed. The IIci can be considered as an upgrade choice because it has a nice open-ended design, and plenty of products are available for it.

Enhanced Functionality

Outside of performance upgrades, which are concerned with speed and with software compatibility, you should also be concerned with feature upgrades, which are the way in which you make your Macintosh do new things. Upgrading the functions of your Macintosh, such as its ability to display higher quality images or to record video to the hard drive, is based upon the *SCSI ports* and the *NuBus slots*. Small Computer System Interface (SCSI) is the Macintosh method for connecting external devices such as scanners, removable hard drives, and other peripherals that enhance the functionality of the Macintosh. NuBus slots are direct connections to the Bus. The *bus* is a bundle of wires that carries data to and from the CPU. It is the main data pathway of the computer and is detailed later in this chapter in "On Technology." The NuBus slot is the main part of the Macintosh modular upgrade design. You can install a special NuBus card, which can speed up the computer or give it a new feature, such as the ability to record video directly to the hard drive.

NuBus slots in Macintosh computers allow you to connect devices called *NuBus expansion cards* that provide new features, some that may be built into newer Macintosh computers. For example, some of the newer Macs have built-in video capture and sound recording. With NuBus expansion cards, available from a variety of manufacturers, you can bring these features to older machines. With such an open-ended upgrade design, Macintosh computers hardly ever become obsolete, as newer machines are introduced. In this way, technology can proceed at a steady pace without leaving you behind. (See *Appendix A* for a list of performance specifications, connection and upgrade options, and the features that are built into multimedia-capable Macs.)

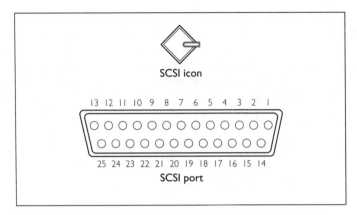

Figure 5.3 *The SCSI port*

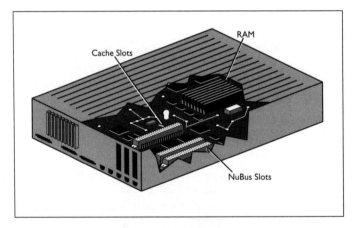

Figure 5.4 *NuBus Slots*

What Makes the Macintosh Tick?

The main component of your Macintosh is the *central processing unit* (CPU), which is responsible for the complexity and speed of your system and how it handles information. Motorola manufactures the Apple CPUs under variations of the style number 680x0. Often you will hear these processors referred to by the last three digits of the number such as 030 or 040. Faster processors are based on the 68040 CPU, which is built into the latest Apple computers on the market.

There are still many machines with the 68030 processor on the market, both new and used, such as the Macintosh II line (IIci, IIfx, etc.).

The 68030 machines are perfectly capable of handling most multimedia applications and are often far less expensive than newer 040 machines. Their only drawback is that 030 machines don't have much of what comes built into some 040 machines, such as 16 bit color, and NTSC video out which allows the AV Macintosh computers to output their video signal to an ordinary television set and record the signal directly to video tape. Fortunately, as mentioned earlier, there are several ways to enhance and accelerate earlier Apple computers, which will be covered later in this chapter.

N O T E

Keep in mind that there is a second determining factor for speed in the CPU called the *megahertz* (MHz). The processor model number determines the overall speed, power, and consequently, the capability of the CPU; the megahertz determine cycles-per-second, or how much information the processor can address at one time. This distinction can be a little confusing, so think of the CPU as a car engine. Newer models will be more efficient, and megahertz make the car faster, more comfortable, streamlined, smoother riding, etc. A 68040 computer running at 25 MHz is faster than a 68030 at 25 MHz, and a 68040 running at 33 MHz is faster than a 68040 running at 25 MHz. Megahertz are easy to overlook but should not be because they can make a tremendous difference in your system's performance. Always remember that the higher megahertz the better.

RAM and System Upgrades

All of the Mac's features that affect performance can be upgraded. And as multimedia software improves, speed and performance will always be issues in the computer as well. Any computer you buy will likely need to be upgraded at some point regardless of its current capability. There are several options that are available to you for enhancing the performance of your Macintosh.

RAM—Random Access Memory

The fastest way to enhance the performance of your computer is to increase the amount of RAM you have installed. RAM is a very fast, temporary storage location for your software that is only available when the computer is running. It allows the computer to retrieve software quickly, without using processing power. Unlike a hard drive, it stops storing information as soon as the computer is shut down. Multimedia software tends to be very large and very processing demanding, so increasing the amount of RAM in your computer helps to improve performance.

RAM is installed in the computer in slots that are located on the motherboard. RAM cards are made of silicon chips that are placed along a piece of plastic called a single in-line memory module (SIMM), which gets plugged into one of the slots. The process is easy to handle and does not require special training. You can buy RAM from most mail order houses that advertise in *MacUser*, *MacWorld*, and other Macintosh trade magazines. A list of RAM configurations of the various multimedia Macs is available in Appendix A.

What RAM is and What It Does

Before you run a program in your computer, it is like a piece of folded clothing in a drawer. It will remain there, occupying space, until you call on it to operate. When you open a program the computer looks into the file and decodes all of the programming information (code) that is there. This program code tells the computer what to display on screen, and the functions of the program that are available to you as the user.

Much of the program's code does not need to be processed by the computer continuously. For example, you may not use all the features of the program every time you use the program. But the computer must keep them on the ready where they can be reached very quickly without taking up processing power from the computer. This temporary storage location is RAM.

As mentioned earlier, RAM is made of silicon chips placed along a rectangular piece of plastic called a single in-line memory module (SIMM). The silicon chips are very fast storage devices (their speed is measured in millionths of a second, nanoseconds) that only operate while the computer is running. Therefore, RAM is necessary for the fast processing of software in that it keeps software handy and quickly retrievable.

The more RAM you have installed on your computer, the faster your software will run. Many multimedia programs are very large, even in their closed state. Therefore, they require a great deal of RAM to run at all and need even more RAM when dealing with demanding functions. For example, three-dimensional graphics and animation programs are typically very large in storage size. When you actually create an image or animation, you trigger a complex mathematical computer function that requires RAM in order to be completed. Naturally, the more RAM you have while running a three-dimensional program, the faster the rendering time of images and animations. (See Figure 5.5.)

Figure 5.5 *Random Access Memory*

Accelerator Cards

Accelerator cards increase the processing speed of the computer by taking over some of the processing tasks normally handled by the CPU. They are installed in the NuBus slots of the computer, or in the case of the IIci, they can be installed in a processor direct slot *(PDS)*, also called the *cache slot*. This improves the speed of your computer and reduces the amount of time necessary for multimedia software processing.

Some accelerator cards have processor chips installed on them, such as the DayStar Digital line of accelerator cards. They offer increased speed, and the ability to run software with certain types of processors. For example, DayStar offers accelerator cards that have 040 processors installed directly on them. This set up can bring computers with 030 processors (such as the IIci) up to 040 speed of the newer Quadras. DayStar also offers a PowerPC upgrade for many of their cards (a quick way to bring the PowerPC to older Macintosh computers at very low expense). (See Figure 5.6.)

Figure 5.6 *The DayStar Digital Accelerator Card*

Motherboard Swapping

The third type of upgrade for the Macintosh involves completely replacing the-motherboard. This options becomes available when Apple introduces a new line of computers or improves an existing line. If there are enough similarities between your older computer and the new line, you may be able to switch motherboards, and in effect, build a new computer. This is the most expensive type of upgrade, and can end up costing about the same as buying a new computer. If you consider the resale value of your used computer and add the cost of a motherboard upgrade, you will probably find it more profitable to invest in a new computer. Contact Apple, or an authorized Apple dealer for information on the motherboard upgrade paths available for your Mac. Usually the cost of the upgrade is the difference between the book value of your motherboard and the retail value of the new motherboard. This cost may be negotiable with a dealer, but not by much.

Installing RAM, Accelerators, and Motherboards

RAM and accelerator cards are installed directly into slots that are on the motherboard of the computer. The process is simple and does not require any training, but there are some things to be aware of.

WARNING

Motherboards are not as straightforward to install as RAM or accelerator cards. Therefore, motherboard upgrades are best left to authorized Apple service centers. You can also send your computer directly to Apple to have them install the new motherboard for you. Go to whoever has the best offer considering both service turnover and expense.

If you install your own RAM or accelerator card, be aware of the following:

✳ The computer should be unplugged and the power supply cord should be disconnected. You can short your computer's motherboard otherwise, and you risk shocking yourself.

✳ You should make sure that you are grounded by touching a nearby metal object before touching anything inside of your computer. This will release any static electricity that can surge from your hand into the computer, and cause data loss. Some RAM manufacturers and dealers ship their products with a grounding band. Before handling Mac components, the band is placed around one wrist. A line that is attached to the band is then clipped to a nearby grounding surface. This discharges any static electricity from the body.

✳ Never force anything into a slot. RAM and NuBus cards must be positioned at very precise angles. If the angle is right, it should clip in easily. If you force the card or SIMM you run the risk of damaging the motherboard, or the item that you are inserting. A broken RAM or NuBus slot clip prevents the slot clip from being used and is very costly to repair. You will also lose the use of your computer until it is repaired.

✳ Never put screwdrivers, paper clips, pencils, or pens into the computer. These items can scratch the motherboard or break some other part of the computer. Metal objects can also short the motherboard if there is stray electricity traveling through them. Some screwdrivers also have magnetic charges that can erase memory in your computer.

✳ Buy a Macintosh repair and installation guide. There are several on the market. These books offer multiple case scenarios and help to trouble-shoot situations specific to your computer and installation.

On Technology

The basic architectural design of Apple Macintosh computers is identical in all models. The circuitry of the logic board (or motherboard) is designed around a bus. As mentioned earlier, the bus is a conduit of wires that delivers information to and from the CPU. The bus branches off to all pathways of input and output in the computer.

Let's look at the keyboard for an example of how the bus works. When you press the letter **R**, this message is sent into the computer, along the bus, and into the CPU. The CPU then sends a signal out to your monitor, which then displays the letter **R** in your word processing software. The design is something like the nervous system: The bus represents the spinal column, the CPU represents the brain, and stimuli and response are sent along a central channel. (See Figure 5.5.) Remember that the bus is a bundle of wires that acts as the computer's nervous system. Information travels all along the bus to and from the CPU and everything else that is connected to the computer.

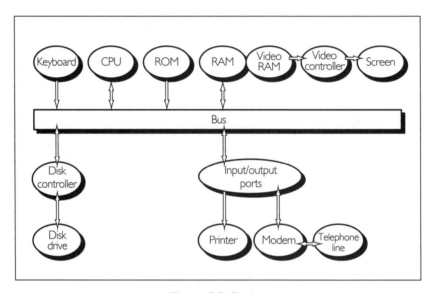

Figure 5.7 *The bus*

The bus doesn't only handle information input from the keyboard. It also carries information to and from the hard drive, RAM, the ports that connect the computer to external devices, and other peripherals such as processor accelerators. Essentially, it is the common thread connecting all parts of your computer.

On System Software

Every Mac comes with a System Folder. In that folder is a program called—simply enough—the System.

What System Software Does

Your Macintosh's *system software* is what makes the computer so easy to learn and use. The system software creates a *graphical user interface* (GUI), which gives everything in your computer an icon that you can directly select. This means that files, software, hard drives, peripherals, etc., are represented by icons on-screen that you select with the mouse by clicking on them.

When you click on a folder or hard drive, a window that displays the hard drive or folder's contents opens. Folders can be stored within other folders so that you can organize the contents of your computer in a way that best fits your needs. Older systems and the IBM disk operating systems (DOS) rely upon your knowledge of particular commands to navigate through your computer to find the documents that you need. The GUI system of the new Macintosh (like Windows, the GUI systems for DOS computers) keeps things very clean and simple. (See Figure 5.8.) The Macintosh GUI allows you to directly select icons that represent files, folders, and the items connected to the computer without needing to know special commands. When you double-click on a folder or hard drive icon, a window that displays its contents opens. You can organize the contents any way you choose. Pull-down menus allow you quick access to commands such as **Cut** and **Paste**, which use the Scrapbook and Clipboard programs to transfer items between programs and are consistent from program to program on the Mac.

Three outstanding features are included in the operating system software: pull-down menus, the Clipboard, and the Scrapbook. *Pull-down menus* make selecting commands in your software and managing your computer's operation easy. The *Clipboard* allows you to use the **Cut** command to remove a portion of a file and then use the **Paste** command to place it elsewhere. The Clipboard will temporarily store any cut item until you **Cut** a new item. The item can also be pasted into the *Scrapbook*, which stores it permanently (even when the system is shut down) and allows you to retrieve it later. These universal features lend familiarity to all software programs on the Mac, even if they are new to you.

Elements of the System Software

There are two main elements to your computer's system software: the software on the disks that come with your computer and the program which is stored on memory modules built into the computer, called its *ROM*. ROM, or read-only memory, is similar to *RAM* in design, but the content of ROM cannot be changed. ROM contains the computer's instructions on how to display windows, how to display the icons of various files, how to copy and paste documents, and how to use the pull-down menu commands and other features that distinguish the Macintosh operating system from others and that give it the Macintosh personality.

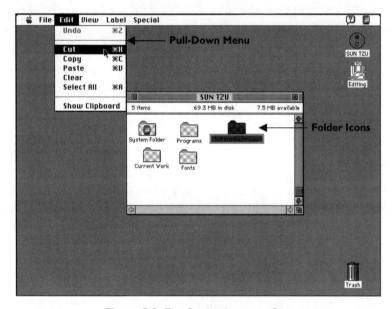

Figure 5.8 *The Graphical user interface*

The system software that comes on the disks with your computer contains the portion of your system that can be upgraded, including the System file and the Finder, which allow you to do things like keep several programs open at one time and switch among them as you work. If system software is the personality of your Macintosh then the computer's ROM can be considered its innate personality, since it cannot be changed. (You can replace the ROM, but this almost never happens.) The disk software can be upgraded to allow for system extensions, and this is the software that designs the overall system interface. Apple periodically improves upon the system software and makes it available to you. If your Macintosh is current enough to take advantage of new versions of system software, then you will be able to upgrade for a fee, or obtain the system software from an authorized Apple computer reseller, or through other channels such as local Macintosh user groups or authorized mail order houses. Call Apple for local user groups and authorized dealers in your area. On-line modem network services such as America Online and CompuServe are also good platforms to get that type of information.

The two current features of the Macintosh system software that are vital to multimedia are *32-bit addressing* and the *QuickTime* extension. 32-bit addressing is what allows your Macintosh to channel the large amounts of information from the large amount of RAM needed for animation and other complex graphics and video. Without this feature, information can get backed up, and impede your multimedia software from flowing smoothly.

QuickTime is the name given to a set of computer instructions that can be added to the instructions already present in the operating system of your Mac. This additional code allows the Mac to display animation, video, and audio—independent of third party multimedia software. Several multimedia programs such as Adobe Premiere and CoSA After Effects can export QuickTime movies into work done in other programs. The QuickTime extension and file format is an extremely useful way to transport animation, video, and audio (in a single file) among applications on the Macintosh platform. More information about QuickTime is available in *Chapters 11* and *16.*

Virtual Memory

Virtual memory is a feature of your Macintosh system software that allows your software to use space on the hard drive as if it were RAM (detailed later in this chapter). It is not useful to multimedia because it is very slow, and multimedia needs a minimum amount of speed to operate properly that virtual memory does not provide.

N O T E

Be careful not to rely on system software to replace actual RAM.

On Bits, Bytes and Binary

Binary is the fundamental language code that the computer understands. It is the way in which all information in the computer is moved and stored. The code works in such a way that everything in the computer, every letter, every number, every symbol, every action, is encoded in a string of 0s and 1s. This is also why the code is called binary, because it consists of only two different characters (0 and 1).

Each 0 or 1 is called a *bit*, or binary digit. This is the smallest unit of data that can be transferred through the computer. Eight bits form a *byte*, every letter is represented by a byte in binary code. The next step up is the *kilobyte,* which represents 1024 bytes. *Kilo* technically means 1000, but binary increases with a base of 2 not 10. As a result, 2 to the tenth power is the closest that binary gets to 1000. It actually equals 1024, thus the discrepancy. The kilobyte is the smallest unit of file size that you will be working with. Binary sizes increase in increments of powers of 2. The next unit is the *megabyte,* or 1024 kilobytes. The next up is the *gigabyte,* or 1024 megabytes, etc. Binary is the language that the computer understands, and is often referred to as the computers *lowest-level language,* or *raw data.*

Aa BbCc
Dd EeFfG
gHhIiJjK
kLlMmO
oPpQqRr
SsTtUuV
vXxYyZz

Chapter

6

Hard Drives and Other Storage Methods

Multimedia programs, and the files that they use, require more storage space than most other types of software. That makes the topic of storage devices a very important one.

Storage Devices

Hard drives and other storage devices are the mechanisms in which you will store your computer files. They are the computer equivalent of a filing cabinet and, as such, are rated by the quantity of information that they can store. Hard drives are also rated by their *access time*, the speed at which information can be retrieved from them. Multimedia systems depend on storage devices because they are the only way to save your work in the long term.

There are two types of storage devices: fixed drives and removable drives. *Internal drives* are fixed because the amount of information they can store never changes. A 230M hard drive will never be able to hold any more than 230M. They are also fixed because they are not designed to be removed from the computer. Some fixed drives are small enough to be considered transportable, but there are better ways to accomplish that goal.

The most important reason for having a fixed drive is that it provides a permanent location for your system software. System software allows your computer to operate and run other software programs, and your computer needs access to it at all times. If you use a removable drive for your system software you cannot remove the cartridge from the drive while the computer is operating, which defeats the removable drive's purpose. You also must have your system software on every disk that you plan to use in the removable drive. A fixed drive keeps the system software in one convenient location.

Removable drives are designed for the portability of information. Your files are stored in a cartridge or cassette that can be inserted in a drive and read just like information on a fixed drive. These drives are useful for archiving your files and for bringing them to other computers.

You can store an unlimited amount of data on removable drives. Even though you are limited by the amount of data that a single cartridge or cassette can hold, you can always supplement the cartridge or cassette with another one. Because their storage capacity is flexible, they are ideal for storing large files and archiving data that you want to access, but don't want to have take up useful hard disk space.

NOTE Use removable drives to store a back-up copy of your system software. This practice provides a greater level of security for your information and ensures that you can continue working if your fixed drive fails. You can start your computer and perhaps even repair whatever caused your hard disk failure with a program like Norton Utilities for Macintosh.

The technology behind the different storage methods is very similar. Information is encoded into magnetic fields and read by either an electromagnetic device or a laser. This technology is easiest to describe while also describing the mechanism of a hard drive. Since all of the drives here are based upon the fundamental design of the fixed drive, you will find most of the technology discussion, including access time, in the section on fixed drives.

Buying your storage devices is not a matter of determining whether you need a fixed drive or a removable drive but rather deciding which fixed drive is your best buy. When making this decision for multimedia systems, keep in mind that removable drives help keep the storage in your main hard drive free and simplify the task of bringing large graphics files to service bureaus to be printed onto video tape or mastered onto CD-ROM. FWB Hammer drives are very reliable. But remember that removable drives are strictly optional as storage media.

NOTE

Capacity and speed are important, but you also need to look for warranty term and software bundles.

Determining how well a hard drive is made is almost impossible because that information simply isn't available without testing. Warranty length is a good sign of the manufacturer's confidence in the equipment because no manufacturer wants to spend money on repairs. Also, study the comparison tests on the latest equipment that are run by trade publications like *MacWorld* and *MacUser*. If you call either magazine, they will tell you when they plan one or sell you a copy of a back issue with the information you need.

Many hard drive manufacturers include software such as computer virus protection, automatic backup (which duplicates your files in case some are accidentally erased), or some sort of hard disk diagnostic software like Norton Utilities. This software can add value to the price of the drive, but you should still pay careful attention to the quality of the drive. The software may be useful, but it doesn't make the drive any better. Look for software, but check the warranty and buy from reliable manufacturers.

What happens when capacities improve? The disks in fixed drives and removable disk drives always have the potential to store more information; it's the read/write mechanism that is improved. As read/write technology becomes more sophisticated, you can store more information on the same surface area of the disk. The magnetic charges that are encoded information on the disk are microscopic. Consequently, as the mechanics of the drive improves, you have much more room to work with. For this reason, floptical disks can store much more information on the same media as a floppy disk, because a laser helps the magnetic read/write head to locate the smaller areas of information. (See Figure 6.1.)

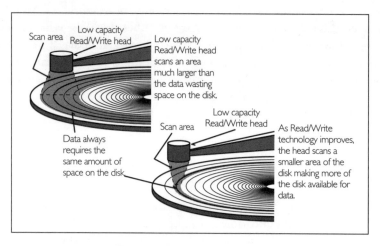

Figure 6.1 *Improving capacities*

On Care and Crashing for All Storage Devices

Shock, dust, and magnetic fields generated outside of the read/write head are the three major causes of hard drive failure.

Shock

Contrary to popular belief, the electromagnetic read/write head does not contact the disk. If it does, the head is likely to damage the disk. The read/write head does come near the surface of the disk, but only close enough to sense the positive and negative charges that define the data. In fact, a thin coating of oil on the platter provides an added measure of protection against contact. The only exception is tape back-up systems which are designed much in the same way that ordinary audio and video cassette recorders are designed. However, they read and write digital information. These drives have other concerns unique to them that are covered later in this chapter.

In all systems except tape back-up systems, shock, or a physical jolting of the drive, can cause what is known as *head slap*, which occurs when the read/write head hits the disk. It can cause physical damage to the platter or cause the electromagnetic head to inadvertently alter the data where it touches. Hard drives and other disk media are vulnerable to head slap when they are saving or opening files, which is when the read/write head is over portions of the disk that are encoded.

Hard drives are designed with *park zones*, empty parts of the hard disk where the head pauses when there is no hard drive activity. Some hard drives have a locking head that takes the read/write head completely away from the hard drive when paused. The function of both is to help prevent head slap and make moving the computer while it is on but not in use reasonably safe. Still, the best way to prevent shock damage is to not move the computer suddenly while it is on, and to not move it at all if you are saving, opening, or otherwise requesting something from the hard drive.

Dust

All storage devices are designed to be as airtight as possible, but because nothing can be truly airtight, airborne particles can sometimes get in. Dust and smoke can interfere with the read/write head's ability to sense and transfer information to and from the media. Like dust on a record album, some of the information will be missed completely, or the dust can cause the head to misread an area.

The dust that can get into a storage device will be microscopic, and the disk is rather sturdy, so dust isn't likely to damage the disk or the information on it. Dust is really just an issue of preventing the hard drive from performing correctly. Removable drives such as SyQuest and Bernoulli are particularly susceptible to smoke and dust because the inner mechanism of both drive and disk are directly exposed to air every time a disk is inserted or removed. The best way to prevent this type of failure is to keep the drive in a dust-free environment. If dust somehow manages to get into your drive or removable disk, you can send it to a service center where it can be opened under appropriate conditions and cleaned properly.

Magnetic Fields

All storage media rely upon very controlled use of magnetic fields to operate. If a magnetic field passes close to the drive, it won't cause physical damage, but it can erase all of your information. You can prevent this type of information loss by keeping your hard drive away from anything that you may even suspect as emitting a magnetic field such as pieces of electronic musical and stereo equipment that aren't shielded.

Solutions

Identifying the exact cause of any problem you are having with your hard drive may be difficult. The software program called Norton Utilities diagnoses these types of problems and even retrieves information that is in danger of being lost for whatever reason, including accidental erasure. Norton Utilities can also help you maintain your drive and intercept any impending problems. Otherwise, you must send your hard drive to a manufacturer-authorized service center where the drive can be checked under controlled circumstances. The sales source of your hard drive can give you more information on service.

WARNING

Hard drives need to be formatted so that they can operate with your computer, which means that they need to be encoded in such a way that allows the computer to search through its contents for the files that you place there. This formatting takes up some of the capacity of the drive, but will be invisible to you on the desktop. Therefore, when you open the drive icon on your computer, you may find that some of the drive's capacity is unavailable even though the drive appears empty. A 1.2 gigabyte drive may end up with only 1 gigabyte of space available for your files. The amount of space required for a drive's formatting data will vary from drive to drive. Therefore, you should ask your hard drive vendor for the *formatted capacity* of the drive you are considering. This will amount to the true, useful capacity of the drive you are buying.

Fixed Drives

On Function

The hard disk drive, or fixed drive, will be your primary method for storing your computer files when you aren't using them. The main benefit of hard drives is that they store information even when the computer is turned off. A hard drive is connected to your computer externally via the SCSI port in the back, or it can be installed internally, in the casing of the computer. (See Figures 6.2 and 6.3.) There is no overall performance difference between internal or external hard drives, although external drives require additional desk space and may be slightly more expensive for the same size drive because they include a case and a separate power supply. Your primary concerns in buying a hard drive are the amount of information it can store (capacity), its speed (access time), and the frequency with which it pauses to check itself for defects (prediction update).

Figure 6.2 *Internal fixed drive*

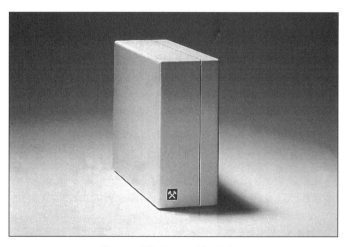

Figure 6.3 *External fixed drive*

The hard disk drive appears as an icon in the upper right corner of the Macintosh computer screen. To open it, double-click on the icon or highlight the icon and press **Command-O**. A window with an inventory of the information that is stored in that hard drive appears on-screen. Once it is installed it should function invisibly, as if it were constructed as part of the computer. (See Figure 6.4.)

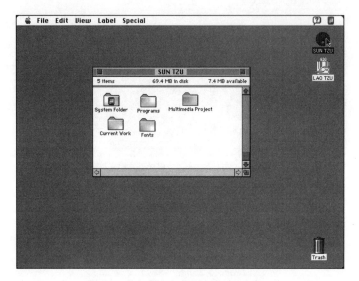

Figure 6.4 *The contents of a hard drive*

Capacity

For multimedia you will need as much hard drive capacity as your budget allows. Multimedia files are large, and you need some place to keep them. Recall that one second of video or animation for a television screen can require up to 30 Megs of storage space. Naturally, the more capacity you have, the more information you can store.

You can also have several hard drives connected to your computer. This configuration allows you to start with a smaller capacity and build on it.

For example, let's say you have an 80M hard drive with 20M of free space and a 230M hard drive with 28M of free space. Simple math says you have 48M of free space, but when your render one second of animation, the computer informs you that you don't have enough space on either hard drive. You will need to either erase files, move files from one drive to the other, or create the animation in a manner that will allow you to store some of it on one drive and the rest on the other.

This may be a minor inconvenience the first few times it happens, but it becomes a major nuisance when it happens every time you try to save something to your hard drive. You should have a hard drive that can accommodate a large amount of information. In this way, you can work as freely as possible on your projects. A good start is a hard drive with at least 200M of storage capacity. Apple offers a 230M hard drive, and several other manufacturers supply hard drives with a similar capacity.

Speed

Speed in a hard drive is measured in milliseconds (1/1000 of a second) and is identified as its access time. Access time is determined by the length of time the hard drive takes to respond to a request. That is, when you click on the hard drive's icon, you request that it open and display its inventory. The period between your click and the window's actually opening is determined by the access time. When this book was written, hard drives averaged 10 to 15 milliseconds in access time. Lower access times are faster, and therefore better.

Considering that the main purpose of the hard drive is information storage (saving files) and information retrieval (opening files), you can readily understand that overall speed is not crucial to the development of multimedia files. However, hard drive speed is important if you plan to produce presentations from your computer, which is how you might use a notebook computer. A slower hard drive can produce a noticeable delay in presentation creating a poorly timed presentation where action and sound are not in synch. Otherwise, hard drive speed affects only the ease at which you work. Because multimedia is more a process of creativity than one of function, you will want a fast hard drive so that you can reduce the amount of time to get things done.

Prediction Update

Your third concern, prediction update, has to do with the mechanics of the hard drive. Read the next section for more information.

On Technology

Hard disk drives function very much like old-style record players. Your information is stored on a platter made of an aluminum alloy or glass (rigid, lightweight, nonmagnetic materials) that is coated with an iron oxide, which can be magnetized. This platter is mounted through its center with a motor that can spin the hard drive at very fast speeds. Your files are recorded and accessed with an electromagnetic device that is moved across the surface of the disk by an "arm" that is also made of a nonmagnetic metal. (See Figure 6.5.)

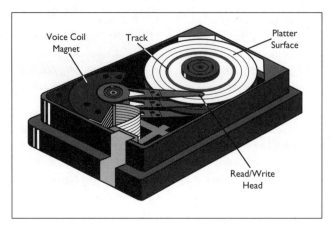

Figure 6.5 *The hard drive mechanism*

Information is stored magnetically on the disk in positive and negative fields. Positive and negative fields correspond to the 0s and 1s of binary code, which is the fundamental language of the computer. The electromagnetic device, or head, produces these polar charges when recording to the hard drive and senses and decodes these charged fields when reading information from the hard drive.

Your data are encoded along a spiral track on both sides of the disk. The track is divide into sectors of no more than 512K of data. The hard drive places information in the first available space. If a file exceeds the 512K limit of a sector, then the hard drives divides the file and continues to write to the next available space.

Because your files are encoded in their most basic form and one file can be subdivided and scattered throughout several locations, your hard drive needs a way of keeping track of where everything is. This is accomplished through a *file allocation table* (FAT), which keeps track of everything that takes place on the hard drive. The FAT is an area along the disk's data track to which the hard drive automatically records an information location and inventory.

The FAT also keeps track of those areas on the disk that are empty or *erased*, and therefore available for new data. Erasing an area of the disk is accomplished when a file is discarded or reduced in size, either by dragging the files icon into the trash and throwing it away or by editing a file in some manner such as deleting a large portion of a word processing document. The data are not actually wiped away, but a notation indicating that the information in that area can be written over is placed in the FAT.

The computer communicates with the hard drive through SCSI, but the SCSI does not ultimately control the drive. The hard drive has its own set of instructions programmed into its own memory module, or ROM which receives and responds to whatever information the computer presents. The ROM determines when to write, read, erase, open, and divide files and do everything else the hard drive does.

The hard drive's ROM also contains an instruction called *prediction update*, which periodically sends the electromagnetic head across the surface of the hard disk to determine if any portion is in danger of becoming defective. It judges areas of the hard drive according to a programmed protocol before a problem occurs. If it suspects any sector, then it copies the information from that sector to the next free area and sends a message back to the FAT indicating that the questionable area is unavailable. The purpose of this program is to protect your information from hard drive failure.

Prediction update is important to multimedia because it temporarily pauses the function of the hard drive from reading and writing data. Some prediction update programming activates every 15 minutes, but the time interval can vary depending upon the manufacturer.

Under most circumstances, the period of pause is virtually imperceptible (about 1 second). For multimedia, however, that pause can still cause a problem because many multimedia applications rely upon extended continuous work on the part of the hard drive. One example is video capture in which you record video directly to the hard drive.

You may have only a few seconds of video to capture, but if you do this when the prediction update is scheduled then you could lose some of your video. Also, there is no way to determine when the prediction update will take place. It may just seem to you that something went wrong and you will just recapture the video anyway, but why have unnecessary obstacles in your work? Some hard drives have prediction update instructions that wait until there is no activity in the hard drive. This is the best way to avoid problems caused by prediction update.

Never attempt to open your hard drive if you are not appropriately knowledgeable about hard drive mechanics.

WARNING

What Is a Disk Array?

Disk arrays are large-capacity hard disk drives that use multiple platters and multiple read/write heads. The platters are stacked one over the other with a spindle running through their middles. Two read/write heads face the top and bottom of each disk reading and writing to the disks simultaneously. The shared work of the stacked disks and heads makes them very fast as both a primary storage method and as a back-up system for large amounts of information, even entire networks of computers. (See Figure 6.6.)

Disk arrays are excellent for capturing video because they can receive large amounts of data very quickly. This is particularly important to multimedia because if there is any delay or error in data transfer at any point during video capture, the entire transfer can be ruined.

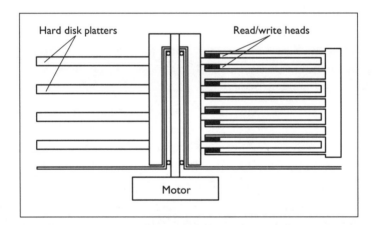

Figure 6.6 *Disk arrays*

Removable Media and Other Storage Devices

All data storage devices serve the same purpose as hard drives: store information and allow access to that information when requested. They all also have very similar considerations: access time and storage capacity. Each device, however, has advantages that the others do not; these distinct characteristics make them useful for different purposes.

Although alternate storage mechanisms may have advantages, there are trade-offs. One storage device may have tremendous capacity but be terribly slow in data retrieval. Another storage device may be portable but be very limited in capacity. Be clear on everything that concerns the operation of your chosen storage mechanism before you make a final decision.

Optical Drives

On Function

Optical drives (also called Magneto-Optical or MO drives) use laser technology to encode and retrieve information. This is the same technology that encodes the CD-ROMs that are used for games or audio; the difference here is that you can rewrite and erase the disks as often as you choose. The main benefits of optical drives are large capacity, portability, and, like audio CDs, durability of the disks. They are best used to store and archive large amounts of data and to master projects for CD-ROM. (See Figure 6.7.)

Figure 6.7 *Optical drives*

Best Media for Shipping

If you are looking for a reliable method to ship data through the mail, optical disks are the best choice. The disks are made of the same materials as CD-ROM and are very resistant to shock damage. Because they are impervious to magnetic fields, they can pass through electronic scanning devices and be stored beside other packages that may have magnetic elements in them. Optical discs also store large amounts of data so you can avoid shipping multiple disks.

Your concerns in buying an optical drive are the same as those for hard disk drives: fast access times and large capacity. Prediction update isn't an issue with optical drives because optical disks are not as vulnerable to failure as hard disks are. At the time this book was written, access times ranged from 19 to 75 milliseconds. Capacities vary depending upon the capacity of the disks with which the drive is designed to work.

Optical drives are increasing in popularity and are quickly becoming the industry standard in mass storage. The general industry opinion is that optical drives will eventually replace magnetic disk drives as the standard in fixed drives. Their major pitfall is that they are very slow in comparison to magnetic hard disks, which makes them impractical for primary data storage and retrieval in multimedia work.

Your information is stored on a disk that is very similar to an audio CD and can be removed from the drive. This serves two purposes.

* Portability—Your data can go with you to other computers that are equipped with a compatible optical drive.

* You aren't limited to the capacity of a single disk. For example, you may have an optical drive that works with disks that can store 650M of data. When you fill one up, you can simply insert another disk and have another 650M of free space.

Optical drives are the perfect way to develop multimedia projects that will be distributed on CD-ROM. CD-ROM playback is different from video tape playback, or even hard disk playback, so projects developed for CD-ROM require special preparation. Basically, if you can make your game or interactive documentary work on an optical drive, then you can make it work on CD-ROM. Conveniently, you can also bring the optical disc that holds the project to the service bureau that will publish your CD-ROM. Using another storage format will require that you rely heavily on special software that emulates the playback of a CD-ROM as well as trust that you are using the proper settings in your multimedia programs.

On Technology

The optical disk is made of a magnetically sensitive metal that is sandwiched in a plastic coating. The laser passes over areas of the disk and fires a highly concentrated beam at a portion of the disk. The heat from the laser liquefies the area.

While the metal is liquefied, an electromagnet passes over the area with a positive or negative charge. The atoms in the liquefied area orient themselves according to the charge and convert to a positively or negatively charged area. When the liquefied area of the disk solidifies again (which happens very quickly), it retains the positive or negative charge, in effect becoming a magnet. The laser later reads the information by reflecting differently off negative and positive areas. (See Figure 6.8.)

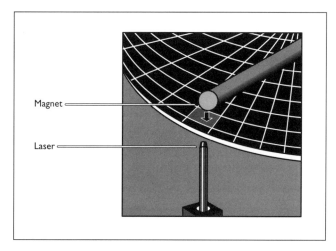

Magnet

Laser

Figure 6.8 *The laser in the optical drive*

Erasing an area of an optical disk is much the same as erasing a magnetic disk. A notation is put into the disk's inventory of contents, FAT. The notation indicates that the "erased" area of the disk is available for new information. When you write new information to that area of the disk, the laser simply melts the area, and the electromagnet recharges it.

Optical disks are the most stable form of data storage in microcomputers because the configuration of the atoms is changed. The only way to change the charges is to melt the metal again, a magnet alone won't do it. As a result optical disks are impervious to magnetic fields. The speed setback is due to the extra steps of melting, charging, and then verifying the charges of the disk, as opposed to a magnetic disk, which simply charges an area, and then verifies the charge.

On Care and Crashing

If you have problems with an optical disk drive, it is probably due to dust or some type of smudge on the surface of the disk. The obstruction prevents the laser from striking an area on the disk. This, and actually moving the drive, can cause the laser to misread the data, or to *skip*.

The solution to skipping due to motion is obvious: Don't move the drive while it is in operation. You can wipe dust from the disks with a clean dry cloth or with a cleaning solution that is available from the same places where you can buy audio CDs. Other than this, you don't need to do much to maintain an optical drive. Just keep it in a dust-free, dry environment; clean your disks periodically; and use an optical head cleaning kit like what you would use for an audio CD player once a month, depending on you usage.

Removable Disk Drives

On Function

Removable drives work the same way that fixed hard drives do except that the disk your information is stored on can be removed from the drive. In the case of cartridge drives, the entire mechanism—read/write head and disk—is in a cartridge that is inserted in a carriage connected to the computer. Removable drives can transport and store large files and large amounts of data.

Removable hard drives are just as fast as fixed drives, and their storage capacity is determined by the limitations of the individual disks. Some may work with 44 or 88M disks; others will work with 150 or 250M disks. Removable drives can be used in place of fixed drives as your main storage space, but this presents several limitations that you should consider.

One limitation is on capacity. You are constrained by the amount of data that a single disk can hold. Presently, no disks are large enough for multimedia files. Ideally, you should have at least 1G of storage on a fixed drive. You can get away with less, but as you become more adept with multimedia you will definitely need more space. You can't get that level of storage capacity on removable disks; it simply isn't available. You should use removable drives to back up, transport, or store your files so you can erase them from your main drive.

The other limitation is system software. System software translates, directs, and presents all of the activity in your computer. Your computer is useless to you without system software, so it must have access to the software at all times. It is not recommended to use a removable drive in place of a fixed drive, because you must locate your system software on one of the disks, and you cannot remove the disk from the drive once the computer is started. Being unable to remove the disk defeats the purpose of a removable disk drive.

N O T E

If you are considering a removable disk drive, be clear on what disks will work with your drive. SyQuest disks work with SyQuest drives, but not with Bernoulli drives. Also, be certain that you know what disks your drive can read and write to. A Bernoulli drive that is designed to work with 150M cartridges can read, but cannot write, to the smaller 44M Bernoulli cartridges. The same drive designed for 150M cartridges can read and write to smaller 90M cartridges, but the 90M drives can neither read nor write to 150M disks. These examples are not unique, so look for these types of issues in the drives that you are considering. It is recommended to use an 88M SyQuest drive that can also work with 44M cartridges because this is the most predominantly used removable media for the Mac.

Disk compatibility is an issue only if you plan to take your data where they may not have a compatible drive or if you plan to use someone else's disks. Also, if you buy an older drive, new or used, it may be on its way to becoming obsolete and disks for those drives may no longer be made. This consideration is not important if all you plan to do is back up and store your files. You should, however, contact service bureaus and anyone else you plan to trade information with and find out what they use before your buy anything.

SyQuest

SyQuest drives are the most popular removable drives on the market. Presently individual disks do not have as much capacity as Bernoulli disks, but their well-established base in the Macintosh world more than makes up for the smaller capacity. (See Figure 6.9.)

You can also be certain that a service bureau, or anyone else using a removable disk drive, will have a SyQuest drive of some sort; you can't be as certain about a Bernoulli drive which was originally designed for IBM/compatibles and is much better established in that arena.

SyQuest manufactures the mechanism inside the hard drive and is sold under many different names. In other words, many companies sell drives under their own name that will work with SyQuest disks. The internal components of the drive are built by SyQuest; all the selling company does is provide the casing and the power supply that helps it operate. The company you choose to buy from will provide the other services such as repair and warranty, so choosing a reliable company is still important.

Figure 6.9 *SyQuest drives*

BERNOULLI

Bernoulli drives are manufactured by Iomega Corporation and are very reliable. Although not as widely used as SyQuest mechanisms in the Macintosh world, they are an excellent choice for archiving and storing files that do not need to be transported elsewhere. (See Figure 6.10.) None the less, you will probably need a SyQuest drive to transfer data among other Macintosh systems, because SyQuest is the defacto standard for the Mac.

Bernoulli drives will write to and read only Bernoulli disks, so you are limited to available Bernoulli drives to retrieve your information. Bernoulli drives are not prevalent in the Macintosh environment; therefore, you should make sure that anyone with whom you plan to trade data has a Bernoulli drive that can read your disks. The reliability and size of individual disks makes Bernoulli an excellent choice for data backup and the archiving of information that doesn't necessarily need to be transported.

On Technology

SyQuest drives function the same way as fixed drives, but the disk is in a cartridge and is removable. An aluminum alloy disk is coated with a magnetically sensitive metal. When the cartridge is inserted, a protective lid moves aside and exposes the disk to an electromagnetic device that reads and writes to it. (See Figure 6.11.)

Figure 6.10 *Bernoulli drives*

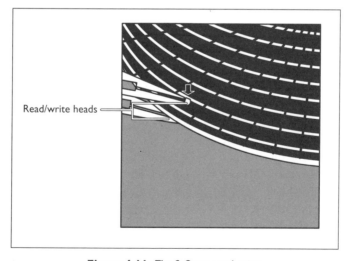

Read/write heads

Figure 6.11 *The SyQuest mechanism*

On the other hand, Bernoulli drives store data magnetically on two flexible plastic disks that are similar to the disks found in floppy disks, only they are larger. The disks are positioned one over the other in a cartridge that is inserted in the drive through an opening in the front. These disks are coated with a magnetically sensitive metal that allows an electromagnetic head to record information on them through positive and negative charges.

There are two read/write heads positioned in the drive—one facing the top disk, the other facing the bottom. When the disks spin in the drive, air moves swiftly between the plastic disks and the read/write heads. This swiftly moving air produces a low-pressure area that pulls the area of the flexible disk directly beneath the read/write head upward. This aerodynamic effect is called the *Bernoulli effect* and is the drive's namesake. (See Figure 6.12.)

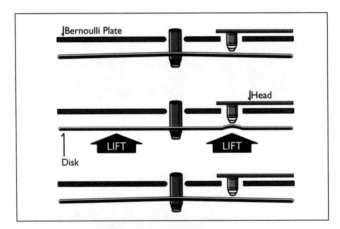

Figure 6.12 *Bernoulli: drive and effect*

The Bernoulli effect brings two benefits to this drive. First, the disk is drawn closer to the head reducing the possibility of misread information. Second, the low-pressure area is present and draws the disk to the head as long as the drive is spinning. This means that gravity won't affect the drive, making Bernoulli drives impervious to shock, even when moved while operating.

Cartridge Drives

On Function

Cartridge drives, like those manufactured by Mountain Gate, are a combination of a removable disk and a portable hard drive. The actual hard disk and drive, including the read/write head, are built into a cartridge that can be removed from a carriage. The carriage is attached to the computer through the SCSI port. The arrangement is somewhat like a car stereo and a Benzi box. (See Figure 6.13.)

Figure 6.13 *Cartridge drive*

You would use a cartridge drive if you needed a great deal of security in your information. They are available in variable sizes so they can be used as your main fixed drive as well. Your concerns in a cartridge drive are the same as those for a fixed hard drive: capacity and access time.

Cartridge drives are somewhat rare so they aren't a good choice if you need to transport information or trade it with someone else. The cartridge carries the mechanism but requires a compatible carriage to operate. Cartridge drives are also bulky and heavy compared to other removable media and even small portable hard drives. Their only practical purpose is if you must remove all data from your computer, as might be necessary in securities, military, or government work. If you want to keep your multimedia work absolutely private, then a cartridge drive is a good choice.

On Care and Crashing

Cartridge drives are threatened by magnetism and dust. Because the cartridge is portable, you must be conscious of anything that may give off a magnetic field. Dust can get into the carriage and onto the contacts that connect the drive to the carriage. You can use compressed air to clean out the carriage.

Digital Audio Tape (DAT) and 8mm Tape Back-Up Systems

On Function

Tape back-up drives store very large amounts of data using the same technology as video and audio tape. They are very slow in comparison to other storage methods because the information is stored on tapes in a linear manner. In other words, the drive must fast forward or rewind to any given part of the tape, as opposed to disk-based drives, which have an arm that can randomly locate any portion of the disk. The benefit of using a tape drive is the ability to store large amounts of information at relatively low expense. (See Figure 6.14.)

Figure 6.14 *Tape back-up systems*

Digital audio and video tapes are much easier to come across than SyQuest or Bernoulli cartridges because you can buy them in just about any store that sells stereo equipment or CDs. They are also less expensive. Consequently, tape drives are a cost-effective method of storing your information. Their slow speed is their only downfall and ultimately what limits them to archiving information. Tape drives are excellent for multimedia because many service bureaus recognized their cost-effectiveness and convenience in transporting multimedia-size files. As a result, many service bureaus are likely to have tape drives. Exabyte manufactures tape drives that are particularly popular in the service bureau circuit.

On Technology

Tape backup drives operate much the same way as audio and video tape recorders. A plastic strip coated with a magnetically sensitive metal is spooled around two spindles in a cassette. The spindles turn, passing the tape over a stationery (*linear scan*) or rotating (*helical scan*) electromagnetic read/write head. Helical scan tape mechanisms are quicker and more efficient than linear scan mechanisms because the head contains two read and two write heads. (See Figures 6.15 and 6.16.)

Figure 6.15 *Linear scan tape drives*

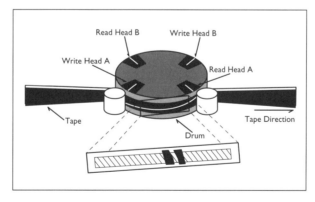

Figure 6.16 *Helical scan tape drives*

The major distinction between a tape back-up drive and an audio or video tape recorder is that the tape back-up drive is *designed* to be a computer peripheral and offers very precise control over the positioning of the tape. The drive contains memory that keeps an inventory of the contents of a tape. This allows the tape to be recorded and erased without endangering any of the information you already have on it.

On Care and Crashing

In addition to the care concerns outlined in the beginning of this chapter, there are other care issues to consider for tape systems. The cassettes you use in a tape back-up drive are no different than the tapes you use in a video or audio deck, so you should care for them the same way you would care for ordinary tapes. Keep them out of extreme temperatures and don't directly touch the magnetic tape strip. You can clean the drive head with the same head cleaner you can find in a video hardware dealership.

Tapes can tangle in the cassette, so this can also be a cause of a crash. Use the same caution in untangling the tape as you would an ordinary video or audio tape. If a tape is creased, it will affect the data on it, the same way creases on audio or video tapes will cause interference. The major difference in a crease on a back-up tape cassette is that the data lost in the crease can affect whether the data before and after it can be read at all.

If you get a crease in a tape, transfer the data little by little to your fixed drive, and then to another tape. Dump the creased tape when you're done. Transferring data in this way is tedious, but you'll be happy you did it.

Floppy Disks

On Function

Floppy disks are the most common method of storing and transporting data for the Macintosh. But their low capacity (1.4 M) and their slow access time (several times that of a hard drive) rule out their use for multimedia projects. Every Macintosh comes equipped with a floppy disk drive, which makes these disks a convenient method for transporting small graphics or other files related to your multimedia work. (See Figure 6.17.)

For larger files you probably will need some type of compression software such as StuffIt or Compact Pro. Compression software allows you to reduce file sizes by 60% or more. You can then divide the compressed file into smaller sections that can be stored on separate disks. When you reach your destination, you can use the same compression software to recombine the separate files and decompress the data to its original form. Albeit inconvenient and involved, it's the least expensive and most accessible way to transport and store multimedia documents.

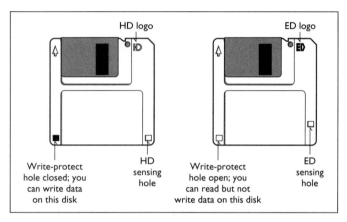

Figure 6.17 *Floppy disks*

Floptical Disk Drives

On Function

As the name suggests, Floptical disk drives combine the convenience of floppy disks with optical laser technology. The disks are in cartridges that are the same size and shape as floppy disks, but they can contain much more information. This technology will probably replace floppy disks as the standard in small data storage and transport. (See Figure 6.18.)

Floptical drives look very much like external floppy disk drives, but can only read floptical disks. All floptical disks use the same technology, but as disk capacity improves today's floptical drives may not be able to read tomorrow's disks. This is a very popular technology. When speaking to the manufacturer of a floptical drive, inquire about the compatibility of upcoming drives and current disks.

Floptical drives are much slower than removable disk drives and even floppy drives; they were not meant to compete on that level. They were designed to be a much higher-capacity floppy disk. They are useful to multimedia because the technology accounts for the larger file size of day-to-day computer work. With a single floptical disk, you can transport a graphic file that would normally require file compression software and several floppy disks.

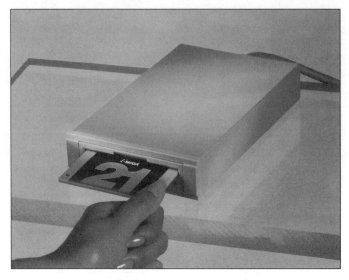

Figure 6.18 *Floptical disk drives*

On Technology (Both Floppy and Floptical)

Floptical disks and floppy disks both use the same type of plastic disk to store information. A magnetically sensitive metal coats the disk, and an electromagnetic read/write head encodes data on this metal coating. The optical technology comes from a laser that precisely positions the read/write head allowing it to be more precise and capable of recording finer tracks of information. (See Figure 6.19.)

The disk has a concentric magnetic track where information is recorded. Beside these tracks are concentric positioning tracks that the laser uses to pinpoint the location of data. The magnetic head follows the laser positioning to locate the position of data.

The laser is necessary because of the large amount of information that is stored in the same surface area of a conventional floppy disk. Magnetic storage devices are more limited by the physical dimensions of the magnetic head then they are by the amount of data that can be stored on the disk. Using a laser to keep track of the data positioning makes smaller data areas possible, which is what allows more information to be stored on a floptical than on a floppy disk.

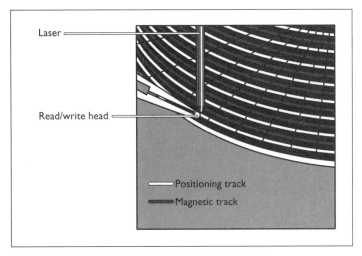

Laser

Read/write head

Positioning track
Magnetic track

Figure 6.19 *Floptical disk mechanism*

N O T E

Floptical disks are not very sturdy, and the plastic disk can damage easily. Like floppy disks, if data are corrupted on a floptical the drive will probably not allow the data to be mounted. Never rely on floptical disks alone to store your data. Either keep your files on a separate back-up disk or keep a copy on your hard drive. As an added measure, use a floppy disk cleaner frequently to keep things clean.

Monitors

Your monitor is the component of your computer system that looks like a television set and displays the activity inside your computer. You could probably argue that no one component of the multimedia system is most important to the work, but the monitor is the most important component to you. (See Figure 7.1.)

For multimedia your greatest concern in a monitor is the quality of the image it displays. A quality image is more than just a good looking image on-screen. It also includes an accurate representation of your graphics and text in both dimension and color. Your projects will be traveling to other computers or will be output to video tape or CD-ROM; consequently, your control over accuracy is ultimately important. The quality of image that your monitor displays is determined by its resolution and sharpness. Magazines, such as *MacUser* and *MacWorld*, frequently publish benchmark tests that measure the quality of different monitors.

Figure 7.1 *The monitor*

Another concern is the size of the display area. Your display area is called the *desktop*, which is an excellent analogy. The more space you have in your display the more things you can have on it at once without getting cluttered. Large screens make working with large images or with a lot of images at once easier.

You can still work with a small screen, but it may become an annoyance because you must manipulate your software to see the parts of images that aren't visible. Working with a small screen is like having the nice big desktop mentioned above but wearing blinders so you can see only part of the desktop at any one time and must move your head to see anything else. Naturally, large screens are more expensive than small screens; you must find a solution that fits within your budget.

A monitor can be particularly difficult to pick out because so many monitors that can be described in a similar manner are available. Prices can also vary dramatically, further complicating this issue because more money doesn't necessarily mean that your getting a better monitor.

Here are some criteria to help you.

1. Make sure that the monitor works with your Macintosh. Dealers selling to the IBM community as well as to other markets often advertise in the same places as Macintosh resellers. Because some may not even sell computers, you can't make an assumption based upon association. Also, be sure to ask about how the monitor connects to your computer; some monitors may require a special interface to work with your Macintosh and will add to the expense. (How monitors are connected to the Macintosh is detailed later in this chapter.)

2. Meet technical requirements; then price shop. The details outlined here will help. Be sure that the monitor provides correct resolution, color depth, and a comfortable display size. Color depth is the only specification in a monitor that can possibly be upgraded. Make a point to know your options.

3. Look at the monitor that you plan to buy. Many monitors display a slightly different image even if they are technically identical. It's really a matter of personal preference, not entirely unlike shopping for a television set. Many dealers have display units on a showroom floor so you can compare them. You may not be able to find a place that has the exact monitors that you are considering set up side by side, but you can at least get an idea. Because you will be staring at this monitor for hours at a time, you should be happy with it. Once you've identified your favorite monitor, buy it from whoever offers you the best deal, including mail order.

Resolution

Resolution is measured in dots per inch (dpi). The *dots* refer to *pixels*, the tiny squares that make up the display image. The higher the resolution of a monitor, the sharper the image. Do not confuse resolution with the screens pixel count or pixel aspect ratio (detailed later in this section).

Most software developed for the Macintosh is designed to equate one actual inch with 72 pixels (or dots) on-screen. This standard is used because the original Macintosh computers had screens with 72 dpi. On a 72-dpi monitor, an inch on-screen will be an inch on paper.

Although resolutions over 72 dpi produce sharper images because more elements make up the picture, they also show items as smaller then they actually are. The screen images are sharper, but the standard between display and output is lost. The graphic on the 72-dpi screen will print or output to video at the displayed size; the other screen will output a larger image then what is displayed.

Multimedia programs allow for the precise control of image size. For example, an image that you have created for video tape is 640×480 pixels in screen dimensions. The image looks smaller on a screen that has a resolution of 82 dpi than it does on a screen that has 72 dpi. That's because the higher-resolution 82 dpi screen has the pixels "packed together" more than the lower-resolution 72 dpi screen. The computer, however, doesn't care about the resolution of the monitor. It stores the image size as 640x480 pixels—regardless of the monitor's resolution.

You should also be aware that most computer monitors have a screen resolution of 72 dpi. If you are working with a monitor that has a higher resolution, you run the risk of producing work that will look different on most other computers. Many monitors with high resolution have the ability to emulate 72 dpi. You can switch between the two settings to be certain that you are getting the screen composition that you desire and still benefit from having the increased screen area.

Pixel Count (Pixel Aspect Ratio)

The *pixel count* identifies the number of pixels on the screen. It represents the width and height of the screen in pixels. For example the standard 13-inch Apple monitor has a pixel count of 640×480. The pixel count, in conjunction with the screen's dpi, actually determines the quality and size of your monitor's active display area. (See Figure 7.2.)

Color Depth

Color depth refers to the number of colors that the screen can display at one time. This number is measured in bits, as in 1 bit, 2 bit, 4 bit, 8 bit, 16 bit, and 24 bit. These bits are the same units used to measure memory and storage in the other components of the computer. Because the computer is based on a binary system, 2 raised to the power of your monitor's color bit value determines the number of colors that the screen displays. (See Table 7.1) For example, an 8-bit display is capable of displaying 256 colors at once; 2 to the power of 8. (2 to the power of 8 can also be written as 2^8. To determine the value, multiply the base number in this case 2, by itself the same number of times as the *power* or exponent, in this case 8. This could also be written in mathematical longhand as $2\times2\times2\times2\times2\times2\times2\times2 = 256$.

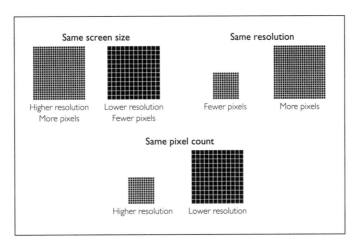

Figure 7.2 *Resolution and pixel count*

Table 7.1 *Bits of color*

COLOR BIT	VALUE	NUMBER OF COLORS AND SHADES OF GRAY
I Bit	2^1	Black and White
2 Bit	2^2	4 Colors and Grays
4 Bit	2^4	16 Colors and Grays
8 Bit	2^8	256 Colors and Grays
16 Bit	2^{16}	65,536
24 Bit	2^{24}	16,777,216

The color capability of your monitor determines the quality of the graphics that you can work with and display. The larger the number of colors, the finer the detail of shading. The world presents our eyes with shades of color that are affected by light; software uses these numerous, subtle changes in color to simulate perspective, dimension, texture, and anything else real.

You can still create highly sophisticated color graphics without having a 24-bit monitor, but you may have difficulty judging whether you are getting the results you want. If you plan to work with three-dimensional rendering programs, video, or photographs, then you need high-level color to be truly effective. You should consider a monitor arrangement that displays at least-8 bit color and can eventually be upgraded to 24-bit color.

Third-Party Monitors and Upgrading Color

Third Party Monitors (manufactured by companies other than Apple), typically will not operate through the built-in video port in Macintosh computers. Third party monitors also tend to have larger display areas that are not directly supported by the CPU. These monitors need to be connected through NuBus cards that connect to the computer through the NuBus slots. NuBus slots are detailed in *Chapter 5*. The NuBus card provides the additional support needed to display to the larger area. (See Figures 7.3 and 7.4.)

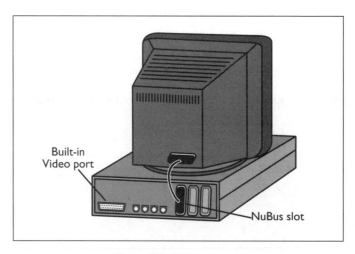

Figure 7.3 *NuBus monitors*

Upgrading color means increasing the number of colors that the monitor can display. The multimedia Macintosh offers two ways to upgrade color: Video

RAM and color NuBus expansion cards. The specifications of your computer determine how you can upgrade color.

Figure 7.4 *Color expansion card and monitor*

Video RAM Upgrades

In older Macintosh computers the RAM responsible for the display is part of the same RAM that is responsible for running the computer and the software. In newer Macintosh computers, Random Access Memory Single In-line Memory Modules (RAM SIMMs) are dedicated to managing the monitor and the display of color. Increasing the amount of this type of RAM in your computer increases the color capability of your monitor.

Video RAM (VRAM) manages the display of monitors that can be connected to the computer through the built-in video port. This may limit the number of different monitors that you can choose from because they must meet this fundamental criteria. If the monitor that you choose does not operate through the built-in video port, then it probably works with a NuBus interface.

NuBus Upgrades

Color for third-party monitors and monitors that cannot be upgraded any further through the built-in port with VRAM must be upgraded through NuBus expansion cards. These cards also have an on-board accelerator that completely frees the processor and RAM from the burden of built-in video. Your monitor can now display the enhanced color without slowing down the display's speed.

Display Area

Screen size and display area are two different issues. *Screen size* is the number that usually is advertised by manufacturers and resellers; it corresponds to the diagonal distance across the screen from one corner of the plastic bevel (frame) to the other. This distance includes a black area that displays nothing at all.

Display area is determined by the pixel aspect ratio and the screen resolution described earlier. For example, let's say two monitors are advertised, one with a 13-inch screen and the other with a 14-inch screen. Upon further examination you discover that both screens have a pixel aspect ratio of 640×480 and a screen resolution of 72 dpi; the 14-inch monitor offers nothing more except perhaps greater expense. The only apparent reason Apple did this was to give the buyer the impression that he or she is getting something more. Your only protection is to know better.

This doesn't mean that you shouldn't consider the 14-inch monitor; there may be other differences that make it the better choice. You should simply be aware that they are technically identical with regard to display area, in spite of screen size. Though magazine advertisements are useful for keeping up with how product releases and current prices, you should never rely upon advertised screen sizes to describe the active display area accurately. Ask for the pixel aspect ratio and the screen resolution and do your own math.

Multiple Displays in the Same Computer

One Macintosh computer can function with several different monitors at once. Use a combination of built-in video and NuBus monitors, or NuBus monitors alone, to accomplish multiple displays. Each monitor can have its own interface with the computer, and each interface can have its own processing power so that it does not affect the overall performance of the computer.

Using more than one monitor generates a desktop that is continuous across all of the displays. This means that you can move the mouse cursor past the edge of one screen and it will continue to travel across the display of the next monitor. It's like having one large desktop with adjacent windows positioned over it.

Using a part of the system software of your Macintosh called the *Monitors control panel*, you can select which monitor will be your start-up monitor. This is the monitor on which your computer will place all of the pull-down menus and hard drive icons when you turn the computer on. You can select any of the monitors that are connected to your computer for this purpose.

This type of arrangement can be useful for organizing your work. You can have a high-quality color monitor that you use for working on graphics. You could also have a low-cost black-and-white monitor for your other programs and as a place to keep the tools that you use in a graphics program. In this way the tool palettes don't clutter up useful space on your color monitor. (See Figure 7.5.)

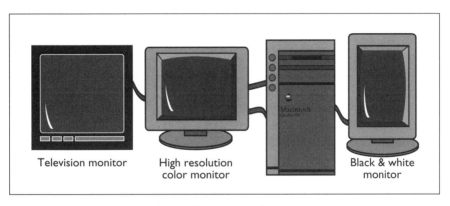

Television monitor   High resolution   Black & white
                      color monitor   monitor

Figure 7.5 *Multiple monitors in the same computer*

Connecting a regular television to your computer is particularly useful to multimedia. The newer Macs, such as the Quadra 840 AV, have video output jacks that allow you to connect a television directly into the computer. However, for Macintosh computers that do not have this capability, you will need a digital to analog transfer card, such as the TruVision Nuvista +. Connecting a television to your computer allows you to preview what your graphics will look like on video tape when they are converted to a signal that the video can record. A television's display is different from that of a computer monitor; therefore, connecting to a television along with a high-resolution computer monitor can help you be more productive. Using a television in this way, you can be certain that you are producing what you want while you can still change it.

On Technology

The image on a computer monitor begins with a digital description of what should be displayed. The program you are working with creates this digital description. Once the display has been calculated, it is transferred to a portion of RAM that is reserved for it.

In earlier Macintosh computers, the RAM that is used for the display is a part of the same RAM used for your programs; consequently, it tends to be slow. On newer Macintosh computers, VRAM is dedicated to receiving and storing the digital display description generated by your program. The same amount of RAM is used for each pixel as is indicated by the color level of the monitor, so 8 bits of RAM are used for each pixel in a monitor that displays 8-bit color or 256 colors at a time.

Once the display has been transferred to the VRAM or the RAM on a color expansion NuBus card, it is converted to a signal that can be displayed on a monitor. This is accomplished through video circuitry that is built into to the motherboard or on the expansion card. From this point it is ready to travel to the monitor through the connecting port. (See Figure 7.6.)

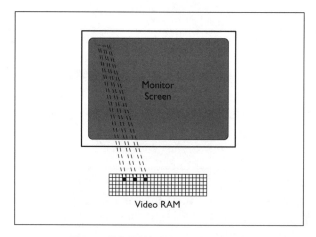

Figure 7.6 *RAM and the video display*

Inside the monitor, the display signal is sent to a mechanism called a *cathode ray gun*. This cathode ray gun fires *electrons* (charged atomic particles) at the back of the screen. Magnets inside the picture tube help to guide each electron beam so that it hits a specific part of the screen.

The back of the screen is covered with a phosphor coating that glows when it is struck by the electron beam. This glow produces the image on-screen. The electron beam travels from left to right, line by line, across each pixel of the screen, starting from the top-left corner and ending in the bottom-right corner. When it reaches the bottom, it starts again from the top-left corner. The process repeats so quickly that the eye can barely detect it. (See Figure 7.7.)

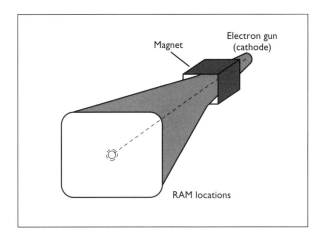

Figure 7.7 *The cathode ray gun*

In black-and-white monitors, each pixel receives only 1 bit of information. That information indicates whether a pixel is lit up for white or left alone for black. So the cathode ray fires only at the pixels that are going to be white.

A color monitor is somewhat more complex. As mentioned earlier, there is an equal number of bits in RAM for each pixel as is indicated by the monitor's color depth. This information is separated into channels of red, green, or blue. Each color channel then continues on to its own cathode ray gun, which fires at a pixel. Each color also has its own phosphor coating on the screen. The different intensities of red, green, and blue combine to create the different colors visible on the screen.

The different complexities between black-and-white and color monitors explain why color monitors are more expensive and heavier as well as why some Macintosh computers can display to a large black-and-white monitor but only smaller color monitors. Now it should be clear why expansion cards that take on the burden of processing the screen image improve the performance of the computer.

NOTE

All color monitors can display in black and white, grayscale, and lower levels of color. If you set the computer to these lower levels when appropriate, then your computer will run faster. Using these lower settings may be helpful when you are developing a project and are just working out ideas.

Grayscale

Grayscale is a monitor performance mode that displays multiple shades of gray. It is faster than color but slower than black and white. Grayscale is useful for work with black-and-white photography and for speeding up processing when you are working out a project.

Grayscale monitors are capable of displaying detail and shading much the same way that a color monitor can, only with varying intensities of gray. Black and white can accomplish detail and shading only by varying the number of black pixels in an area that simulates darker patches. Grayscale is a good median between the quality image of a color monitor and the speed and low cost of a black-and-white monitor.

Most images that are displayed in grayscale need only 8 bit video, which provides 256 shades of gray, to be effective. Color monitors can display grayscale, and there are dedicated grayscale monitors that cost less than color monitors. Use this mode to preview graphic shading if you don't have a high-level color display. However, it isn't recommended to use a grayscale monitor as your primary monitor because color is extremely important to multimedia.

The Difference Between a Computer Monitor and a TV

Computer monitors and televisions are physically quite similar. They both employ a cathode ray gun that fires an electron beam at a phosphor coating that glows and produces the screen image. The differences are in the treatment of color and the screen's resolution.

Televisions are designed to display a signal that is not digital in origin and is, therefore, not as precise as a computer's image. This signal is based upon the NTSC signal, which was named after the National Television Standards Committee that established the transmission standard in the United States and affiliated countries. The NTSC standard was established for black and white trasmission in the early 1940s, the standard for color was established in the early 1950s. As detailed in *Chapter 11*, the transmission standards in other parts of the world are called PAL and SECAM.

This standard signal combines the red, green, and blue signals into one signal, reducing the complexity and cost of the mechanism needed. The lower color capability and resolution of the screens allows for an adequate television image but would not suffice for computer work. This is why television sets are so much less expensive than comparably sized computer monitors. This is also why connecting a regular television to your computer along with your high-resolution monitor is useful. You can see how the lower resolution and color will affect you graphic images if you are producing for video.

On Eye Strain and Operating Conditions

Every time the cathode ray guns in a monitor display the screen image, it temporarily blanks out and then reappears. This is called the *screen refresh*. Even though it is almost entirely imperceptible, the eye detects it, and the muscles in your eye respond slightly every time it happens. This continuous eye movement can produce fatigue and potential loss of visual acuity due to strain.

Remember your mother telling you to get away from the television set? She was right. The other type of potentially harmful effect that your monitor can have is glare, which can have the same effect as staring at a light for too long. Because you will be spending a great deal of time staring at a computer screen in multimedia work, it's important to be aware of what can happen. There are simple ways to reduce the risk of both situations.

You can prevent damage due to strain simply by being aware that your eyes are getting a mini work-out while you are looking at the screen. Like any other muscles in the body, your eye muscles can't do this for extended periods. Protect your eyes and take frequent rests from the computer. Otherwise, colors will appear distorted and you will lose the ability to perceive your work clearly.

Glare screens that reduce the glare that a monitor puts out are available. Glare screens are placed over the monitor screen. If you use one, be aware that it changes the way colors and some graphics appear on-screen.

Keep a safe distance away from the monitor (2 feet) and set the contrast and brightness controls to a comfortable setting. Some people even recommend controlling the room lighting to the extent of taping down switches when you have your optimum condition. Whatever you do, be conscious that you will spend a lot of time at your computer and that it can have a harmful effect on you if you aren't careful.

Your eyes and the monitor will never be as accurate as the software and the computer. Trust the settings that you place in your software and be sure they are precise. Computer-related injuries are a relatively new phenomenon; consequently, a great deal of information isn't available just yet, but you should still take advantage of what is already known.

On Care

You care for computer monitors the same way you care for television sets. Dust them and clean them with the same household cleansers used for windows. First, spray the cleanser onto the cloth that you are using to clean. If you spray it directly into the screen, it may trail down past the edge and into the monitor.

Another thing that can damage your monitor is screen burn-in. This occurs when the phosphor in your monitor permanently shows a faint display, even when it is turned off. Burn-in is caused by having the monitor on for too long with only one display that doesn't change.

You can prevent burn-in by not leaving your monitor on and idle for long periods of time or by graying down the screen, which entails setting the monitors brightness to its minimum. If you use a modem that you like to leave on all the time or work with three-dimensional artwork that may require long periods, even days, to render a single image or animation, then turn your monitor off while you are away from it. This will also speed up the computer's processing.

You can also use software called *screen savers*, which produce a moving image on-screen if the computer is left idle for a predetermined period of time. When you do something, such as move the mouse or press a key on the keyboard, the computer "wakes up", the screen saver disappears, and you are back in whatever program you were working with before. Make sure the screen saver you select is compatible with the multimedia software that you plan to use; some will prevent your software from functioning when the screen saver activates.

Input Devices

Input devices are the tools you use to interact with your computer and software. They allow you to type text, enter numbers, draw graphics, and control the other devices connected to your computer. The most common input devices used for the Macintosh computer are the keyboard and the mouse.

Input devices are connected to the computer through the Apple desktop bus (ADB) port in the back of the computer. The ADB port leads directly to the computer's bus, which is the nerve center and main data pathway of the computer. When you press a key on the keyboard or move a mouse on a pad it sends information along the bus, which causes changes on the computer screen and can make software react. The bus is detailed in *Chapter 5*.

ADB devices (input devices) can be *daisy-chained*, which means that one can be connected to another. The first in the chain, usually the keyboard, is connected directly to the computer. The only exception is the mouse that is included with your Macintosh, which does not have an outlet for other ADB devices to be connected to because it requires a full range of motion to work efficiently. Daisy-chained ADB devices all send their information through the devices ahead of them along the chain to the computer. (See Figure 8.1.)

For example, the keyboard is connected to the ADB port of the computer and the mouse is connected to the ADB port of the keyboard. Since nothing can be connected to the mouse, an ADB splitter produces two ports from the keyboard allowing the mouse and a digitizer tablet to be connected to it. More devices can be connected from the digitizer tablet on.

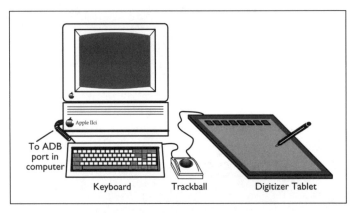

Figure 8.1 *Daisy-chained ADB devices*

As already mentioned, the keyboard and the mouse are the most common input devices, all others are variations of these two basic forms. For example, a digitizing tablet allows you to use a pen on a flat panel to perform the same functions as a mouse, but with the free-form control of a pen or pencil. You can work just as effectively with a mouse and with a keyboard that has a numeric keypad as you can with a digitizer tablet. A digitizer tablet like the Wacom tablet will, however, provide you with greater control and precision when using graphics programs—especially paint programs such as Fractal Design Painter. (Numeric keypads are detailed in this section.)

Some input devices are not used for the development of multimedia projects but are useful for the presentation of your project. For example, a touch screen can allow someone to use a presentation kiosk and navigate through your information simply by touching the screen. Another example is a bar code reader, which can be swept over a bar code so that it instantly enters information into the program. At a trade show, the bar codes could contain vital contact information; you could also encode security information if your project must be accessible only to a few people. An infra-red remote mouse is also useful for presentations because it can control the computer's pointer from a distance. It works just like a regular mouse, but you don't need to work right in front of the computer, where you may be obscuring the view. (See Figures 8.2 and 8.3.) Keeping these types of devices in mind can help you to create very effective and streamlined interactive multimedia work.

Figure 8.2 *Alternate input: touch screens*

Keyboards

The Apple keyboard is the most fundamental input device for the Macintosh. Some Macintosh computers include one, but you may need to purchase one with the higher-end models.

Standard computer keyboards are designed exactly like the same keyboard used in typewriters. A few additional keys give them greater functionality, but the letters and numbers are organized in the old familiar QWERTY layout.

QWERTY represents the layout of the first six letters from left to right on the top line of a conventional keyboard. There is also a **Shift** key which, when pressed simultaneously with another key, produces the capital of the letter on the face of the key or the character that is printed on the upper half of the key. For example, the **Shift** and **Y** keys produce a capital *Y*, and the **Shift** and **7** keys produce an ampersand (&). If you know how to type, then you can use the standard computer keyboard.

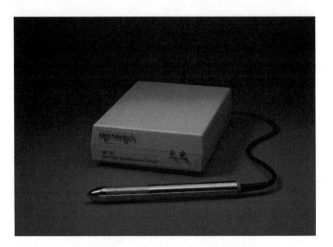

Figure 8.3 *Alternate input: bar code readers*

The Macintosh keyboard also contains several function keys that produce differ-ent preprogrammed results when pressed in combination with other keys. These keys are located in the lower left of most keyboards and on both the lower left and lower right of the main keyboard on some. Two of the control keys are labeled "Control" and "Option"; the **Command** key is labeled with the Apple logo and a symbol that looks like a clover leaf. Specific key combinations using the **Control**, **Option**, **Command**, and **Shift** keys can produce streamlined operation such as quickly saving, opening, and closing files. The function keys (**F1**, **F2**, etc.) along the top of the keyboard can be programmed to execute groups of commands with a single keystroke. The arrow keys, in the "inverted T" layout can be used to move the cursor and graphics small distances on screen. Some keyboards include a built-in numeric keypad on the far right-hand side, but they can also be purchased separately. The key to the top right of the keyboard can be used to turn the computer on in the higher-end models. (See Figures 8.4 and 8.5.)

Figure 8.4 *The Apple adjustable keyboard*

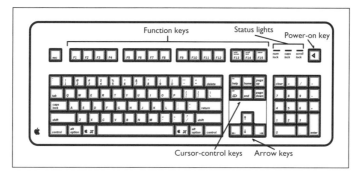

Figure 8.5 *The keyboard layout*

The function that these combination keys play is designed into the programming of the software that you use. Some key combinations are specific to the software, and some are universal to all software. All programs allow some commands to be executed quickly by pressing combinations of keys. The function that a particular combination of keys plays is usually reflected in the pull-down menus of the program.

In drop-down menus, the symbols and letters to the right represent key combinations that execute the command to the left. For example, all software programs have a **Save** command in their Edit menu. When selected, it records a copy of the file that you are working on to the hard drive. Next to the word

Save in the pull-down menu is the key combination **Command-S**. If you press the **Command** key and **S** at the same time, you will save the document. This is true for all Mac programs. (See Figure 8.6.)

File	Edit	View	Inse

New	⌘N
Open...	⌘O
Close	⌘W
Save	⌘S
Save As...	⇧F7
Find File...	
Summary Info...	
Print Preview...	⌘⌥I
Page Setup...	⇧F8
Print...	⌘P
Print Merge...	
Video	
CD-ROM	
Scanners	
Input	
Quit	⌘Q

Figure 8.6 *Key combinations*

In addition, pressing the **Command** key and **N** produces a new file, pressing **Command-O** will open an existing file, and pressing **Command-W** closes an open file.

Key combinations like **Command-S** are consistent throughout different programs. The common ones are detailed in your Macintosh owner's manual; the specialized ones will be detailed in your software's literature. Their purpose is to help streamline the work process. Utility programs like QuicKeys by CE Software allow you to define your own key combinations to expand upon the Macintosh interface in your work environment.

On extended keyboards, you can write a program for the function keys so that they execute any command or combination of commands that you wish. For example, you could write a program so that a single function key performs the same "save" that pressing **Command-S** accomplishes. These user-programmed keys are called *macros* and require a special software program called a *macro editor* to accomplish. They can be extremely useful once you have established a routine in your work and know what would improve your productivity.

Most keyboards also have arrow or cursor keys, which you can use to move the cursor or a graphic small distances on-screen. These keys are typically laid out in a row or in an inverted T with the left, down, and right arrows in a row in that order, and the up arrow positioned directly over the down arrow. These arrow keys are good for the graphics work in multimedia because they are helpful in the fine manipulation of graphics.

Alternates to the keyboard are available for Macintosh computers, but nothing that can serve you too much better. For example, there is a keyboard based upon key combinations to create letters and numbers, like chords in music. (See Figure 8.7.) Conventional keyboards are fine because you are probably already familiar with the layout and speed typing is not an issue to multimedia.

Figure 8.7 *The Bat keyboard*

Many conventional keyboards have ergonomic designs, which can reduce the chances of injury such as carpal tunnel syndrome and other muscular disorders that are caused by bad positioning and repetitive actions such as typing for long periods. The Apple adjustable keyboard is one such keyboard. Using keyboard rests that raise the back of the hand and provide a cushion can also help.

Numeric Keypad

Numeric keypads are used to input numbers; they have a layout similar to that of a calculator. All keyboards have number keys, but a numeric keypad makes entering numbers much easier. These keypads are often built into more elaborate keyboards in an area off to a side. They are also available as separate ADB devices to supplement smaller keyboards and Powerbooks. Because you frequently enter numbers to edit video and animation clips and to create precision graphics, they are useful to multimedia. The extended keyboard comes with a numeric keypad built into it. (See Figure 8.8.)

Figure 8.8 *Numeric keypads*

The Mouse and Other Pointing Devices

ADB Mouse

The mouse makes the Macintosh easy to learn and use. It allows you to manipulate programs simply by pointing at objects and selecting them by pressing the button on the top of the mouse. It has made the computer a tool for everyone, reducing its operation to a simple process of pointing and clicking. For multimedia the mouse has been essential because many of the people who now use computers for multimedia are artists with little or no computer background. (See Figure 8.9.)

Figure 8.9 *The Mouse*

The mouse is a simple tool that operates as a pointing device by controlling a small free-floating arrow on the screen. The form of the actual pointing graphic may vary from program to program, but the overall function in multimedia is the same: to select and manipulate objects.

The mouse registers the movements of a ball that protrudes from a small opening in the bottom. When you move the mouse across a flat surface or mouse pad, a small ball in the mechanism rolls against two rollers, one horizontal, one vertical. When the rollers turn they send a signal to the computer. These signals register how far the mouse has moved in a given direction. The computer then responds by moving the position of the pointer on the screen. The pad that you move the mouse on represents the screen of the monitor except that you use it on a flat, horizontal plane.

Apple manufactures the most commonly used mouse for the Macintosh and ships it with all new computers. Alternatives from other manufacturers are available; they usually vary in ergonomic design or have some other functional difference, such as one mouse that is connected to the computer via an infrared remote. (See Figure 8.10.) The remote feature allows the mouse to be used without the limitation of a connecting cable. Choosing a pointing device for multimedia is really a matter of preference, but the Apple ADB mouse is the most convenient and serves the purpose well.

Figure 8.10 *Variations of the mouse: Infrared remote*

Trackballs

Trackballs are similar to an inverted mouse with a much bigger ball. They are also ADB devices and serve the same function of selecting and moving objects on-screen. The difference is that the ball that rolls against the position-sensitive rollers is exposed through the top and can be moved directly. (See Figure 8.11.)

Figure 8.11 *The trackball*

The major operational advantage that a trackball has over a mouse is precision of movement. The major physical advantage is that it does not need to change position in order to move the cursor. In other words, you need only move the ball in its socket, the rest of the mechanism stays in place. With a trackball, you can work with limited desk space, which makes using the pointer easier across the longer distance of the larger screens preferred for multimedia. One of the greatest benefits of the trackball is that it uses different hand muscles than the mouse, and it requires that you change your hand positioning constantly. This is essential in the prevention of carpal tunnel syndrome—a severe stiffness of the hand muscles that is caused by holding the hands in the same position for too long a period of time.

Digitizer Tablets

Digitizer tablets provide for the functionality of a mouse with the control of a free-form artist's tool. They serve as pointing devices by tracking the movements that you make with a penlike device across a flat plastic panel. The panel has sensors built into it that allow the cursor to be controlled from any point on the surface. These devices are excellent for multimedia because they combine the functionality of a mouse or trackball with the familiarity of a pencil or drawing pen. (See Figure 8.12.)

Figure 8.12 *Digitizer tablets*

The latest digitizer tablets have a pressure-sensitive feature that registers how much pressure is being applied to the pen. Some graphics software takes advantage of this feature, allowing their tools to be affected by pressure. For example, an air-brush tool in a paint program produces a strong wide line with greater pressure and a soft line with less pressure. This feature allows you to use digitizer tablets to simulate more traditional painting and drawing tools.

Pressure sensitivity and freeform technique are not particularly essential to multimedia because the software is designed to work with the mouse and keyboard. There is usually no assumption on the part of the software developer that you will be working with anything else. You should have the same control over multimedia software with the mouse and keyboard as you do with any other kind of input device. Other input devices may provide some advantage, for example Wacom tablets are quite easy to use. They are also precise, and are often bundled with software. However, these are not essential for the operation of multimedia software.

Part III

Multimedia Peripherals

The type of peripherals you choose determines the capability of your multimedia development system. The computer alone can serve only as the central processing unit and storage space as well as a display for your completed projects. Peripherals, however, transform a Macintosh into a multimedia development system.

You can use each peripheral mentioned in this section for all multimedia development. Understanding the purposes of each peripheral will help you know the best place for you to start. Essentially, a multimedia peripheral has a focused function: It brings image or audio into you computer for software manipulation and inclusion into your multimedia work.

Of course, the scope of each peripheral differs in some ways. For example, a scanner brings in images, but only still, single images. Whereas video gives you full motion as well as sound, given the appropriate equipment. Clearly both capture images, but they do so in distinctly different ways.

At first glance scanners may appear to be limited in comparison to video, but in fact they are not. Scanners produce a much clearer image than video does and are therefore the better choice where clarity is an issue for single images. On the other hand, besides offering motion images, video is not bound to the desktop and can "scan" three-dimensional objects. Both items have benefits and limitations that you must be aware of before you make a decision. Once you know what you want to accomplish with your work, and who will be viewing it, then you will be much closer to identifying the peripherals you need.

Buying Peripherals

Basically, the rules for buying peripherals are the same as the rules for buying the computer system itself. Peripherals are marketed in much the same way as hard drives and monitors. You can find them in mail order houses and authorized dealerships or buy them used. The only exception may be video equipment. The video capture interface can be treated as any other peripheral, but the tape decks and cameras are a slightly different story. Video is a complete industry in itself and does not depend upon the popularity of computers for its success.

Fortunately, the differences in buying video equipment work in your favor. The video industry has been around longer and is somewhat more stable than the computer industry; consequently, video equipment doesn't fluctuate or rapidly decrease in value the way that computer equipment can. To introduce video images to your work, all you really need to start with is an analog-to-digital capture card and a video source such as a VCR or video camera. This is all covered in greater detail in the *Chapter 11*.

If you are interested in using video extensively in your system, then you must take into account the fact that there are considerable differences between video and computer equipment. There are also varying degrees of video integration into a multimedia system. *Chapter 11* addresses the differences among the levels of video integration in a multimedia system. It goes into detail on how to digitally manipulate video using *only* computer equipment with a single video source for input and output. The multimedia category that involves a great deal of video, and video specific peripherals, is generally referred to as *desktop video.*

Video peripherals and equipment can also be purchased through similar channels as computer equipment. The difference is that mail order houses and information will be listed in one of the many video-specific trade magazines available on newsstands. Video dealers also tend to deal only with video equipment and computer systems that are designed to function more as a peripheral to the video equipment than vice versa.

Consider Your Future Needs When Buying Peripherals

The peripherals discussed in this section are designed to bring image and sound to your projects in varying degrees. Ultimately, you will want to distribute or otherwise display your completed projects. Although the final product is really a function of the software that you choose to work with, you must still consider the capabilities and limitations of your equipment. CD-ROM, for example, does not perform as fast as a computers processor. You must take this fact into consideration if you are developing interactive titles for CD-ROM. You also must be aware that even high-quality CD-ROM players can be limited by inadequate processing power of some of the lower level Macs such as the LC and the Classic. CD-ROM playback can also be effected by the amount of RAM installed in the computer. The important point here is that your CD-ROM project can easily perform very differently depending upon the system on which it is played.

Using CD playback emulation software might help you overcome this limitation, but you could also buy a CD-ROM WORM (Write Once Read Many) drive, which allows you to create your own single CD to test how it plays back. Then you could use the emulation software to accommodate the many different systems on which the CD could play.

Video also has a similar concern associated with it. Playback on video tape can be quite different from playback on a computer screen. You can help to avoid problems here by using an analog-to-digital interface card that not only captures video but also outputs it to tape. Buy a VCR that receives digital image frames accurately and then preview your productions for video until you get your desired result. When you are happy, you can send your files, with all the correct software settings, to a professional output service bureau for printing to video tape.

Development for playback on a computer screen is really subject to the computer system itself. You must take into consideration any limitation that the system you are developing for may have. On-screen presentation is really only a question of the software you are using and the configuration of the computer.

Taking development and future output into account is important so that you don't buy less than what you need. For example, you may buy a video capture card that can only capture, but not output to video tape. This function may be all that you want to accomplish for now, but you will need to buy a whole new card with that added feature when you do want to output to tape.

Although buying only what you will immediately need and use is wise, you should not create dead ends for yourself. Look at everything that you will want to accomplish and be aware of what is needed to accomplish it. You may discover that spending a little extra money now will save you a great deal later. The only exception for this rule occurs when you are positive that you will not need any more functionality than the equipment that you are buying, at least not for 6 months to a year. If you find a remarkable deal on a piece of equipment, buy it. However, chances are that costs will be low enough when you do need the added functionality to make buying it any earlier foolish. All your output considerations are covered in *Chapter 19*.

Multimedia Peripherals

CD-ROM

Chapter 9 covers CD-ROM discs, which are compact laser discs that have made possible the inexpensive distribution of complex programs that use large file sizes. You can use CD-ROM to bring prerecorded audio, video, and still images to your multimedia projects. You can also use a CD-ROM player to view the work of other multimedia artists to help you develop your own titles.

Scanners

Chapter 10 covers scanners, which bring high-resolution still images to your multimedia work. The images can be manipulated in image-editing software and then used in your multimedia software. Using a scanner is the best and only way to bring photographs and other still images that aren't digitized into the computer with high-quality results.

Video

Chapter 11 covers video, which brings full-motion images to your multimedia work. You can use the video files in the computer exclusively within your multimedia software and presentations. You can also manipulate the video in a number of different ways for output back to video tape.

The multimedia-capable Macintosh can produce work that can effectively be broadcast on television. Video peripherals allow you to preview your work that will eventually be broadcast. They also provide you with a broader base of distribution as many more people own VCRs than own computers or CD-ROM players.

Digital Still Photography

Digital still photography serves a similar purpose to conventional photography, except that the images are captured electronically as opposed to chemically. The technology falls somewhere between scanners and video. This subject is covered briefly in *Chapter 11*.

Sound Input

Sound completes the multimedia experience. You can use it to create a mood or influence the viewer's perception of the images you have created. You can never underestimate the power of sound—voice-over and narration, sound effects, and music. Sound is one of the most important elements in multimedia work. *Chapter 12* gives you some information about how to bring audio to your multimedia work.

Chapter

9

CD-ROM

CD-ROM discs are discs that are similar to audio compact discs but store computer files and programs and require a special player to function. They can be used to store graphics, sound effects, programs, music, and virtually anything else that can be stored on a computer's hard drive given the appropriate equipment. Aside from being the best way to distribute very large multimedia and interactive presentations, they are an excellent way to introduce music, professional graphics, and prerecorded video to your multimedia work.

CD-ROM has truly opened the door for multimedia and interactive authoring in the mainstream markets. It allows for the packaging of large amounts of information at little expense. You can easily store hundreds of megabytes of information on a single disc, which permits you to include sophisticated graphics and sound in the programs that you plan to distribute. CD-ROM discs also allow you to take advantage of complex sound and graphics that have already been published on CD and are available for you to use in your own work. (See Figure 9.1.)

Figure 9.1 *CD-ROM discs and player: NEC multimedia bundle*

N O T E CD-ROM discs and drives allow you to read information from the discs, but you cannot write back to them. Optical disks and drives are the closest comparative method of reading and writing information to a laser media. The price difference between the two is also tremendous.

Optical disks require a formatting procedure that is similar to the formatting procedure for hard drives, and can be done with an optical disk drive connected to your computer. CD-ROM discs require a different formatting procedure that allows them to be read by CD-ROM drives. The CD-ROM formatting procedure is unique to CD-ROM and is encoded onto the disc when it is originally created with a CD-ROM recorder. CD-ROM is basically the best method to transport multimedia files, but they can be encoded to only once and then read repeatedly; they cannot be written to. The differences between optical disks and drives and CD-ROM discs and drives are what make CD-ROM discs less expensive, even though they are created with similar procedures and materials.

Why CDs Are So Popular

CD-ROM is considered to be one of the best ways to transport and package software. There is very good reason to favor and encourage its growth. For example, CD-ROM discs are sturdy and impervious to magnetic fields. Therefore, CD-ROM information is more reliable and longer lasting than diskette information. They can also store large amounts of information, so that they can hold large applications and multimedia-sized files. Consequently, distributing large multimedia files and programs at low expense is easier. Apple now offers a CD-ROM drive option for all of their computers and includes CD-ROM programs with the bundle, which has greatly increased the installed base of CD-ROM drives in home computers, and has boosted the entire CD-ROM industry.

Information is encoded as the same digital data that are stored in any other computer storage method. Therefore, integrating a CD-ROM drive into your Macintosh computer system becomes a simple matter. There is no need for special translators, but discs must be formatted in a manner that allows a Macintosh, IBM/compatible, or any other system to read it.

Since CDs can store large amounts of information, producing a CD with separate areas that are formatted for different systems is possible, given adequate space on the disc. This means that you can produce a CD project that can be stored on a single disc that you can use on Windows systems, Macintosh systems, and any other system that will fit on the disc. The storage capacity of CDs makes them perfect for software developers, many of whom now develop for multiple computer platforms.

Software on CDs

Many software developers now offer their products on CD-ROM. The cost to manufacture remains the same, and often they will offer some additional incentive, such as bonus software bundles or clip art. Very often the cost of a program on CD will be less to you then the cost of the same program minus any bonus incentives as shipped on diskette.

The difference in development cost exists because applications are now very large and usually need to be compressed onto several diskettes in order to be shipped. Placing their programs on CD allows the developer to encode it, without any compression, on one convenient location. Plenty of room remains on the disc left for developers to put other goodies at no additional cost to you or them.

If the software on a CD is copy protected you'll want to drag it from the CD onto your hard drive. That's because a copy protected program usually forces you to enter a registration number before the program becomes operational. You can't write information onto a CD, so there's no way to enter this number. Copying the program to your hard drive remedies the problem.

Files that do not require some type of code to operate can simply be read directly from the CD. This can keep the space on your hard drive free. In fact, you may have software now that includes many files that take up useful space on your hard drive and are rarely used. The CD version of the same software requires that the application along with files for the system folder are the only things that you actually need to copy onto your hard drive. You could use the CD with the remainder of the files to access the other software options that you need. This can easily save dozens of megabytes of hard drive space normally taken up by just a couple of programs.

The downfall of this setup is that you must have that CD-ROM in the drive whenever you use that program. If you intend to use other CDs, as you would when working with multimedia and interactive programs, you must have all files essential to that program's operation available to the computer at all times. Although transferring minimal application files to your hard drive may be economical, you must be cautious that you aren't restricting yourself in any way.

Overall, if you own a CD-ROM drive, you should take advantage of the bonuses offered with CD versions of software. You will invariably get much more for less money. The software is just as operational, and CDs are much more durable than diskettes so you will never need to create a back-up copy of your software.

Clipmedia on CDs

Clipmedia CDs are collections of animation, music, sound effects, complex graphics, and QuickTime movies. These media clips can be used, often times royalty free, in your multimedia presentations and other projects. These CDs are published with either random clips or with specific themes in mind, such as business and medical clipmedia, the way you would expect to find clipart for document layout programs.

Ultimately, you will probably produce everything associated with your projects, but clipmedia CDs are a good place to find material to get you started. They can also save you time if you need a QuickTime movie or animation that depicts a specific theme for a presentation. Clipmedia CDs can also help you to develop new ideas and to learn how to use unfamiliar multimedia software.

N O T E

Many of the companies that distribute video and audio collections claim that the clips theycontain are royalty free. That means that you can alter the clips and use them in your own productions, without paying a fee. If you do intend to sell your multimedia program, though, carefully read the fine print of the documentation that accompanies the movies and sounds. If you intend to use a media clip in a product frim which you'll profit, you might be requested to include information about the copyright in your final program or pay a fee.

Developing Games and Other CD Programming

The variety of CD titles is increasing rapidly. This means three things to you.

* You will have plenty of titles to choose from to use with a CD-ROM drive.

* You can use the example of what has been successfully done in developing your own projects.

* There is a growing market for your multimedia projects on CD-ROM. Most of what is available is either for entertainment or education such as interactive encyclopedias and video games.

Listings of CD titles are available from dealers and directly from the several growing CD title publishers.

The greatest benefit in developing interactive projects for CD-ROM is that you do not necessarily need a knowledge of programming. You can develop your projects using authoring software, such as Macromedia Director, which simply requires that you develop the logic pathways of your project and provide the music and graphics files that you intend to use. The large capacity of CDs allows you to work with these graphics and sound files intact, instead of needing to describe them through a programming code.

In developing for CD-ROM, you must take into consideration that CD-ROM drives are approximately 10 to 20 times slower than hard drives. Therefore, multimedia projects that play well from a hard drive might not necessarily play well from a CD-ROM drive. The varying performance levels of host machines is a determining factor towards the quality of CD-ROM playback. You must address these considerations through CD-ROM playback emulation software and in the authoring code that you write into your interactive presentations. Another technique for developing CD-ROM programming is to use a *WORM drive*, which allows you to encode CD-ROM discs. You can create test prints of your program and then send the master files to a mass production facility when you achieve your desired results. This is all covered later in *Chapter 19.*

The Various Types of CD Drives

All information on the various types of CDs is stored as digital information, in the same way that information is stored on a hard drive. The differences among types of CDs lies in how information is organized on the disc. Each type of CD has a section that includes the disc's format and identifies what it is. Compatible players read this portion of the disc and use it as a guide to the information encoded on the disc.

Some CD players can read several different types of CDs, such as Kodak photo CDs and CD-ROM discs. All CD-ROM drives can read audio CDs. These players translate the format of different discs. Once identified, the player adjusts its own performance to accommodate the disc's format. The Macintosh requires that you install system extensions that allow the computer to access information from CDs other than CD-ROMs. For example, you need to install an extension called CD Audio Access to listen to audio CDs on your Macintosh CD-ROM player. Some CD players have stand-alone features that allow them to be used without the computer, but these are exceptions. The CD Audio Access extension ships with the Macintosh system software and is frequently included with CD-ROM drives.

Using Audio CDs in Your Presentations

Some CD-ROM drives are so similar in operation to audio CD players that they can stand alone as a stereo component. Music and other sounds from audio CDs can be channeled into your computer through these CD-ROM drives. (See Figure 9.2.)

You must have a sound utility program that allows you to record sound to the hard drive from the CD-ROM. This is just as essential as the need for specific software to capture video to the hard drive. This sound utility software also allows you to convert the raw sound data to a file format that your multimedia and interactive programs recognize. One such program is Macromedia SoundEdit Pro.

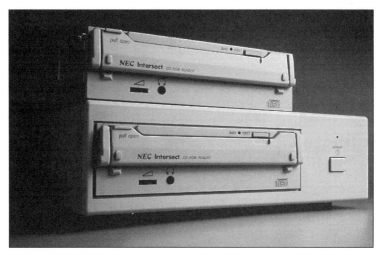

Figure 9.2 *Stand-alone CD-ROM player*

This capability to use sound from professionally recorded CDs can be quite tempting, considering that you can also edit the sounds once they are in the computer, but use caution. Music is copyrighted the same as writing is, so that you must contact the owner of the music rights to get permission to use the work or make other similar arrangements. Sometimes you may find that a short passage of music can be drawn from copyrighted work free of royalty charges; however, the owner of the rights or their legal agents have that information. If you intend to use captured sound for any type of professional endeavor, you must be certain that everything is cleared first.

Why CD-ROMs Are More Expensive Than Audio CDs

Audio CDs contain only audio information, which is far less complex than the information stored on a CD-ROM. Information can be lost or damaged on an audio CD with little or no consequence to the performance of the disc. You may get a "skip" in playback, but an audio disc rarely ever crashes and stops operating completely.

CD-ROM drives, in contrast, depend upon every bit of information on them being intact. CD-ROM data are also much more complex than then the data encoded on an audio CD. There can be no data damage on a CD-ROM because any data loss can easily cause the CD-ROM drive to misread the disc.

Understandably, drives designed to read CD-ROM discs require more sophisticated features than those in an audio disk drive. CD-ROM drives have sensitive error-correction features and are designed to provide additional functionality, such as passing their data into a computer as well as through speakers. The greater capability, complexity, and sensitivity of CD-ROM discs and drives justify the greater expense.

Kodak Photo CD

Kodak Photo CD is a technology that prints your photographs to CD format. The service works very much like sending your film out to be developed, except that it comes back on a CD-ROM. You can send the CD back to the service bureau to have additional photographs included until the capacity of the disc is full. (See Figure 9.3.)

Figure 9.3 *Kodak Photo CD*

Photo CDs have a specific format, which also means that you must have a player that can read them. There are photo CD television players, but you must have a photo-CD-enabled player and photo-CD-enabled image-editing software, such as Adobe Photoshop, to use these CDs with your Macintosh. Both software and CD-ROM players that can use Kodak Photo CDs are easy to find.

Each photo CD actually has multiple versions of the same photographs encoded on it. The multiple versions are available in different sizes and resolutions to accommodate the different players and software that can use them. For example, there is one version of the photographs for the player that can be connected to your television, another for the software that allows you to preview thumbnails of the images simultaneously on-screen, and another resolution for the image that you can open in photo-CD-enabled image-editing software.

You will need to be certain that any CD-ROM player that you select be capable of reading Multisession photo CDs. You can return photo CDs to the service bureau to have new photographs encoded on them. These new photographs have their own directory on the CD; it's like having multiple CD programming on the same disc. Your CD-ROM player must be capable of recognizing this multiple-level programming on a photo CD.

Philips Interactive CDs, 3DO, and Other Markets

Many other technologies ship programming on CD-ROM besides the computer, video game, and audio industries. Two such markets are the Philips CD-I (Compact Disc-Interactive) and the 3DO (Three-Dee-Oh) system for interactive players and programming for your television. 3DO is the company that developed the technology of the same name, and licenses the technology to other companies. 3DO is a joint venture between Panasonic and AT&T. It is a perfect example of media and communications companies having strong interest in multimedia and the CD market. Currently, both 3DO and Panasonic have developed players for the 3DO system. Many of these CDs will be developed using the same tools that you will be using for your multimedia and interactive programming on the Macintosh. Incidentally, these interactive players for the television also double as audio CD players, increasing their overall value. (See Figures 9.4 and 9.5.)

Developing CD Projects for Markets other than the Macintosh

It may be possible for you to develop for these markets. You must follow a specific protocol when programming your work in order for it to work with their machines. The manufacturing company provides you with this protocol and specifies what software produces the best results.

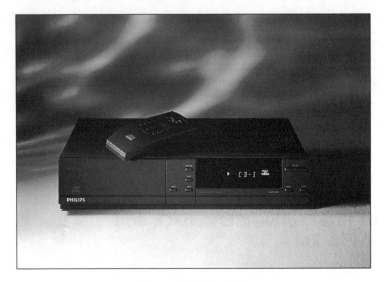

Figure 9.4 *Philips CD-I*

Figure 9.5 *3DO (Panasonic player)*

One of these other development possibilities for you is the IBM-compatible Windows market. Some of the authoring software available for the Macintosh also have versions available for Windows machines or players for Windows machines that will run your program. Simultaneously developing your interactive programming for both the Macintosh and the IBM is possible as a result of this software. It is even possible to have one CD-ROM programmed with both the Windows- and Macintosh-formatted versions of your program.

Choosing the Right CD Drive

CD-ROM drives are the mechanisms that you can connect to your Macintosh to allow you to use CD-ROM and other types of discs in your computer's software. They function in much the same way as a hard drive with regard to accessing the information on them. There are several factors you'll want to be familiar with in order to purchase the proper CD-ROM drive. (See Figure 9.6.)

Figure 9.6 *CD-ROM drive*

Transfer Rate

Your primary concern in purchasing a CD-ROM drive is its *transfer rate.* Transfer rate is the speed at which information passes from the CD-ROM drive to the computer and is identified in kilobytes per second. Often this is included in the name of the drive where the number after the manufacturer's name represents the transfer rate.

Faster transfer rates in a drive allow you to take advantage of complex CDs, but this faster rate must be matched with a machine that can take advantage of a high-performance drive. Having a lightning fast CD-ROM drive with a very slow machine doesn't make much sense; there won't be any difference in performance against lesser drives. The newer programming demands better transfer rates so that faster drives will be necessary in the future. The slowest and first transfer rate for computer data is called Redbook and transfers data at 150kb per second. This is the same transfer rate as ordinary audio CDs. Faster CD-ROM players will transfer data at some multiple of the Redbook convention. The fastest transfer rate for a CD-ROM drive on the market when this was written was 4× Redbook, which is 600kb per second.

CD Compatibility

Most drives can play audio CDs as well as CD-ROM discs, but some may have the ability to read other formats. One such format is the Kodak Photo CD. The more formats your CD-ROM drive can handle, the greater your possibilities in working with programs from different manufacturers. Besides having greater functionality with your drive, you can examine the work of others to help you improve your own work.

Block Size

Data are read from the CD-ROM in blocks of kilobytes. Currently these blocks range from 2 to 10 kilobytes each, depending upon the drive. The larger the block size, the less work is needed from your drive because it is getting much more done with each pass. Larger block sizes improve the overall performance of your drive, especially when more demanding programming becomes available. Although block sizes are not generally advertised, you can ask for them from a CD-ROM drive dealer or manufacturer. This will help you choose the best performance drive.

Cache Size

The cache of your drive is a holding area for data that the drive anticipates you will want next. The drive selects the data based on frequently executed commands in a program. An example is a word processor; when you scroll, the drive anticipates that you need the next page in the sequence in your document.

CD-ROM drives do the same thing for multimedia programming. They read information into the cache through the slower block rate and then feed it to your computer's RAM at a much greater rate. Larger cache sizes can hold more information; therefore, they are somewhat faster than those with smaller cache sizes.

Dust Prevention Features

Dust is the biggest problem in a CD-ROM drive. Look for features that prevent dust interference. Part of the problem is that the optical lens in a CD-ROM drive is delicate and can be damaged easily.

Look for a drive that has features that prevent this problem. Some may have a secondary door so that the interior of the drive is never directly exposed to air when inserting or removing a disc. Others require that you use a *caddy*, which is a casing that you place the CD-ROM disc into before inserting it in the drive. Some of the better drives have automatic lens-cleaning features that keep the sensitive lens free of dust at all times.

Stand-Alone Features

Many CD-ROM drive manufacturers have taken advantage of the CD-ROM's similarity to audio discs and drives in their design. These drives have control panel features that allow you to use them the same way you would use a stereo component, with and without having the computer on. This dual capability is like getting two machines for the price of one.

Some machines are also portable. They have battery operation capability that makes them independent of the desktop system. You can use these to make presentations on the road or even to use as a portable CD player.

Upgrade Path

Some manufacturers offer an upgrade path for their CD-ROM drives, which allows you to trade up to the newer machines as they are introduced. Trading up will cost a discounted fee, but it will still cost less than the equipment without the trade up. Not all manufacturers offer this option.

On Care

As already mentioned, the greatest threat to the performance of a CD-ROM is dust. Some drives are designed to prevent dust interference by having a secondary door that prevents air from entering the drive or an automatic lens-cleaning mechanism that keeps the optical reading device clean. The best way to prevent dust damage is by keeping your CD-ROM drive in a clean, dust-free environment.

Even though compact discs are particularly resilient, the mechanisms within the drive are not. You must be cautious about anything that you do that affects the inside of the drive. Because the lens is especially sensitive, you should not use anything that touches it directly unless it is expressly meant to. In other words, if you plan to use a cleaning method of some sort, you must be certain that it is designed to work with CD-ROM. There are cleaning methods that are available for audio CD drives, but these can potentially cause damage to a CD-ROM drive. Ask the developer of the cleaning system if it is appropriate to use with CD-ROM.

On Technology

CD-ROM uses an optical technology to encode information in binary code. A laser melts areas of a disc, and a magnet then polarizes those areas so that they retain a negative or positive charge. The negative and positive areas represent the 0s and 1s of binary code, respectively. CD-ROM drives read the information encoded on the disc by firing a laser onto the surface. The laser reflects differently off of positively or negatively charged areas, thus deciphering the code. This reflected information enters a lens into the mechanism of the drive, which then passes the information into the computer.

An important factor in the operation of CD-ROM drives is the speed at which they spin the disc. The disc must rotate at a constant rate, so that the speed will alternate accordingly depending upon where the laser is on the disc. If the laser is near the center, the disc spins slower; if it is near the edge, it spins faster.

Another important point is the format of the disc. This factor does not concern the drive as much as how the information is organized on the disc. Different drives can decipher the format of different types of CD-ROM by reading the format information encoded on the disc. This capability enables certain CD-ROM drives to read multiple formats.

Scanners

Scanners are like computer photocopiers. You place a still image—a photograph, drawing, or slide—on a panel or use some other method that exposes it to the scanner's mechanism. Then, either you or the scanner passes a light reader across the image, which converts it into digital information. A scanner stores the image as a computer file that can be used in your multimedia software, whereas photocopiers cannot store images. There are three basic types of scanners: hand-held, slide, and flatbed.

In most scanners the first image that is produced on-screen is a low-resolution preview that can be used to determine the part of the image you actually want to scan. You then create a graphic bounding box around the area of the picture that you want to scan and make any adjustments to the settings of the scanner to produce the most desirable image. This feature is not available in hand-held scanners because you cannot reliably get the same scan twice.

You can use the still images that you scan in presentations and illustrations. One use for a still image is as a background for a presentation. Still images are also used as *textures* in multimedia software. Textures are graphic files that create the surfaces of three-dimensional graphics in multimedia composition software. For example, a photograph of tree bark can be a scanned and used as the surface of a tree trunk made in a three-dimensional graphics program. Another example is placing a photograph of an executive on a square that floats across the screen of your presentation while information about the executive is displayed.

Once a photograph or other still image is scanned into the computer, you can manipulate it with image-editing software such as Adobe's Photoshop, which is detailed in *Chapter 14* and on the enclosed CD-ROM. With a program like Photoshop you can distort, alter, and improve images with a tremendous range of possibility. For example, you can take a photograph of a car and combine it with a cliff top and panoramic background. The entire image can be seemlessly generated with separate photographs right on your desktop.

The important factors to consider when selecting a scanner are the size of the image that it can scan, the maximum resolution of the image that it produces, and the quality of the reproduced image. Dimensions and resolution are available in the technical specifications of the scanner, but the quality of image produced can be determined only by a side-by-side comparison with other scanners.

Scanners typically ship with an image-retouching software package. While this doesn't determine the quality of the scanner, it is certainly something to be figured into the overall value of the scanner. Bundled software usually means that the software company endorses the equipment, which may indicate a good scanner. Nevertheless, you must make sure the scanner meets your quality standards and technical specifications, such as color capability, resolution, and the ability to scan film.

Hand-Held, Slide, and Flatbed Scanners

Hand-Held

Hand-held scanners are small devices that look something like a hand-held vacuum. You run a scanner along the surface of what you want to scan, and it digitizes the image into the computer. They are usually low-resolution and are typically used to scan text documents or simple graphics. For multimedia they can prove to be unreliable because they require a very steady hand to get a good scan, but they are the least expensive scanners on the market.

Slide

Slide scanners are designed to work with photograph slides and other types of film and transparencies. You insert the slide, or other type of film, through a slot in the scanner either directly or indirectly by positioning it in a carriage that is then inserted in the scanner. These scanners are perfect if you plan to do a lot of work creating presentations for products. Often uncovering slides of a product is much easier than finding printed photographs.

Slide scanners usually produce the best results because they shine light through the image as opposed to reflecting light off of it. You get a good scan because you are working with an earlier, and therefore better, generation of the image (you're working with the film instead of a print generated from the film). You are also working with a purer form of light because it directly enters the scanner instead of first striking a surface. Reflecting off a surface first may interfere with the actual image. These scanners are excellent but will not allow you to use a flat photo or picture from a magazine.

Flatbed

Flatbed scanners are broad, flat devices, which are about 2 feet in length, 1 foot in width, and 6 inches in height. On the surface of a flatbed scanner is a glass plate on which you position your photograph or drawing. They can scan an area as large as a foot-and-a-half in length and 10 inches in width, which means that they can definitely scan a much larger area than hand-held scanners (which only scan an area about 6 inches wide) and slide scanners (which are limited to the small dimensions of film slides). These scanners may be the best choice, depending on your needs, because they produce a good image, are less expensive than slide scanners, and allow you to work with a wide range of image sizes. They allow you to scan any flat image that can fit on the scanner's surface. Some flatbed scanners can scan film as well, but this is usually an option that is available for an additional fee. Ask the scanner manufacturer or dealer about this option. (See Figures 10.1, 10.2, and 10.3.)

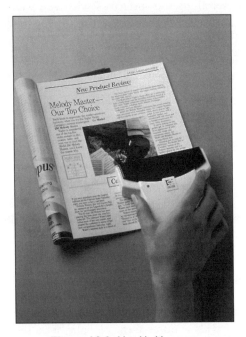

Figure 10.1 *Hand-held scanner*

Figure 10.2 *Slide scanner*

Figure 10.3 *Flatbed scanner*

Color Scale

Like monitors, scanners come with the ability to produce an image in black-and-white, grayscale, or color. Color scanners can also produce grayscale and black-and-white images. Black-and-white and grayscale scanners are limited to black-and-white and grayscale color ranges, respectively, but they are usually much less expensive.

For multimedia, color scanners are best not only because they produce a more dynamic image but also because they allow for a greater level of control over the image produced. Color scanners also come with color image-editing software, which will have a wide range of functionality.

Although it is not recommended for multimedia, you can keep cost down by purchasing a noncolor scanner. With grayscale the results are good, and the shading frequently makes up for the lack of color. Black-and-white scanners are generally used only for simple line art and for scanning in text. You can compensate for the lack of color by using color graphics that you create in your software or by treating the grayscale scans with color in image-editing software.

NOTE There can be a discrepancy in color accuracy among different scanners. Not all scanners "see" color the same way. You may not be able to determine the difference unless you compare the output of different scanners simultaneously. Color saturation, hue, and luminance can be washed out or inaccurate when compared to the original image. Yellow may still be yellow and red may still be red to your eye, but these same colors will be different from one unit to another. This discrepancy may not be important because you can always treat the colors with software in the computer.

Resolution

Resolution determines the sharpness of the image that the scanner can reproduce. Computer images are composed of large numbers of small picture elements called *pixels*. These pixels are composed of the colors that make up the image, as they are grouped together they generate the image. The resolution feature of a scanner is measured in dots (pixels) per inch with higher numbers yielding finer results.

Scanner resolution can range from hundreds to thousands of dpi. Scanners provide the option to scan at any resolution lower than the maximum of the scanner. Clarity of image means that the lines do not *alias*, or form "steps" along the edges. Like what older computer graphics looked like. Higher resolution allows for a wider range of flexibility with the image in your graphics software. (See Figure 10.4.)

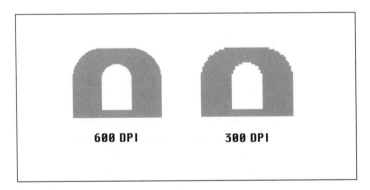

600 DPI   300 DPI

Figure 10.4 *Higher vs. lower resolution*

WARNING

Images scanned at high resolution require large amounts of storage space on you hard drive. Very high resolutions may not be necessary for much of your work. First test lower resolutions until you get the results you want rather than simply scanning at the highest resolution for your scanner.

Actual vs. Interpolated Resolution

Scanners are sometimes offered with two separate maximum resolutions: *actual* and *interpolated*. The actual resolution is the scan of the image as it has entered through the lens, whereas the interpolated resolution is a magnification of the image—usually through the built-in programming of the scanner. What actually occurs during interpolated resolution is that the data translated from the light image are recalculated and artificially improved. This difference is a concern only if you intend to use your work for high-quality printed output. Usually all it means to multimedia is that you may be able to get a high-interpolation resolution scanner for less than the cost of a scanner with the same actual scan capability.

Scan Area (Dimension)

The scan area of a scanner represents the maximum size of an image that can be scanned. In slide scanners this area is limited to the size of the slide or other compatible film or transparency. In hand-held scanners this area is limited to the width of the optical head at the end of the scanner. In flatbed scanners, the scan area is the size of the glass platform where you lay your picture and is represented by the size of a sheet of paper that can be placed completely on it, such as a full-page scanner. Variable sizes are available, but full-page (8.5×11), or legal standard (8.5×14) are the only set standards. You need to look at what is currently available to make a determination.

NOTE Scanners equipped with similar specifications often have different prices. Although this difference may be due to the reputation of the scanner's manufacturer, a difference in price usually means a difference in the quality of the components used. This price difference has to do with the quality of the electronic circuitry, the quality of the moving parts in the scanner, and other features that are not immediately evident. If you encounter a difference in price in similar scanners, ask the manufacturer or dealer what the justification is. It may be worth the extra cash.

On Technology

Scanners work like video capture devices that can capture only still images. They function in much the same way as video cameras operate, but the electronics currently used in scanners are much more sophisticated then those used in most video cameras so that they can produce remarkably clear, high-resolution images. Of course, scanners can capture only still, flat photographs and drawings. The scanner's similarity to video essentially ends at technology and makes them distinct from video in function.

Scanners can be connected to the computer through any port that can transfer digital information. The fastest scanners currently available are connected through one of the NuBus slots, but they also tend to be the most expensive. Most scanners are designed to function through the SCSI port, which is a perfect compromise between cost and speed.

Technology in all scanners is very similar. An optical device shines a light either against or through an image. The light then passes through a lens which delivers it to a charge coupled device (CCD). Here the image is stored electronically.

A CCD is an electronic chip that is also found in video cameras. The CCD receives the light image and stores it as charged cells of electrical energy that vary in intensity. This electrical image then passes through a converter, which translates the electrical intensities into digital information, the 0s and 1s of binary code. From here the image passes into the computer where you can use it in your software.

Hand-Held

Hand-held scanners basically serve the same function as flatbed scanners. The major difference is that these scanners replace the precise and controlled mechanical movement of the optical devices in a flatbed with what you can manage with your arm. Otherwise they use light, lens, CCD, converter, binary, computer, and your software in the same way.

Slide

These scanners are also called *transmissive scanners* because the light passes through the image instead of reflecting off it. They are very steady and produce a very clear image. The technology remains the same, except that they do not reflect light off the image. (See Figure 10.5.)

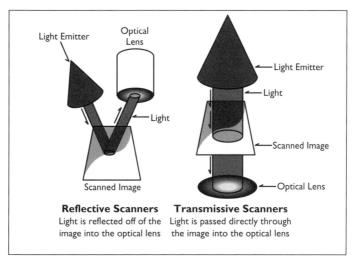

Reflective Scanners
Light is reflected off of the
image into the optical lens

Transmissive Scanners
Light is passed directly through
the image into the optical lens

Figure 10.5 *Transmissive vs. reflective scanners*

Flatbed

Flatbed scanners function by running an optical device beneath a glass plate along the length of the scanner. The optical device shines a light onto a flat image that is laid on the glass. These scanners are also called *reflective scanners* because the light reflects off the surface of the image and back through a lens in the scanner.

Chapter 11

Video

Video is a powerful electronic media that allows you to capture moving images on magnetic tape the way that you can capture moving images on film. The tape can be played through video tape recorders, which can be connected to a television monitor. You can use video technology to bring moving images into your multimedia work.

You can use video to enhance on-screen presentations and CD-ROM programming or to transfer computer graphics and sound files onto video tape to enhance a video production or to distribute alone. To manipulate these on-screen images, you must use digital transfer cards that convert the video signal into a form that the computer can understand. Once the video has been successfully transferred into the computer, you can bring it into your multimedia software for manipulation and playback.

Unlike other computer functions, video is a very complete media that has its own set of technical considerations and peripherals. Essentially, bringing video into your multimedia work means combining two distinctly different environments. Your understanding of how video works will greatly support the quality of the work that you produce.

One of the best things about video for multimedia is that you are not restricted to using the computer to prepare for your production. Of course, you could use your computer to do everything from editing your video to applying special effects. This is very memory- and processing-intensive for the computer, but it is still possible. You could also create complete productions using dedicated video editing and special effects equipment and later bring these already edited clips into the computer for your multimedia work.

Generally, multimedia work that is heavily weighted in video peripherals and editing equipment is known as *desktop video*. Technically this work is still multimedia, but you need to know much more about the mechanics of video than you might need for most multimedia work. Some Macintosh based systems, such as the Avid and the Imix Video Cube, are designed specifically for desktop video. These systems are used to edit video entirely within the computer—so that they have a great deal of storage space and have accelerated CPUs. Although these systems are powerful and are used to develop high quality multimedia productions, you don't need one of these to develop effective multimedia. If you are just beginning to work with multimedia, then you can build a system modularly, and later consider a powerhouse system like the Avid.

For beginning multimedia, all you really need to know is how to get the video clips into your computer. Next, you need to know how to manipulate the video files, and, finally, you need to know how to use the video files in your multimedia software. It's also important to know how to prepare computer graphics and sound files properly for output to video tape, but that is covered in *Chapter 19.*

As you become more advanced, you may want to add more details to your work and introduce specialized video-editing equipment. This equipment allows you to create sophisticated video productions that you can integrate in a variety of ways with your computer. Later in this chapter is some information on the options that are available to you in that area.

Analog vs. Digital

Video signals (*analog*) are very different from computer data (*digital*). Knowing how these signals differ is important because a big part of multimedia is the use of video for distribution. The difference between analog and digital is that analog is the waveform of a video signal, and digital is the same signal converted to the fundamental computer language of binary code. That is, analog is the video signal when it is broadcast over air waves, when it is stored on video tape, or when it is in the form of electronic waves passing from the video tape to the monitor. Digital is the binary representation of the wave after it goes through analog-to-digital conversion. The digital representation of video is no longer a waveform—it is a series of numbers stored on your hard drive or stored in RAM. It can later be reconverted to video or analog form. While the signal is digital, it is composed of the same type of data as any other stored computer information. Most of the equipment available for your Macintosh can simply be connected to your computer and used after a few minutes. Video is a bit more complex; consequently, you can easily make assumptions about compatibility that will be wrong.

WARNING

Digital video tape does not mean that the recorder can simply be plugged into your computer and you will be able to output that beautiful animation onto tape. You still need analog-to-digital conversion equipment.

The concept behind analog and digital is simple, but it is one of the most difficult properties of video to grasp. The raw explanation is this. The video is analog when it is on video tape or inside the camera. The video is digital when it is inside the computer or otherwise goes through a translation into binary code. Both are still the same video, but analog is the actual video signal, and digital is a numerical representation of the video. The numerical (digital) representation must go through a deciphering in order to be viewed. The analog signal can simply be fed directly through video equipment.

Analog

Analog information is in waveform. Video starts out as waves of light entering the lens of a video camera. The camera converts the light waves to electrical signals. Next, the signals are stored in magnetic form on a video tape. The process is reversed when you play a video tape on a VCR. The analog information in its magnetic form is read off of the tape and converted to electronic information, then finally transformed back to light when it is displayed on a television's screen. The signal is called analog because the signal, while in a different form than the original information, is in various versions of a *waveform* that accurately represents that information. The various states of this waveform (light, electric, magnetic) are analogous to each other and to whatever was video taped.

In order to be recognized by your Mac, the analog video signal must go through a translation into the fundamental computer language of binary code. This binary code is a digital form of the signal. Once it is translated, it is then converted into one of the digital video formats that are available for the Macintosh and will be discussed later in this chapter.

Digital

The video becomes digital when it leaves the state of a wave form and becomes purely numerical data—more accurately the 0s and 1s of binary code. The signal must be reconverted to an analog state in order to be video again, but it is stored and transferred as code.

The binary code describes the video signal in much the same way that it describes anything that is created on the computer. The code forms patterns that represent the amplitude, frequency, and other properties of the video wave form. Because the video signal is now a code, it is more easily stored and changed without quality loss.

Every time you record a video signal from one tape to another, a little clarity is lost, some of the audio becomes muffled, and the colors are less vivid. In its digital form, the video remains intact regardless of the number of times that the data are transferred. The numbers remain the same.

You can manipulate a digital signal as often as you choose, adding special effects and transferring it into other files. All you are doing is changing the patterns of numbers. When this is brought back into a video form, it is translated back into the analog wave form. In this way, it can be viewed on either the computer's monitor or a television screen or recorded back to video tape. All these forms require an analog signal to display the video image. The computer's monitor is included in this category because it operates in the same way that a television set does. The only difference is that the transfer device in a computer's monitor converts digital information to analog, whereas a television works with television airwaves or signals across a cable. The monitor is able to display the computer's information because there is a digital-to-analog converter built into the circuitry that leads to the monitor. (See Figure 11.1.)

Digital Video Tape

Digital video tape formats, such as D1, D2, and D3, are high-grade quality professional systems that use a digital encoding process to record video onto tape. Digital video recorders and cameras have built-in analog-to-digital transformers that convert the analog signal to digital information. In effect, digital video equipment uses video tape the way computers use tape back-up systems. In playback, the digital signal must be converted back to analog information in order for it to be viewed.

The advantage of digital video is that it can be processed multiple times, and does not lose image quality. This is because, like digital information in a computer, the information that is being altered is binary and will not change. The disadvantage is that the tape will eventually wear out and is particularly susceptible to damage. So, while digital video tape is invulnerable to image quality loss due to multiple generations of recording, it is still vulnerable to data loss due to the frailties of the media.

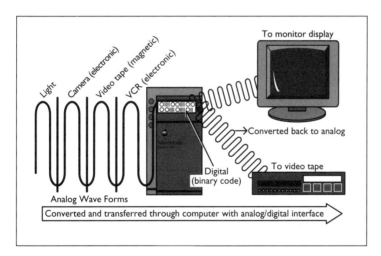

Figure 11.1 *Analog to digital, the difference is the computer*

Digital Video Tape and the Macintosh

Information stored on digital video tape is similar to binary information within a computer. The difference is that you cannot simply download data from digital video tape into a computer. Most digital video recorders and players are equipped with an RS-232 port that allows them to communicate directly with IBM/Clones that are also equipped with an RS-232 connection. RS-232 is the equivalent of SCSI in the Macintosh environment. As yet, there is no direct connection for digital video equipment for the Macintosh. Therefore, you should use the analog video output capability of digital video equipment, coupled with the video input option on the Macintosh. An example would be an analog/digital transfer NuBus card, or in higher end Macs, such as AV models, the direct video input capability.

Video Frame Rate

Video, like film, is comprised of a succession of individual images that are presented so quickly to the eye that the images appear to move. The number of frames that video or film display within a second of playback is called the *frame rate*, or *frames per second (FPS)*. For example, the frame rate for NTSC video, which is covered later in this chapter, is 30 FPS. Technically, the illusion of movement is achieved at 22 FPS, but the design of video requires the faster rate.

Frame rate is important to you if you plan to transfer files onto video tape from your computer. If you create 1 second of animation on your computer, it may play at different rates depending upon the machine that you use. You can be certain that if you create 30 frames of an animation that it will run for exactly 1 second of video time, regardless of how long it takes to play back on your computer screen. If you adhere to the 30 FPS convention, you'll be fine.

Although motion is perceived at 30 FPS in video, there is a noticeable flicker at this rate on a television's screen. This is because the television image is scanned onto the screen from the upper-left corner to the lower-right corner, line by line. Although this happens very quickly, there is still a moment between scanned images that the eye notices.

The solution for this problem is to display more images per second, but this requires more information to be transmitted over airwaves for broadcast video. A worthwhile compromise is for each frame to be split into two different *fields*. Fields are alternating lines of the screen. First the even lines are scanned, then the odd lines are scanned. This division of the image scan is called *interlace scanning*, and eliminates the screen flicker of video at 30 FPS.

If you are a multimedia developer interested in developing video, you will need to be certain that you output your video to tape in fields, otherwise you will see the flicker in your video playback. Most analog/digital transfer cards such as the TruVision NuVista+ offer the option to output in fields. Using this option produces the best quality video from computer output.

Video Capture

Video capture is the process involved in translating video to a digital form that the Macintosh can read. Once the video is passed into the computer it is converted to a computer graphic file format. From there, the video can be imported into a multimedia program like Adobe Premiere to have special effects applied. These effects include transition effects, titles, addition of sound effects and music, and any other treatment that would be applied during conventional analog video editing.

Since the video is now in digital format, you can also treat it as any other digital graphic file formats, such as PICTS or PICS. You can alter the colors, cut out parts of individual frames, or use a program like Adobe Premiere or Photoshop to apply graphic filter effects like the fish-eye lens.

Once treated in the computer, the video is exported from the multimedia composition program in a digital file format such as QuickTime or PICS. The newly edited video can also be output back to video tape through use of an analog/digital transfer card and a video recorder. The digital video files can also be imported into other multimedia programs where they can be combined with other titles or integrated into interactive presentations with a program like Macromedia Director.

Macintosh Computers with Built-In Video Capture

Some of the higher-end Macintosh computers, such as the Quadra AV Macs, are designed with direct video input and output jacks. These computers are equipped with the necessary translation circuitry for analog-to-digital conversion. You can connect and capture video from just about any camcorder or video tape deck to these Macs, which adds a whole new value to the overall expense of the higher-end machines.

These Macintosh computers work with video in *real time*. In other words, the computers record video to the hard drive as the video tape is running through the VCR or camera. Normally you can't use the Macintosh to control a video source through only the video input and output jacks. You'll use the controls on the video source, such as a VCR, instead. With the right software tools you can, however, let the Mac control the video source. The Abbate Video Toolkit is one such software tool. The Video Toolkit controls several types of compatible video decks and cameras with a serial cable and software interface.

The fact that the built-in video capability of the higher-end Macs is real-time makes them unreliable for output of long or complex video or graphic sequences to video tape. This is because what is recorded to video tape is subject to the computer's on-screen playback. Several different factors must be measured here. Video playback requires a fast CPU and a lot of RAM. Even then, the computer is doing a great deal more than simply displaying video, though technically this is all you have directly asked it to do. The system is constantly performing tasks—such as loading information into RAM—that can interfere with the playback of video. You may be recording a simple three minute sequence of video to tape in real-time and the computer may skip only a fraction of a second of it, nonetheless, this will ruin the entire sequence and you will need to start again. This is the sort of thing that makes real-time recording from an unaccelerated or otherwise enhanced Macintosh unreliable. Macs can output video and graphics sequences, but they must use a program like Macromedia Director, or Adobe Premiere and QuickTime. The computer files are recorded to video tape at the same rate and quality as what is displayed on the computer's monitor.

Real-time video recording to video tape depends heavily on the performance level of the Macintosh you are using. Granted, the higher-end machines may have the ability to record graphics to video off of the hard drive at 30 FPS, but you will not get the same quality as what you can achieve by recording your computer graphics and video to tape frame-accurately. *Frame-accurate* recording is achieved with the use of a digital-to-analog output device and a video tape deck that can operate frame-accurately. This topic is covered later in this chapter.

The Video Capture Card

Video capture cards are fitted into the NuBus slots of Macintosh computers and allow you to record video and graphics to and from the hard drive and a video recorder. Some of these cards transfer only video in and out of the computer. Many also transfer audio information, so you can bring in sound and music from existing video footage or transfer audio information to video tape from your computer.

Video capture cards vary according to the complexity of their function. As mentioned previously, some may have audio capability. Others may have extensive connectability with a wide range of video equipment. Other decks have the capability to transfer video to and from PAL or SECAM video, which are broadcast methods that are used outside of the United States. They are described later in this chapter in more detail.

If all you plan to do is have a few QuickTime movies in a multimedia production that you plan to show from your computer, then you can use a simple video capture card. Of course, if you want sound transfer capability as well, you must determine whether the card has that capability. Some cards allow you to produce sophisticated effects such as *Chroma-Keying*, which allows you to combine video seamlessly as well as graphics from two different sources. This technique is used to put the weatherman in front of the satellite photographs that are constantly changing in the background. (See Figure 11.2.)

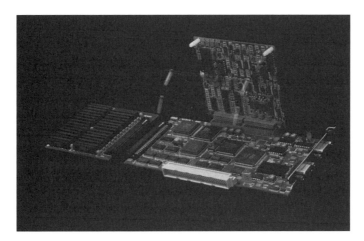

Figure 11.2 *Video capture card*

Outputting Computer Files to Video Tape

Once you have all of the appropriate equipment for video transfer, namely an analog-to-digital transfer method and a video camera or video tape deck, then you have several options available for recording to tape. One option is real-time recording as stated previously. This method records your graphics and other digital files to the video tape at the same rate that it appears on the screen. As discussed earlier in this chapter, real-time recording is not particularly reliable because the computer may interfere with playback at any time. This is because, unlike dedicated video equipment, the computer is processing more than just the video playback data.

In order to record digital files to video tape effectively, you need to conform to image size requirements. What this means is that your graphics must be an appropriate size in order for them to look good on tape. The size of your graphic images for video should be determined by the format you plan to use. For example, NTSC video requires that each frame be 640 × 480 pixels in size. If you don't conform to this requirement, then you will get video graphics that are either constrained to a small window playing in the middle of the screen or too large for the screen.

If you have a fast Macintosh, then this is not as much of an issue. Many software programs have a *print-to-tape function* which allows you to use a video capture card or Macintosh built-in capture capability the same way that you work with a printer. You select the file that you want to transfer to tape and start your video deck recording; the software transfers the files onto the video tape as they appear on the screen.

You can get better quality graphics if you use a *frame-accurate recording deck*, such as the AG 9650 SVHS VCR from Panasonic, and a digital-to-analog transfer card with frame accurate capability, such as the NuVista series of NuBus cards from TruVision. Together with your Macintosh, this equipment can transfer single frames of graphics to video tape separately. This type of recording deck allows you to transfer exactly one frame of an animation for each frame of video so that you have better control over timing and precision. By using a frame-accurate method, you will be certain that 30 frames of graphics will take exactly 1 second to play on video tape. Otherwise, you may fall victim to the arbitrary figure that you may get with a method that depends on the playback performance of your computer alone. Frame-accurate recording is much more tedious and time consuming than real-time recording, but the quality of the results are far better.

You also must be aware of other preparations for your graphics and other digital files. These preparations optimize the digital files for quality transfer to video tape. Since this requires a certain familiarity with multimedia software, preparation for output to video is covered later in *Chapter 19.*

VHS and Other Video Tape Formats

Video formats are the way in which information is recorded to the tape from the electronics of the video recorder or the camera. A wide range of formats is available, but you must be concerned only with what is called the *consumer formats.* These video formats produce professional results and are relatively inexpensive.

VHS

VHS is the most common video tape format that is recorded onto half-inch tape cassettes. It also happens to produce the lowest-quality output, but you can be certain that if you produce something on video tape that you will be able to play it anywhere. It may be a better idea to create the *master*, or original version of your project, on a better format, but VHS is the best choice for distributing your multimedia work on video tape.

SVHS

SVHS is a higher-grade version of VHS and is the most commonly used consumer-level format for professional applications. The video tapes used are the same half-inch variety, but they are specifically designed to work with SVHS recorders. The half-inch tape is currently the safest video media to work with because it is very popular and more people own VHS video decks than 8mm video equipment.

SVHS equipment will be able to play and record VHS video, but VHS equipment cannot play or record SVHS format video tapes. Since SVHS format video plays only on SVHS recorders and players, it's a good choice for mastering but not for distributing work. SVHS is a better choice than VHS because you always have the option to record your work in VHS format for distribution.

SVHS is the best deal considering price, quality, and potential distribution base. A lot of editing equipment and other options are available for SVHS. Another benefit is that you will have no problems with integrating clips from other video sources such as footage from rental tapes that you have acquired permission to use. (See Figure 11.3.)

Figure 11.3 *SVHS VCR*

8mm

8mm is a growing video format that is most popular in the home camcorder market. The tapes are compact, as is the equipment. Most people who own 8mm camcorders generally use the camera itself to view the tapes. The greatest benefit of this format is its compact size, which makes toting the camcorder around as easy as carrying a regular camera.

The downfall of this media is that it is still not quite as established in the main-stream video market as VHS is. You can certainly find plenty of 8mm equipment, but it operates only with 8mm tapes. This can make working with VHS tapes diffi-cult, unless you also want to buy VHS equipment to complement your 8mm equip-ment. This format is the best choice if you intend to buy a camcorder and just want a quick and easy way to get video into your multimedia productions.

Hi8mm

Hi8mm is the high-grade version of 8mm. It produces a better image than any of the other consumer-level formats, but its small tape size can be inconvenient. This is the best consumer-level format to work with, but you probably should include a quality VHS or SVHS recorder to have a system that is completely compatible with other systems and video sources.

Plenty of Hi8mm editing equipment is available, so that you won't be at a loss for options in the event that you choose to go with this video medium. The compact size of Hi8mm camcorders is preferable because it is lightweight and easy to transport. If you plan to buy editing equipment as well, Hi8mm is a good choice. If you aren't planning to buy editing equipment, then finding ser-vice bureaus equipped for Hi8mm can be a task. (See Figure 11.4.)

VHS-C and SVHS-C

VHS-C (VHS-Compact) is a variety of VHS that has all the properties of VHS, except that the cassettes are about the same size as 8mm cassettes. As a result, VHS-C camcorders are quite compact and lightweight. SVHS-C is the Super VHS version of the same compact media. The cassettes can be played in regular VHS and SVHS tape players with the use of a caddy that the smaller cassette is posi-tioned into before being inserted in the player.

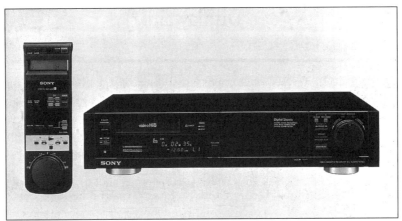

Figure 11.4 *Hi8mm VCR*

This format combines the compact size and lightweight properties of 8mm with the accessibility of VHS equipment and services. It isn't considered a format for professional applications, as regular SVHS is. This is true primarily because of the unconventional tape size for a VHS format, but the image quality is good and the compact size makes it easy to work with on the desktop. (See Figure 11.5.)

Figure 11.5 *SVHS-C camcorder*

NTSC and the Video Display and Transmission Formats

Video display and transmission formats are standards set by national agencies that define common elements for all video signals. These standards make possible the reception of transmitted video signals by any television set designed to work with that standard. NTSC is the standard in the United States; it is named after the committee commissioned to establish the standard, the National Television Standards Committee.

These standards define the amplitude, frequency, and other elements of the signal that is transmitted from stations. It also defines the technology in compatible television sets. It is somewhat like the AM and FM frequencies of radio. The signals may have been created on different types of recording equipment, but the standards allow them to be sent along the same airwaves.

PAL (Phase Alternating Line) and SECAM (Sequential Color and Memory) are the other prominent standards and are used in other parts of the world. In order for a video signal to be recorded, displayed, or transmitted, it must use equipment and methods that all adhere to the same standard. An NTSC video tape will not play on a PAL or SECAM VCR and television set, but with conversion equipment you can translate video created with one standard into another standard.

WARNING

Do not confuse transmission and display formats with tape formats; they serve different functions for video. Tape formats are concerned only with how the image is captured and recorded onto tape. Transmission and display formats are concerned with how the signal is prepared to be sent over airwaves and the design of the equipment it will be received by. There are NTSC SVHS camcorders and VCRs, just as there are PAL and SECAM SVHS camcorders and VCRs.

Transmission Standard Concerns for Multimedia

Transmission standards are unimportant to Macintosh multimedia development unless you plan to produce video to be used in countries that use something other than NTSC. All you really need to be concerned with is that your digital-to-analog transfer method and recorder conform to the standard with which you plan to have your project operate. Other than that, transmission and display standards are a purely video (non-computer-related) concern.

What is important is that the frames of any image that you plan to transfer to video conform to the pixel aspect ratio of that standard. This means that the height and width of graphics, animation, or anything else you create on your computer are created with a specific frame size. For example, NTSC requires an image size of 640 × 480 pixels to create one full-screen image. PAL and SECAM have their own dimensional considerations.

As long as you are certain that you are creating your multimedia projects in the appropriate size for your intended standard, then you are doing all you can to create graphics for video properly. Of course, you should also keep in mind the 30 FPS convention of video. Properly preparing your multimedia files for output to tape in all standards and tape formats is covered in detail in *Chapter 19*.

S-Video and Composite Video

S-Video and composite video are different methods for connecting video components to each other and to video capture cards. The major difference is that S-Video is only one connection that transfers video and audio along the same cable. Composite video separates video and audio channels into separate cables with separate connections.

All video equipment has composite connections; only some equipment has the S-Video connection. The general consensus in the professional video industry is that S-Video produces a better video signal, but most people can't tell the difference for most multimedia applications. The newer AV Macintosh computers have both composite and S-Video connectability.

QuickTime and Other Digital Video Formats

When video is captured into the Macintosh, it is converted into a digital file that you can open in your multimedia software. You usually have the opportunity to choose the type of file format that is used, or to convert these files into the format that you need. The digital video formats are Sequential PICT, Sequential TIFF, PICS, and QuickTime.

Sequential PICT and TIFF

Sequential PICT and Sequential TIFF can be grouped under the same category because they achieve the same result. They are a series of image files that are assigned sequential numbers in their names. PICT and TIFF (tagged image file format) are file formats used primarily in desktop publishing, fine art, and illustration application; they have been expanded to this capability through multimedia software.

When you use these file formats, you tell your multimedia software to save each frame of the video as a single graphic file, like a scanned image. When you save and name the file, the program attaches a number at the end of the name. In this way, when you use the file in another program, it recognizes the file as being part of an animation or video sequence and looks for the other images.

PICS

PICS combines all the sequential images of an animation or video clip into a single file. This consolidation makes transporting and keeping track of multimedia files easier. Consider that storing just a few seconds of video or animation as separate files for each frame could easily mean hundreds of individual files.

PICS files separate into the individual files of which they are composed when they are opened in your multimedia software. Since a PICS file is a single file, it also uses a data compression method that makes it smaller than the separate individual files that it contains. It does this by recognizing areas of an animation that do not change from frame to frame and then does not repeat that information for separate frames; it repeats only the areas that change.

N O T E   PICS files do not contain audio information, only video and graphic data. If you create a presentation that contains sound in a program that can save the presentation as a PICS file, the audio information is discarded during the conversion.

QuickTime

QuickTime is a Macintosh system extension that uses software compression to combine video, audio, and animation into a single file. QuickTime files can be used in programs such as Adobe Premiere and Macromedia Director, or they can be played through the QuickTime player application that is available from Apple Computer. This file format is the best choice to use for multimedia because it keeps audio and video information synchronized even if you bring it into different multimedia programs. The alternative is to reorganize audio and video every time you introduce a new software tool.

One of the best aspects of QuickTime is that it allows for several data compression methods that optimize playback and storage space. These compression methods can be used to create animation that will work best with CD-ROM, when transferred out to video tape, or even if the files are to be played back for an on-screen presentation. QuickTime is covered in detail in *Chapter 16*. (See Figure 11.6.)

Figure 11.6 *The QuickTime file format and player*

Strictly Video

As mentioned earlier, video has a large selection of peripherals designed to work outside of the computer. Consider using these peripherals to create more complex productions before introducing them to the multimedia work in your computer. These peripherals can also be useful for editing graphics and animation into existing video footage.

Because video is a complete subject in itself, each item here is covered in a cursory manner. The intention here is to make you aware of the options available to you. If you are interested in getting very involved with video, you may enjoy browsing through some of the dozen or so video trade magazines that are available at most newsstands. Video, as it more directly pertains to multimedia production, is covered in more detail in *Chapter 19.*

Camcorders and Cameras

Video cameras allow you to create original video footage for your multimedia work. You may find that having one will be incredibly useful as they permit you to grab images quickly for spot presentations and other uses. For example, you could very easily take a video "snapshot" of a person's face that you want to highlight in a presentation. Of course, you must have a video capture method in your computer in order to accomplish this.

Camcorders are a combination of video camera and VCR. This is the best type of camera to purchase for multimedia, because it allows you to play existing video tapes as well as video tapes that you create. Camcorders are designed format-specific, so you can buy one that is SVHS, Hi8mm, etc. (See Figures 11.7 and 11.8.)

Figure 11.7 *SVHS camcorder*

Figure 11.8 *Hi8mm camcorder*

If you plan to use existing video footage, VHS formats are best because most easily accessible video footage is on VHS tapes.

N O T E

Lighting

Cameras and camcorders are not as sensitive as your eyes, so you will probably need additional lighting for many applications. This can range from a single light mounted on the camcorder to powerful lights on stands positioned on a set. Your camera's sensitivity to light will determine what type of extra lighting, if any, is needed for your intended use. If you do choose to buy a camcorder, speak with the manufacturer about its abilities and limitations with light.

Editing

Editing video can involve using two separate video recorders, camcorders, or both, to combine video footage from different sources or to remove unwanted video footage. Essentially this means dubbing select areas of video footage, which requires very precise record and playback equipment. Using video-dedicated editing equipment can help you create stunning presentations and allows you to preview video and animation footage intended for professional broadcast.

Edit Controllers

Using edit controllers is the only way to get professionally edited video. They are connected to the separate video desks and are used to define what video is transferred from tape to tape and where. Very often they come with editing effects such as transition effects that bring one portion of the video to another in a graphically interesting manner. Transition effects are covered in greater detail in *Chapters 16* and *17.* (See Figure 11.9.)

Figure 11.9 *Edit controller*

Signal Control Devices

Signal control devices are video peripherals that help to monitor and adjust the quality of the video footage that you are manipulating. They are generally considered necessary only if you intend to do heavy and professional video work. The type of signal control devices that you choose depends upon the type of video you use.

Video Special Effects Equipment

Plenty of components are available for video editing; they can help enhance the editing system and the quality of your productions. For example, there are components that produce transition effects, visual effects such as splitting the screen image, and titles in multiple fonts. You can produce many of these effects in the computer, but using these components is often quicker and cheaper.

Monitors

If you are going to use video extensively, then you need editing monitors. They are similar to television sets but do not have a receiver that receives channels. As a result they are usually cheaper than regular televisions. On the other hand, many also have connections and image controls that are much more sensitive than a regular television's, so don't be surprised if they are the same price or even more expensive than comparably sized television sets. You could also use regular televisions for video editing, but they are not as reliable for image accuracy. (See Figure 11.10.)

Figure 11.10 *Video monitor*

Linear vs. Nonlinear Editing

The difference between *linear* and *nonlinear* editing is the difference between editing on video-dedicated equipment and editing captured video inside the computer. Video equipment must fast-forward or rewind to find the areas of the tape that you want and is therefore linear. Inside the computer, you can randomly access any part of the digital video footage, which makes editing in the computer nonlinear.

Generally, getting professionally setup to edit video inside the computer and then output back to tape is less expensive and faster to accomplish in the long term, but it usually means dedicating the entire Macintosh to the purpose of editing video. Capturing video to a hard drive consumes large areas of storage and requires a great deal of power. Most Macintosh systems must be heavily accelerated to accomplish digital editing as effectively as dedicated linear editing equipment can. If, however, you intend to do only small amounts of video editing—such as combining a couple of seconds of video from two tapes—consider using your Mac. This is covered in Chapter 16.

Macintosh Desktop Video Editing Systems

Several companies such as Avid and Imix offer preconfigured Macs with all the acceleration and storage capacity that you need to edit entire video productions. These are considered desktop video-editing systems and can also be used for multimedia applications. If all you want to do is multimedia and interactive, you can get away with lesser machines. (See Figure 11.11.)

Figure 11.11 *Macintosh based desktop video-editing system*

Digital Still Photography

Digital still photography falls somewhere between video and scanning devices. It is similar to conventional photography in that the cameras are compact devices that are used in a point-and-click fashion to produce still images; some even come equipped with a flash. The difference is that the image is stored in an electronic form as opposed to a chemical form.

Digital still photography is a quick means of bringing still images to your multimedia system, without being bound by the desktop. The image is captured into a CCD chip (detailed in *Chapter 10*) that is the same as those found in video cameras and scanners. Some digital still cameras store the image in the CCD memory until it is downloaded to the computer and then purged. Other cameras have their own form of disk media that allows the images to be used in players and printers designed specifically for digital still images and equipment. These cameras are connected to the computer via the serial port (printer or modem ports).

The usefulness of these devices is in their portability. They are as easy to transport as cameras, but they eliminate the need to first develop and then scan images before being able to use them in your multimedia software. They are excellent for quick presentations and product or personnel shots where time and expense are considerations.

Another excellent aspect of these cameras is that there is no waste. The electronic media, be it disk or a solid-state CCD, is reusable. There is never a need to replace film.

Image Quality Concerns

As is true of scanners, your concerns in a digital still camera are color depth and resolution. They can range in color depth from black and white to millions of color, and resolutions can also vary. You can generally apply the same rules here as you would to a conventional scanner.

The number of pictures that you can take with a digital still camera depends upon the settings that you use for picture quality. Naturally, if you are looking for the best quality possible with the camera you are using, you must take the minimum number of pictures allowed by your camera. For example, the camera pictured here, the Dycam Model 4, is capable of taking from 8 to 32 pictures with a maximum range of 24-bit color and a resolution of 496 × 365 pixels. (See Figure 11.12.)

You can also find features in digital still cameras that are identical to those you might look for in a conventional camera, such as automatic focus and built-in flash. Digital still photography is truly a convenient integration of many different media.

Figure 11.12 *Digital still camera: Dycam Model 4*

Chapter

12

Audio Input Options

Audio is one of the most powerful features that you can bring to your multimedia productions. By strategically placing music and other audio elements in your production you can create a mood, emphasize a point, or describe something where image alone fails. Ignoring the importance of sound is virtually impossible, and introducing it to your multimedia system really isn't difficult.

Ways to Use Audio in Multimedia

Music

Music can help to make a presentation more interesting in a number of different ways. You can also use it to influence the viewer's perception of the images that you have created. Learning to exploit music in your presentations and other multimedia productions can greatly improve the quality of your multimedia work.

Movie scores use theme music to create a mood—one theme for a villain, another for the hero, and still another for suspense. You can use music to the same end for multimedia. If you want something to be exciting to the viewer, use music that suggests excitement. You can never underestimate the influence of music.

Most music can be categorized for different results; classical music connotes sophistication, where as rock and other pop music can express a contemporary feel. You can change your score based upon your audience and intentions. Just look at how television commercials use music depending upon the audience.

Another important use for music in multimedia is to make inactive portions of interactive presentations more interesting. For example, you may have a "Help" portion of your interactive project that presents text information on how to use your program. By including background music, you can make these less active portions of the presentation more interesting. Background music at these points also directly associates these less active moments with the more active portions.

Sound Effects

Sound effects are sounds that are used to emphasize or enhance events in your multimedia productions. Selecting a choice sound effect to play during a particular event in a video can promote the illusion of reality. An explosion is an example of a sound effect. Combining music and sound effects in your multimedia work makes it more detailed and professional.

Sound effects work best in places where music alone doesn't work. For example, you may have an animated logo that sweeps across the screen. You could use music to create drama, or you could use sound effects to create a "sweeping" sound for the logo in motion. The combination creates a more complete experience.

One of the most important uses for sound effects in interactive presentations is *user response confirmation.* In other words, when a button is pressed, the user hears a click or some other tone that signals that the action was registered. You can use sound effects for other interesting confirmations, such as tones for correct and incorrect responses in a game.

Voice-Over and Narration

Voice recordings bring a human element to your multimedia productions. They can be used to give instructions or to provide a narration. Of all the forms of audio that you can use in your productions, only this one communicates directly with your audience.

Voice recordings in interactive programs can be used to prompt a response of some sort from the user, such as making a selection. They can also be used to read off text information, like help windows and instructions, while the text is presented to the user. Overall, voice recording can make your presentation clearer and more direct.

The built-in Macintosh speaker is rather limited because it is small. If you want a quality of sound output that is comparable to the quality of sound that you are using in your projects, then you must add speakers. Many multimedia bundles that come with CD-ROM players include these types of speakers; you can also find them sold separately. Another option is to connect your Macintosh to a stereo via the computer's audio output jack. (See Figure 12.1.)

Ways to Get Audio into Your Computer

Audio is similar to video in that most audio sources are analog in form, which means that audio is an electromagnetic waveform. In order for your Macintosh to be able to use audio, it must first be translated into a digital form. *Chapter 11* provided the information about the relationship between analog and digital information.

Once the raw digital audio information is imported, or *sampled*, into your Macintosh, it must be converted into a file format that your multimedia software can understand. Some audio-digitizing methods allow this to happen automatically. In order to use all available options, you must be certain that you have a digital audio-editing method that allows you to open and save raw digital audio as Macintosh digital audio formats.

Figure 12.1 *External speakers for the Macintosh*

Digital Audio Capture Card

These cards operate the same way as a video capture card, except that they transfer audio information only. As a result, they are invariably less expensive than video capture cards. This option gives you the widest range of audio input options.

Audio capture cards are NuBus devices; consequently, they are the fastest way to bring audio in or out. This means that you can work with high-quality audio information, which requires more data to be transferred effectively. You can connect virtually any audio source to them, including tape deck, video audio output, and television audio. You can also connect a microphone to these devices to record your own voice.

Usually these cards capture only raw audio data, so you must have audio-editing software to use the files elsewhere. You may find an audio capture card that comes bundled with the software you need. No matter what the method, the end result must be the file formats that works with your multimedia software.

Built-In Audio Recording and Microphone

All new and some of the older Macintosh computers have a built-in audio jack that allows you to record sound to the hard drive. This method allows you to record System Sounds, which are placed directly into the system file. You will then be able to select the sound in your Sound control panel as the system's alert sound.

While built-in audio is convenient, it is limited. That's because you cannot use the audio files it produces without conversion software. Built-in audio is an excellent way to bring short voice-overs and sound effects into the system for conversion and then export to other software. You can record only simple, short, and vocal audio with this method. Other types of audio, such as recording from a stereo speaker will not produce very good results.

MacRecorder Sound Digitizer

The Macromedia MacRecorder is probably the best all around deal for audio input for multimedia. It works with all Macintosh computers and records from a wide range of audio sources, including vocal. The MacRecorder also comes bundled with audio-editing software that allows you to manipulate and then save files into most of the major Macintosh digital audio file formats.

The MacRecorder brings audio capability to Macintosh computers that do not have built-in audio. The MacRecorder comes bundled with SoundEdit Pro, which allows you to edit the System Sounds mentioned in the previous section (SoundEdit Pro is shown in some of the screen captures in this chapter). The MacRecorder is connected to the Macintosh via the serial ports (modem or printer ports); as a result, it isn't quite as fast as NuBus audio capture cards. This means only that you may lose some audio information if you record very high-quality and complex sounds such as CD audio. Nonetheless, even with these sounds you get excellent results.

If you connect two MacRecorders to your Macintosh, you can produce stereo sounds. You must have stereo output to take advantage of this. Most Macintosh computers require a sound expansion card and stereo speakers for this to be effective, but the option is always there. Newer Macs, like the Quadra 840 AV and Power Macintosh Computers have stereo output capability. Overall, the MacRecorder is the least expensive, most versatile, and most effective way to quickly introduce original and prerecorded audio to your multimedia work. (See Figure 12.2.)

Figure 12.2 *MacRecorder audio digitizer with SuperMac spigot and Sound Pro audio and video capture card*

Compact Disk Input

As discussed in *Chapter 9*, you can use a CD-ROM player to record audio from compact discs to your hard drive. This method is the simplest and most direct way to bring detailed audio into your multimedia work. You have the option of using audio from clipmedia disks or ordinary audio CDs, the same that you would use with a stereo.

Many electronic publishers are now offering clipmedia CDs for multimedia developers. These CDs contain sound effects and music that is royalty-free beyond the purchase of the disc. This is an excellent source for prerecorded sounds for three reasons.

✳ The sounds are already in a file format that your multimedia applications will recognize, eliminating the additional step of using software for file conversion.

✳ After verifying that the sounds are indeed royalty free, you can use the sounds as freely as you choose in your productions.

✳ They provide detailed libraries of sounds created with professional recording equipment and are often organized in libraries of themes. This makes finding a sound effect or music recording that best fits your presentation, interactive program, or other multimedia production easier.

Audio CDs, on the other hand, can be quite tempting because they are easy to come across, and finding music that a broad audience will recognize and like isn't difficult. You must consider a few things before you pop an audio CD into the player and record away. First, audio CDs output only the raw audio information, so you must have an audio-editing program to convert them into files your software can use. Second, royalties are a big issue with audio CDs, and the agents in charge of keeping track of this will be quite strict about it, especially if the music you use is from a popular artist. Make sure you are aware of the policies of the companies behind the recording rights of the music you plan to use; it will undoubtedly save you headaches.

MIDI

Musical instrument digital interface (MIDI) is a method of controlling musical instruments with a code. It is widely used in the music industry and can be used with your Macintosh with the use of a MIDI interface. This is not a method of recording music to the hard drive, but rather simply controlling the instruments that create the music. The music can then be passed through a sound digitizer into the computer for playback off the hard drive.

MIDI is actually a set of instructions that are passed along through all the MIDI-compatible instruments connected to your controlling device. The code stores all the properties of the sounds that you want to have played from the instruments. The code also stores information about tempo and other orchestration properties.

MIDI software allows you to organize these instructions with tremendous detail. With instruments like synthesizers, you can generate a multitude of different sounds and in effect have an orchestra at your fingertips. The results that you can get out of MIDI with a single instrument can be astounding.

Some multimedia software allows for execution of MIDI instructions from within a presentation. For example, you may have a very sophisticated and lengthy composition in a MIDI code that will cause a synthesizer to play the music. Compatible multimedia software allows you to have a direct connection to the MIDI code so that when it comes time for the music to play, it will trigger the MIDI code and the connected instrument.

Using MIDI in this way can save computer storage space, but it is much more complex then simply digitizing a recording. You can create the music with you computer and MIDI control, so that it will still sound great. You can then digitize the orchestrated sound onto the hard drive, making it easier to transport with your multimedia projects.

One of the advantages of MIDI in conjunction with multimedia is that it offers impressive sound quality. The playback from a MIDI tool with stereo speakers undoubtedly is better than playback from the Macintosh speaker. You must have a MIDI converter connected to your Macintosh in order to integrate MIDI, as well as a MIDI sequencer so that you can connect the instruments. (See Figure 12.3 and 12.4.)

Digital Audio Editing

Digital audio editing is the altering of sound in the computer. With digital editing software you can select a portion of the audio's waveform and remove it, filter it, move it to another portion of the waveform, or duplicate it multiple times. After the sound's waveform has been sufficiently altered or enhanced, you can save it in a file format that can be used in your multimedia programs. These file formats can also be reopened in your audio-editing software for further manipulation.

By editing digital audio, you can refine the sounds you record until they provide you with desired results. Often in audio recording to hard disk, you may also record a short period of silence before and after the noise; this silence can be clipped off. You may also find that you want only a portion of a sound, such as a single phrase out of a lengthy speech. Digital editing software allows you to view the audio waveform, locate the portion that you want, and edit it accordingly.

You can also manipulate the duration of a sound. You can create an animation and then create sounds that last for a precise length of time. Later, you can synchronize the sound and images in a multimedia assembly program such as Adobe Premiere or Macromedia Director.

You can create custom sound effects with audio-editing software. For example, you could record your cat purring, reverse the waveform, add an echo, and then repeat the altered waveform several times into a loop. The result can be a terrific sound effect that simulates a pulsing mechanical sound. Experimentation can yield incredible results.

Figure 12.3 *MIDI interface*

Figure 12.4 *MIDI sequencer*

Some multimedia software allow for basic manipulation of audio files. This type of editing is generally limited to duration and placement in the composition. For detailed control you must have software designed specifically for audio editing. (See Figure 12.5.)

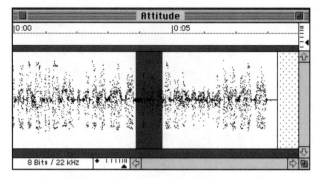

Figure 12.5 *Digital audio-editing software SoundEdit Pro*

Macintosh Digital Audio Formats

The digital audio formats for the Macintosh are the form that your audio files must be saved in to be understood by your multimedia software. Some file formats are specific to the programs that create them, but they may not be understood by all multimedia software. When you create an audio file it's important that you are certain the audio file is universal enough to be brought elsewhere.

There are two main Macintosh audio file formats: QuickTime audio and audio interchange file format (AIFF). There are other audio file types besides these two, but you will most likely find that all Macintosh multimedia software accepts at least one of these two. If you choose to work with sounds in another format, always have the option to convert the file if necessary. (See Figure 12.6.)

Figure 12.6 *Open QuickTime audio file*

Kilohertz, Compression, Bits, and Sound Quality

Sampling Rate

The *sampling rate* is the amount of audio information that is captured into the computer per second. It is measured in kilohertz (kHz) and is directly related to the quality of the sound. Higher kilohertz produce a better sound.

N O T E

While higher kilohertz may produce better quality sound, it also produces large files. Take this into consideration when you choose the sampling rate of your sound files. Higher sampling rates may not be entirely necessary for lower-quality sounds, so first try lower sampling rates.

If lower rates are insufficient, you can gradually increase the sampling rate until you get your desired result. A good formula to calculate the amount of storage space that a sampled sound requires is Sampling Rate × Number of Seconds in the Sample. For example, a 30-second sample at 22 kHz requires approximately 660K of storage space, 22×30.

In determining the sampling rate that is best for the sound you plan to capture, you can make an accurate assumption based upon the source of the sound. For example, CD audio is recorded at 44 kHz, whereas 11 kHz is sufficient for speech. Currently most Macs and most multimedia software produce sounds up to only 22 kHz, but you can still design your applications with higher-quality output. The Quadra AV and Power Macintosh computers are designed to work with 44kHz, but the general consensus is that the Macintosh still has difficulty working with the CD audio quality rate of 44 kHz, although many people claim to have had no problems. The current limitations, if any, are almost undoubtedly temporary. (See Table 12.1.)

Table 12.1 *Sampling rates*

SAMPLING RATE	BEST USES
5 kHz	Lowest acceptable for simple speech
7 kHz	Lowest recommended for speech
11 kHz	Recommended for speech and short segments of music
22 kHz	Current Macintosh normal playback rate better music
32 kHz	Broadcast audio standard
44 kHz	CD quality audio playback
48 kHz	Digital audio tape (DAT) playback

Compression Rate

Many audio sampling devices offer the option to compress the data on the hard drive. This option decreases the amount of storage necessary for your audio files. While this may yield better space management, it also degrades the overall quality of the sound. You may want to try the sound first compressed and then decompressed to see which works best for you.

The standard compression method on the Macintosh is called the *Macintosh audio compression/expansion* or *MACE* and is used by many Macintosh-based audio-sampling devices. MACE uses two different ratios of compression: 3:1, which is sufficient for music recordings, and 6:1, which is adequate only for speech. Different hardware and software tools may have their own compression methods, so that the method depends upon the tools you choose.

Audio Bits

Bits are the amount of information that is reserved for each sample. The two options in the Macintosh, are 8 bits per sample and 16 bits per sample. The bit depth of the audio depends upon your sound digtizer's ability to sample sound.

Currently Macintosh computers are capable of playing back only 8 bit audio. The 16 bits per sample is the bit depth for CD audio quality recordings. You can work with higher bit depths for digital output to a media that can play back higher bit depths.

Part IV

Starting with Graphics

The development of Macintosh graphics has been cumulative. The tools present in early programs were improved and included in more sophisticated software as time went on. In other words, if you know the very basics of Macintosh graphics software, becoming proficient with advanced multimedia software is easier.

Macintosh graphics have opened the door of graphic art to non artists. You can produce professional quality results with little or no graphic arts experience. This incredible software is certainly no substitute for the other skills you may acquire in professional training, but using it gives you the necessary technical proficiency. All you need are good conceptual skills to be effective.

Most graphics programs produce only single still images, which was more than enough for their original purpose—graphics for desktop publishing. Multimedia software uses these still graphic images by allowing you to import and incorporate them into your multimedia projects. In multimedia software you can apply a variety of effects to these still images, but you still need to understand how these simple programs work. The bottom line is this: The better you are with basic graphics, the better your work looks, and that is where most of your project's quality resides.

The Basics

There are two basic types of programs and one that straddles basic and true multimedia. The first basic type falls into two categories: Drawing software, which is covered in *Chapter 13*. The next basic type is Paint and Image editing programs, which are covered in *Chapter 14*. The third, which approaches multimedia, is three-dimensional rendering and animation software which is covered in *Chapter 15*. The progression of these three categories marks the path to what is now considered multimedia software. Understanding these programs will facilitate the creation of your multimedia productions and make them much more effective.

Drawing Software

Drawing software programs are also known as object-oriented graphics programs. They allow you to create graphics with very controlled lines and other detailed features. These programs are much easier to master than other graphics programs because any mistakes you make can easily be corrected, but you need an image-editing program to convert these files into a format that is compatible with most multimedia software programs. The reasons for this are detailed in *Chapter 13*.

Drawing programs create graphics on-screen by using equations that map lines and shapes on the screen (as opposed to describing each pixel separately). This capability allows you to create a line, move it, edit it multiple times, and return to your original arrangement. Drawing programs are an excellent place for beginning graphics users to start.

Paint and Image-Editing Software

Paint software is also known as bitmapped software. You produce graphics in these programs by editing the color and other properties of every pixel, or group of selected pixels, that compose a graphic. It can be somewhat difficult to master, but absolutely essential because most multimedia software accepts only bitmapped graphics. (These issues are considered in detail in *Chapter 14.*)

Image-editing software combines the bitmapped graphic capability of paint programs with the ability to edit and transform graphics in sophisticated manners. Image-editing software also allows you to work with graphics that already exist, such as scanned photographs. Having an image-editing program is very important, even if you are not using it to create graphics, because it also serves as a graphics translator. This feature allows you to integrate graphics created from a variety of sources, regardless of direct compatibility, into your multimedia productions.

Three-Dimensional Rendering and Animation Software

Three-dimensional programs (Also called *Three-D*) use object-oriented capabilities to create objects in three-dimensional space. You create shapes, apply surfaces to them, position lights and other effects in the scene, and then render the image. These programs also provide you with the capability of creating animation. This software category is covered in *Chapter 15.*

Using Three-D programs is similar to working in actual three-dimensional space. You can place objects in the scene with depth, like placing them in a room, more specifically, a photo studio. You frame the scene by positioning your view point, which is also a camera. You can apply such effects as wide angle and zoom to the camera.

Animation is the simple process that consists of creating keyframes, which are pertinent moments in your animation. The Three-D program does most of the work. This is the first step into multimedia, because it introduces motion to your work. You also can use graphics created in drawing, paint, and image-editing programs in your Three-D compositions as surfaces.

Three-dimensional programs are not the only programs that have animation capability, but they are the only graphics programs that also incorporate animation. Creating animation with two-dimensional programs entails importing their images into multimedia composition software, such as Macromedia Director and Adobe Premiere.

Chapter 13

Drawing Software

Drawing software is designed to create graphics with very precise lines and shapes. It was originally designed to provide a computer solution for commercial graphic artists and industrial designers of all sorts. Lines and shapes created in drawing programs can be twisted and resized any number of times without affecting the rest of the image they belong to.

The tools in drawing programs are designed to simulate a traditional drafting environment; they allow you to create perfect geometric shapes and lines. The results are more accurate than using a compass, straight edge, or any other type of real-world drafting tool. Of course, no software can provide you with the skills needed to perform as a technically trained and professional graphic artist or architect. It cannot give you knowledge of structure or proper use of color, but it certainly can make producing profession-al-quality looking artwork easier. Artistically, all you need to use these programs effectively is conceptual skill and patience.

Drawing Programs

Drawing programs create graphics on-screen via mathematical equations that are invisible to the user. This process is similar to using calculus to determine an area or the slope of a curve. When you manipulate a graphic in a program, the program is actually altering the parameters of the equations that make up the image. This is called *object-oriented* programming.

One of the major benefits of object-oriented graphics is that they are easy to manipulate. Another benefit is that file sizes are smaller than other graphic file formats. They're smaller because they contain only the equations that make up the image. Also, you can resize object-oriented graphics freely and still maintain smooth lines, proportions, and small file size.

When you open an object-oriented graphic, the program evaluates the equations and then presents the image on-screen. Compare the simplicity of this process to that of bit-mapped graphics where information for every bit of data contained in each pixel of the image is saved. You read about bitmapped graphics in *Chapter 14.*

Drawing File Formats

All drawing programs have their own method of encoding the numerical data of images created in them. Usually a file saved in one program's native format can-not be opened in another program. For example, a graphic saved in Aldus Freehand as a Freehand document cannot be opened and edited in Adobe Illustrator unless you use a program like EPS exchange by Altys, which acts as a translater. This is because each program has its own code signature that the pro-gram must recognize before the file can be opened.

Some drawing file formats have been around for a while; consequently, most programs give you the option to save in formats other than the native for-mat. This capability allows you to open these documents elsewhere and edit them. One such file format is called *encapsulated PostScript* (EPS).

Encapsulated PostScript (also called simply *PostScript*) is actually a programming language for describing graphic information. PostScript was designed by Adobe and is the native format of Illustrator. Many other drawing programs also allow you to save your work as PostScript.

PostScript files can be opened as text documents, which allows one to edit the code directly without using the tools in a drawing programs interface. One can directly change size, color, angles, and very precise details of you drawing program graphics. PostScript programming is really a desktop publishing application, but you can also use it for multimedia if you are creating images for your projects in a drawing program using PostScript. PostScript programming is a complex issue and is just like learning any programming language. If you're interested in knowing more about PostScript programming, plenty of publications on the subject are available.

PostScript is a universal graphics and printing language, but it only retains object-oriented properties in the program in which PostScript images are originally created. This means that if you create an image consisting of a circle and a square in Adobe Illustrator you will be able to edit the circle and the square separately if the image is open in Illustrator. If you save the file as a PostScript document and open it in another PostScript compatible program, such as Aldus Freehand, you will see the image as it appeared in Illustrator, but you will not be able to separate the circle and the square. The PostScript file will give the appearance of the original image, but not the level of editing control. That information is still retained in the PostScript file, but it is written in a code that only Illustrator understands. The same is true for any other program that creates PostScript files. If you want to change the appearance of an object-oriented graphic outside of the original creation program, you will need to open the file in another image editing program. In this case, you will be working with the image as a bit-mapped graphic, not an object-oriented graphic. Bit-mapped images and programs are covered in detail in *Chapter 14*.

Drawing Programs and Multimedia Production

You use drawing programs to create any graphics that require very precise edges, shapes, and spacing as well as to create graphics that incorporate text. A logo is a perfect example of when to use a drawing program.

Chapters 15 through 17 explore how to use graphics created in drawing programs to enhance three-dimensional and multimedia applications. For example, you could make a label for a bottle with a three-dimensional graphics program, which would result in a very realistic-looking bottle.

Once a graphic has been applied in this manner you can use all of the other tools available in that program in further manipulating the image. Therefore, if you decide to create an animation using that bottle, the label behaves as if it really is a label applied to an actual bottle, moving and rotating with the bottle.

One very important use for drawing programs is to aid in creating the graphic interface used in presentation. You might use these programs to create the buttons that are incorporated within your games and other interactive designs. Basically, drawing programs are useful for creating easy, precise, and sophisticated two-dimensional graphics as well as for accenting and illustrating graphics made in other programs and for enhancing your multimedia presentations.

There are inexpensive programs, such as Adobe Dimensions and Ray Dream Add Depth that can open PostScript files and extrude then, or rotate them into three-dimensional images. This is a convenient way to quickly and easily get three-dimensional effects out of drawing programs. However, these programs don't provide the same level of image control, quality, and realism that you can get from a three-dimensional graphics program. On the other hand, Dimensions and Add Depth cost less than half the amount of three-dimensional programs.

NOTE　Most multimedia programs can import only bit-mapped graphics, such as PICT files. For this reason, object-oriented graphics created in drawing programs need to be converted into bit-mapped graphics in order to be used in multimedia prog rams. You can easily achieve this conversion by opening the object-oriented graphic in an image editing program such as Adobe Photoshop. You can then save the image as a bit-mapped graphic, with which your multimedia software will interface.

You should not expect an object-oriented drawing program to work directly with your multimedia software. Always assume that you need some sort of image-editing program to bridge this gap. All you need to do is verify that the drawing and image-editing programs are both PostScript-compatible, which simply means that they can save and open PostScript documents. All image-editing programs for the Macintosh save PICT files, at the very least. If the image-editing program you are considering can open PostScript documents, then you are right on track. Image conversion is discussed in more detail in *Chapter 14.*

Object-Oriented Graphics

Object-oriented graphics consist of lines, curves, and geometric shapes. You can combine and layer these graphic elements to create detailed images. Although you can combine elements in this way, they always retain their own characteristics and can be separated from the rest of the image at any point, unchanged.

There are several effects that can be applied to an object-oriented image, such as filters that will change the colors in the image. However, there are two basic properties in all object-oriented graphics: **Stroke** and **Fill**.

Stroke and Fill

The individual elements of an image can be edited by their *stroke* and *fill* properties. Stroke refers to the thickness of lines and curves and the outlines of shapes. Fill refers to the property applied to the interior area of a shape and to a curved line and can be a pattern, color, or *gradient* (cycle of colors). You can also apply a value of **None** to either stroke or fill. In which case the outline of the object is defined by the area of its fill. If fill is set to **None**, then you can see other objects through it, and the object consists only of its outline. If both properties are set to **None**, then the object is invisible. (See Figures 13.1 and 13.2.)

Tools of the Trade

Several tools will be common among different drawing programs. An understanding of these basic elements will not only improve your productivity but also make learning new programs easier. Many of these tools are also incorporated in other types of graphic and multimedia software, so knowing how to use a drawing program effectively will really support you in becoming proficient with more detailed programs. (See Figure 13.3.)

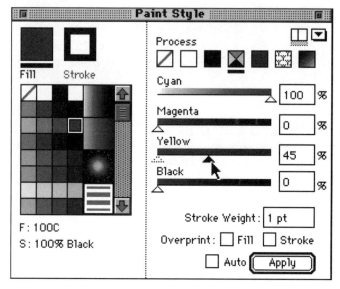

Figure 13.1 *The paint effects palette (Adobe Illustrator)*

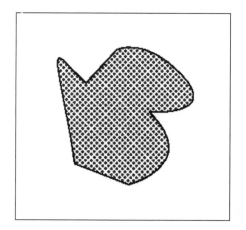

Figure 13.2 *An object showing stroke and patterned fill*

Type

Drawing programs offer tremendous control over the use of type. The type, or text, can float freely or follow along a line that you create. You can edit the type in drawing programs in much the same way that you edit type in word processing programs that can change typeface and style.

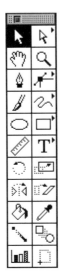

Figure 13.3 *The Adobe Illustrator tool palette*

You have the option of converting the type into an outline. This process converts the text into a graphic that has its own fill and stroke. While this options adds an additional level of control over type, it converts the type into lines and shapes that cannot be edited.

On the other hand, converting text into outlines makes exporting object-oriented graphics to other programs, especially those located in other computers, easier. This is true because you must have the typeface used in the graphic available in any machine in which you intend to open that file before converting the type into an outline. Converting the text to its outlines makes the type an object-oriented graphic that can be imported to a compatible program just as easily as a circle or a line. (See Figures 13.4 and 13.5.)

Figure 13.4 *Type along a path*

Figure 13.5 *Type converted into outlines*

Shape

The shape tools allow you to create perfect circles, ovals, squares, rectangles, and other polygonal shapes quickly. All you need to do is select the tool on the tool palette and drag across the area where you want the shape to appear. You can create the shape either from the center out or from corner to corner. (See Figure 13.6.)

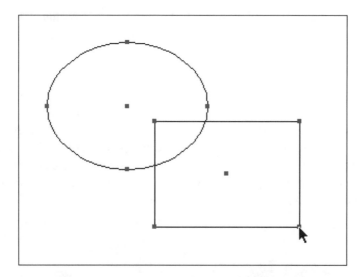

Figure 13.6 *Default oval and rectangle*

Freehand

The Freehand tool allows you to create free-flowing lines the way you would with a pencil. You can then select and edit the line with the control points that are automatically located at the curves that you create while drawing the line; in effect, the line becomes one continuous series of Bezier curves. Although this tool is the most like a real-world instrument, it is the least controllable because it requires you to use the mouse as if it were a pen or paper. It actually works quite well if you incorporate a digitizer tablet such as the Wacom tablet detailed in *Chapter 8.* (See Figure 13.7.)

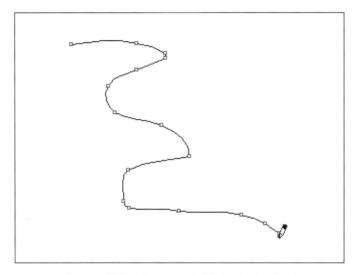

Figure 13.7 *A line created with the Freehand tool*

Pen

You use the Pen tool to create perfectly straight lines and very controlled curves (Bezier curves) and to place control points for a line or a curve. As you place control points, they can be connected to each other by either straight or curved lines depending upon the options that you choose. You can then use the Pointer tool to select the line and any of its control points for editing. (See Figure 13.8.)

Direct Selection

The Direct Selection tool looks like the arrow cursor and is used to select objects in your graphics. An object's control points appear when the object is selected and can then be used to change the object's shape or other properties. For example, you must first select an object with the pointer before you can apply a fill or a stroke to it. Holding down the **Shift** key and clicking (shift-clicking) on different objects selects multiple objects. Any changes made then affect all of the selected objects until you deselect them by clicking elsewhere in the image without using the **Shift** key.

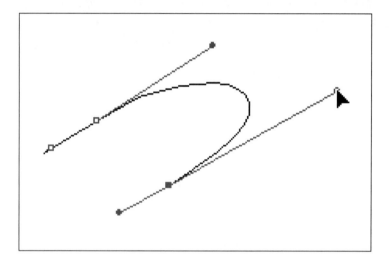

Figure 13.8 *A Bezier curve with control handles created with the Pen tool*

Templates

Templates are actually graphic images that you use as tracing guides for your drawings. You open a graphic image as a template and then use the tools available to you to duplicate the image using the image's lines. For example, to create a drawing of a car, you can scan an image of the car into the computer and then use it as a template. This feature allows you to create technically accurate and attractive images by using real-world objects. Templates are not saved as a part of the image when exported; all that appears in other programs are the drawing objects that you use to trace over the original image. (See Figure 13.9.)

Just a few of the elementary tools are available in drawing programs. Many of the other tools and functions are detailed in the interface tutorial for Adobe Illustrator, which is on the CD-ROM included with this book. The Adobe Illustrator program is also included on the CD so that you can have first-hand experience using a drawing program.

Figure 13.9 *A graphic used as a template (Adobe Illustrator)*

Chapter
14

Paint and Image-Editing Software

Paint and image-editing programs are designed to simulate traditional artistic techniques, such as those created with paint brushes and markers. They control how the program's tools affect every pixel of the image. These programs are more difficult to master than draw programs, but the end result can look much more realistic and less like it was created with a computer.

Aside from the graphic capability of the paint tools found in both paint and image-editing software, the additional tools found in image-editing programs are absolutely essential for multimedia. These tools allow you to convert an existing image's file format or to alter its dimensions. If you frequently transfer images from one program to another, a good image-editing program helps ensure that you never have a problem moving these images.

Bitmapped Graphics

Bitmapped graphics are graphics in which every pixel that makes up an image is treated separately. A good analogy is a lighted billboard, like the one in New York's Times Square. The lighted billboard is a grid of lights, each of which displays a color. When a group of adjacent lights of the same color are turned on they give the illusion of form, but each light is still separate and can be treated that way by replacing it with a different colored bulb. Bitmapped graphics work in much the same way.

Paint Programs

Paint programs, such as Claris MacPaint, Aldus Superpaint, and Pixel Resources PixelPaint Professional, are the oldest form of art program developed for the Macintosh. As a result, a wide range of capabilities in the programs are available. For example, MacPaint from Claris was the first paint program on the Macintosh, but it still uses only black and white. Now you can find programs that take advantage of the full color and performance capability of Macs, and many include scanned image-editing capability.

Some paint programs are difficult to categorize because they include image-editing capability and perform both functions very well. An example is Fractal Design's Painter, which has natural paint effects that are so realistic that you would be hard pressed to identify that the image was generated on a computer. Usually these advanced paint programs can provide natural media effects because they include image-editing capability.

Image-Editing Programs

Image-editing programs, such as Adobe Photoshop, Electronic Arts Studio 32, and Fractal Design Color Studio, use the same technology to create images as paint programs do; they allow you to manipulate the individual pixels that comprise the graphics that you create. However, they also include features that allow you to apply special effects to your images through tools such as filters. Two other important aspects of image-editing programs are that they allow you to manipulate scanned images such as photographs and to convert the file format of already existing images to file formats that you can use in your multimedia software. For example, you can convert EPS, TIFF, or MacPaint files to PICT files.

Most paint programs on the market include some image-editing capability, which varies in scale depending upon the quality of the program you choose. Of course, the programs with the most features are more expensive, but remember that when you buy an image-editing program you get all of the tools that come with a dedicated paint program, and usually much more. For example, Adobe Photoshop provides extensive image editing and conversion capabilities while also providing very detailed paint tools that can be customized. The paint capabilities of Photoshop can also be extended by using software like Kai's Power Tools which provides interesting and unusual visual effects, or Xaos Tools' Paint Alchemy, which provides a large variety of natural media paint effects. (See Figures 14.1 and 14.2.)

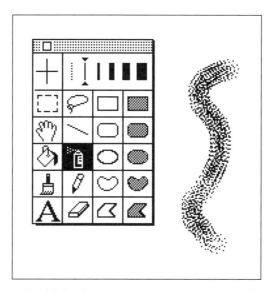

Figure 14.1 *Tool palette from a paint program and a line drawn with the Spray Can tool (Claris MacPaint)*

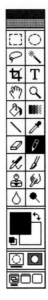

Figure 14.2 *Tool palette from an image-editing program (Adobe Photoshop)*

Common Paint Program Tools

Selection Tools

Since bitmapped graphics do not have individual shapes that can be selected, paint program selection tools are designed to select groups of pixels. Three common selection tools are the Rectangle Selection and Oval Selection tools, which allow you to select a rectangular or oval area, and the Lasso tool, which allows you to select irregularly shaped areas. Once selected, a group of pixels can be moved, deleted, or otherwise manipulated with the other tools and features available in the program. (See Figures 14.3 and 14.4.)

Paint Brushes

Paint program brushes are designed to simulate natural media effects, such as oil paints, spray cans, and airbrushes. They accomplish this by creating pixel patterns on the screen that approximate the way things work in the real world. For example, the Airbrush tool produces a dark area of color at the point of brush concentration and a finer, sparse effect at the edges; a paint brush produces an even, dark effect, but the edges are irregular.

Figure 14.3 *A selection made with the Rectangle Selection tool*

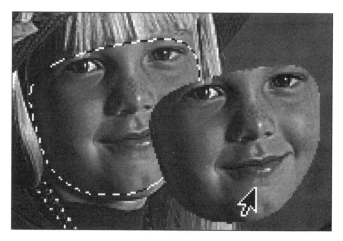

Figure 14.4 *A selection made with the Lasso tool and then moved*

Brush sizes, shapes, and patterns are editable within the programs. This capability allows you to control the type of effect that each tool produces. When you use these tools effectively, you can produce very realistic results; you can also use them to touch up or otherwise manipulate scanned photographs. (See Figures 14.5, 14.6 and 14.7.)

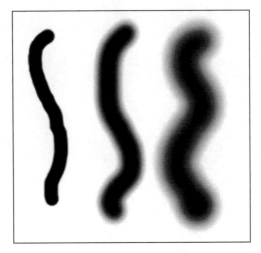

Figure 14.5 *Painted lines from left to right: paint brush with a hard edge, paint brush with a soft edge, and air brush*

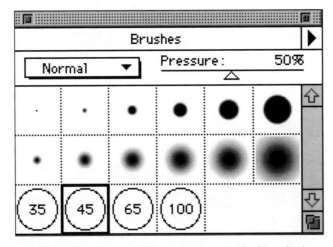

Figure 14.6 *The default brushes palette (Adobe Photoshop)*

Paint Bucket

The Paint Bucket tool is used to treat large areas of a bitmapped image with a color, gradient, or pattern. You click over the area that you want to treat. All adjacent pixels of the same color as the pixel clicked over are affected by the Paint Bucket tool. (See Figure 14.8.)

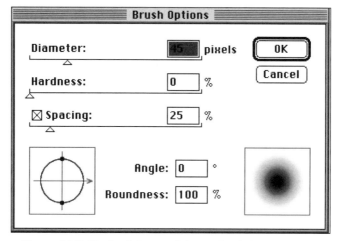

Figure 14.7 *The Brush Options dialog window (Adobe Photoshop)*

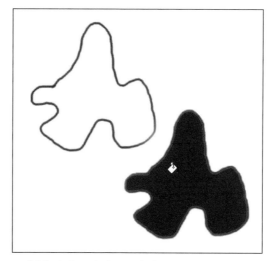

Figure 14.8 *A shape before and after using the Paint Bucket tool*

Masks

You use masks in image-editing programs like Adobe Photoshop to isolate an area so that you can use one of the other tools and affect only the area of the mask. You can also use masks to protect areas of an image from being inadvertently altered when you use a tool nearby. Masks are also useful for creating well-defined edges with the otherwise difficult to control brushes such as the spray can. A good real-world analogy is a stencil. (See Figure 14.9.)

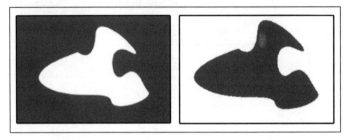

Figure 14.9 *A mask used to protect an area and fill another area*

Gradient Tool

You use the Gradient tool to create a cycle of color over an area. The Gradient tool can affect the entire area of a graphic or only a selected area. This is an excellent tool for creating textured backdrops for multimedia presentations. (See Figure 14.10.)

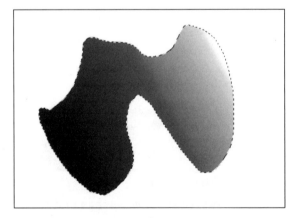

Figure 14.10 *An area filled with a grayscale gradient*

Eyedropper

You use the Eyedropper tool to sample a color from an area of an image. You can have only one color active in a paint brush at a time. For example the eye-dropper will help you find a specific color that you have already used. When you use it on a pixel in an image, it makes the color of that pixel the active color for your brushes. This capability is particularly useful when working with photographs in which pinpointing the exact color of a pixel with your eyes alone may be very difficult.

Pencil

You use the Pencil tool to treat single pixels in an image. Some programs, such as Fractal Design Painter and Sketcher, have various types of pencils besides this common form, such as pastel pencils or editable pencils that can produce a heavier line that spans more than one pixel. For the most part, you use this tool for fine retouching of bitmapped images. (See Figure 14.11.)

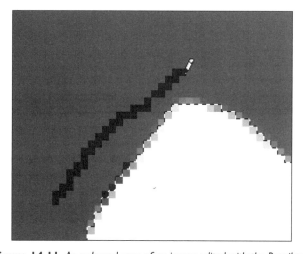

Figure 14.11 *An enlarged area of an image edited with the Pencil tool*

Using Text

In most programs on the Macintosh that use text, you can highlight text on the screen whenever you like and alter different characteristics of the text, such as font, size, or style. This process is a bit different in a bitmap graphics program because you can no longer use conventional text editing techniques on text within a bitmap graphic. This is because the text itself is converted into a bitmap graphic, or a group of pixels that only look like text. Once the text is placed in a bitmap graphics program the only way to edit it is to change each pixel, the same method with which you would alter any bitmap graphic. (See Figures 14.12 and 14.13.)

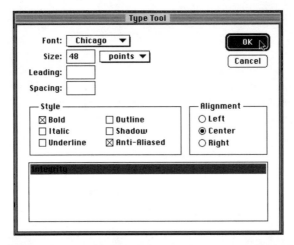

Figure 14.12 *A text entry window where text can still be edited (Adobe Photoshop)*

Figure 14.13 *Text placed into a Bitmapped Image*

Common Image-Editing Features

Image Conversion

The most fundamental feature of image-editing programs is the ability to convert an image from one file type to another. You will use this feature often. It behaves somewhat like a translator for your graphics files and ensures that you never have a problem with graphic file transfer in and out of your multimedia software. This capability is a necessity for any multimedia developer.

You will also use the ability of these programs to change the size of graphics. You need this capability to accommodate the many different places that your graphics can be seen. For example, if you develop a presentation to be shown on a computer other than your own, you can recreate your graphics to accommodate the screen you use during your presentation. You also need control over image size for applications such as development for television, which requires very specific image sizes.

Color conversion is also an important feature of image-editing programs. This feature allows you to alter the color depth of graphics to accommodate the different display capabilities of different monitors. This feature is necessary for television, which requires a different color code than that used for computer monitors.

Filters

You use filters to treat the entire image or only a selection of the image with a special effect. For example, the Gaussian Blur filter that comes with Adobe Photoshop causes a hazy effect that looks very cinematic. Filters are also sold separately through third-party developers and are called *plug-in* filters, because they can be installed in existing software and become available in the host program's menus. (See Figures 14.15 and 14.16.)

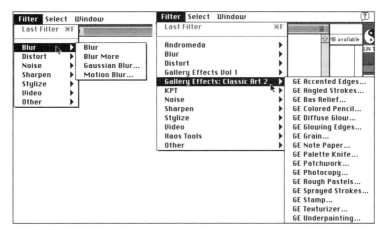

Figure 14.14 *The Filter menu before and after the installation of third party plug-in filters (Adobe Photoshop)*

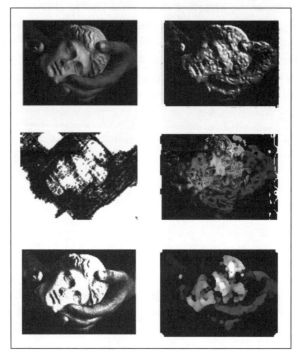

Figure 14.15 *An image (upper left) with filters applied to it. Clockwise: Craquelure, Ripple, Water Color, Film Grain, Charcoal (Filters from Aldus Gallery Effects, Libraries 1 and 2)*

The Alpha Channel

An alpha channel is information stored in image editing programs, such as Adobe Photoshop, that represents the shape, but not the colors in an image. Currently, an image can have up to 16 channels, but most have five or less. For example, an RGB image has three channels; red, green, and blue. The alpha channel is an optional channel that can be used as a mask for the graphic.

The alpha channel can also be used to determine transparent areas of an image. It will render the darker areas of an image opaque and the white areas transparent. This is tremendously valuable in digital output to video tape, because the alpha channel is what makes it possible to have one graphic superimposed over another—without completely obscuring the first image. (See Figure 14.16.)

Figure 14.16 *The alpha channel image (left) produced by an image (right)*

Three-Dimensional Graphics Programs

Three-dimensional graphics programs are designed to simulate scenes out of the real world by automatically reproducing the effects of perspective, detail, and light on surfaces and colors. This means that they take into account the third dimension of depth, which the two-dimensional drawing and paint programs are unable to do automatically. You place objects into a scene, arrange lights and other effects, and then render the scene, which results in a bitmapped image that you can place into other programs or use alone. (See Figure 15.1.)

Figure 15.1 *Three-dimensional program tool palette (Strata StudioPro)*

Three-dimensional programs create shadows and subtle shadings automatically, just by using the general settings that you specify. The resulting images are for the most part difficult to discern from actual photographs. The power here is that in essence you have a virtual photography studio in your computer where you can control every element and detail.

Another very important feature of many three-dimensional programs to multimedia is animation. All you actually do is create the origin and destination scenes of the animation, determine how long the animation will take place, and then render the animation. The program creates all of the intermittent frames. This is called *key framing*.

Three-D in Multimedia

You use three-dimensional programs to produce photo-realistic art for interactive presentations such as creating a user interface. You can create buttons and backgrounds that look as if they are made with real-world materials such as marble and metal. You can also use these programs to create animation for television and other video and multimedia applications. The openings of most news programs and sports events include some sort of three-dimensional animation, as do station identification spots.

WARNING

Three-dimensional programs use a lot of RAM. The minimum recommended by many three-dimensional software developers is 8 megabytes, but rendering animation and very detailed images will require much more. A better amount would be 20 megabytes of RAM. With 8 megabytes of RAM, you can familiarize yourself with the software. However, you will most likely need to increase your RAM when you are ready to start rendering animation projects.

Three-dimensional files also require large amounts of hard drive space, especially if they are animation files. Again, the more RAM you have, the better. Finally, most three-dimensional programs operate only on Macintosh computers with a 68030 processor or better. The lowest configuration on which you can reasonably expect to run these types of programs is an unaccelerated IIci with at least 8 megabytes of RAM and a minimum of 120 megabytes of hard disk space. It is also a good idea to have some way of backing up your files to clear up space on a full disk.

Modeling

Modeling is the process of creating the geometry of the shapes you want to have in your scene. This can be virtually anything. You can create a shape and then, using the tools available to you, create fine details to represent objects in the real, or imaginary, world.

You create models by working with *wireframes*, the framework representations of the objects in your scene. You can think of this procedure as something like working with chicken wire or clay. You mold and shape the frame until it is properly shaped. Later you cover the surface of these objects with images that help to provide a sense of realism.

Default Shapes

Default shapes are available on the tool palettes of most three-dimensional programs. These are typically simple geometric shapes such as spheres, cubes, and cylinders, which are the three-dimensional equivalent of the Circle and Square tools of drawing and paint programs. (See Figure 15.2.)

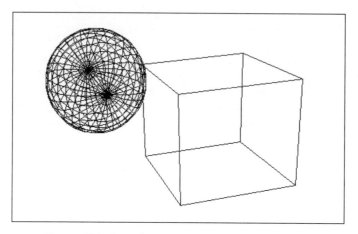

Figure 15.2 *A wireframe sphere and cube: default shapes*

Once default shapes are placed in a scene, you can edit them. For example, if you need a snowball, you can use a sphere and then shift the shape here and there to create an irregular surface. You may also find that arranging groups of default shapes creates more complex shapes. This does not necessarily increase the complexity of the file, because when you actually render the scene, the only surfaces that you see are those that are actually visible, not those that are embedded in other shapes.

Creating original shapes from scratch involves using a variety of procedures. You start with the same tools that you use to create two-dimensional drawing images and then use new tools to convert those two-dimensional shapes into three-dimensional objects. In fact, some programs such as Strata StudioPro and VIDI Presenter Professional actually permit you to import EPS artwork, which you can then use to create three-dimensional shapes. This feature is useful, because drawing programs are better equipped to create those types of designs and allow you greater control over those elements.

Lathing

Lathing, or *rotating,* is the process of taking a two-dimensional design and rotating it around an axis. The three-dimensional program then creates a three-dimensional object along the rotation's path. For example, if you create a 180° arc and rotate it 360° on its open end, you create a sphere. You can also rotate a shape any scale of degrees; therefore, if you rotate that same 180° arc 180° on its open end, you create a dome. (See Figure 15.3.)

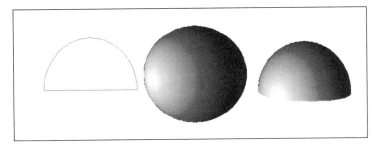

Figure 15.3 *A 180° arc (left) rotated into a sphere (center) and a hemisphere (right)*

Lofting

Lofting, or *skinning*, is the process of connecting two-dimensional cross sections to create a three-dimensional surface. This process has the appearance of a vacuum cleaner hose in which fabric or plastic is stretched over concentric wire circles to create a tube. The difference here is that you can create any shaped cross section and connect it to others. All you need to do is determine which cross section you want connected to which. (See Figure 15.4.)

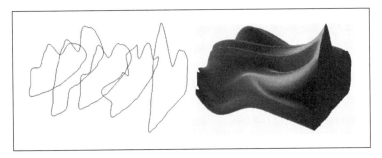

Figure 15.4 *Cross sections (left) lofted (right)*

Extruding

Extruding "pulls" two-dimensional shapes into the third dimension. If you extruded a circle, you would create a hollow cylinder. This is how three-dimensional text is created. You type text into the scene, which is converted into a two-dimensional graphic geometry and then extruded into the third dimension. You determine how far you want the depth of the extrusion to go. (See Figure 15.5.)

Figure 15.5 *A two-dimensional shape extruded into the third dimension*

Placement

You navigate objects in three-dimensional space the same way you would in a two-dimensional program. You select the object with a pointer tool and then position the object. If you want one object to appear behind another, you need to place it there in three-dimensional space. That means literally moving the object deeper into space and placing it behind another, just as you would with real-world objects. (See Figure 15.6.)

Surfacing

Surfacing, also called texture mapping or shading, is the process of adding to the appearance of an object. All three-dimensional models have a default surface that is visible when the scene is rendered, but this consists of a simple color. You can apply surfaces that give the appearance of wood or marble, or even use a graphic that you create in another program. Surfaces are also commonly called *textures*.

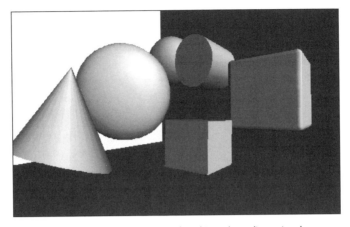

Figure 15.6 *Geometric shapes placed in a three-dimensional scene*

All three-dimensional programs offer a set of built-in surfaces, such as the wood and marble mentioned above. You can also create your own textures by either editing an existing texture, or importing a graphic and applying it to an object's surface. For example, you can use surfacing to create a label for a product or wallpaper for a room. (See Figures 15.7 and 15.8.)

Figure 15.7 *A texture palette (Strata StudioPro)*

Editing Surfaces

You can alter the appearance of a surface by manipulating the parameters of the settings associated with it. For example, you can change the reflective property of a surface so that it reflects surrounding objects. You can create a mirror or a shiny metal surface in a scene.

You can also change a variety of other surface properties, such as an object's opacity. You can use this capability to make an object transparent like glass. You can also change the refractive properties of an object so that it behaves like a prism or a jewel. Use this type of tweaking of a surface's properties coupled with fine-tuning geometry to create truly photo-realistic images. (See Figure 15.9.)

Figure 15.8 *A PICT graphic applied to a three-dimensional object as a surface*

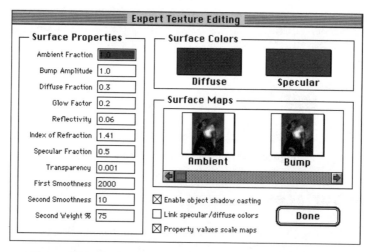

Figure 15.9 *The Expert Texture Editing dialog box (Strata StudioPro)*

Arranging Lights

Light is an important property of three-dimensional graphics because you use it to create shading and shadows. This property is divided into ambient light and object light. Using both types effectively enhances realism.

Ambient Light

Ambient light is the light that exists in a room when there is no obvious light source. It's the light that allows you to see in a room with no windows or artificial lights. The intensity of this light is usually quite low, but you can use it to create a natural-looking scene because it doesn't produce highlights and creates soft shading of surfaces.

You cannot edit the source of this light, because it is omnidirectional. You can, however, make it stronger. You can also edit its color. For example, you can create a landscape at sunset in which the sun is no longer shining directly on the scene but everything is washed in a warm red glow.

Object Lighting

Object lighting is lighting that is produced by objects that you place in the scene and that represent and behave as lights. With these lights you can edit color, direction, placement, and a variety of other properties, such as the effect of gels and filters applied to light. Your lighting effect options will depend upon the type of light you are manipulating. There are three different types of object lighting: directional light, point light, and spotlight.

Directional Light

Directional lights produce parallel rays of light from a distant, unseen light source. You can edit the direction, intensity, and color of this type of light. The shadows produced by this type of light are strong, and all point in the same direction in the scene. Use directional light to create an effect similar to that caused by the sun. (See Figure 15.10.)

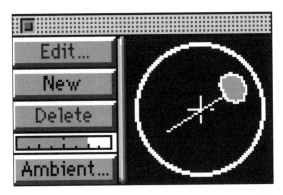

Figure 15.10 *The directional control palette (Strata StudioPro)*

Point Light

Point light is created by actually placing a light into a scene. You can edit the color and intensity of this type of light, but its field of effect is always omnidirectional. Point light behaves like a light bulb. (See Figure 15.11.)

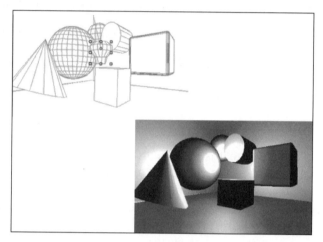

Figure 15.11 *A point light placed in a scene*

Spotlight

As the name implies, *spotlight* is positioned in a scene and then directed at the objects you want illuminated. It produces a circle of light in the scene. Aside from color, intensity, and direction, you can also edit this light's cone angle and the intensity of the light at the center or the beam as well as the edges. You can use this light to produce a dramatic, theatrical effect. (See Figure 15.12.)

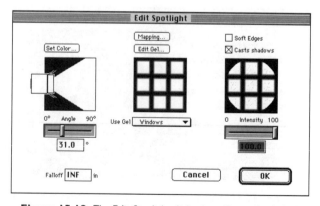

Figure 15.12 *The Edit Spotlight dialog box (Strata StudioPro)*

Other Lighting Effects

Some programs, such as Strata StudioPro, Pixar Typestry and Pixar Showplace, allow you to apply other treatments to light to produce a dramatic effect. For example, some allow you to apply gels to a light, like those used in photography and cinema. For example, you can produce an effect similar to light shining through window panes or venetian blinds. The artificial obstructions are incorporated in the light and create a realistic quality in the light. (See Figure 15.13.)

Figure 15.13 *A scene rendered with a window pane gel applied to a spotlight*

Another effect that some programs allow is applying a texture to a light. This produces an effect similar to that of a slide or movie projector. You can use this effect to apply a graphic to a light or anything else that you want to project onto the entire scene.

Animation and Keyframing

Animation is the process of creating a series of successive scenes that have similar content, but slight changes. When the images are presented to the user at a rate above 20 images per second, the eye perceives those slight changes as fluid motion. This is caused by a neurological process in the eye called *persistence of vision* in which an after image of one scene is still present in the eye when a new image is presented to it. The simple definition of animation is motion over time.

Many computers are incapable of playing animation at 20 frames per second, so animation must be created at slower frame rates for playback from a hard drive. 4 frames per second is the slowest playback on a computer that still produces the illusion of motion. The motion is quite staggered, but it is acceptable. The other setback is that higher frame rates require greater storage space the more individual images you have. Therefore, lower frame rates also help to economize disk space. QuickTime files play well at rates as low as 12 and 15 frames per second. As computers get faster and storage media becomes less expensive, animation playback will begin to near the fluid motion range of 20 frames per second. You can, of course, circumvent the problem by using accelerator devices and large hard drives. However, you might want to look into the machine configurations of those to whom you plan to distribute.

You create animation in three-dimensional programs by creating *keyframes*, which are scenes that represent the origin and destination locations of the objects in the scene. (This process is also called *keyframing, tweening,* or *in-betweening*.) For example, if you want to animate a ball flying across the screen, you first create the scene of the ball at the right side of the screen. Then you select a later time on the time line of the program's animation control and create the scene with the ball on the left side of the screen. Finally, you render the animation. (See Figure 15.14.)

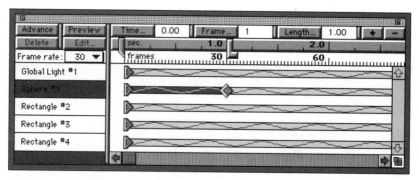

Figure 15.14 *The animation time line and palette (Strata StudioPro)*

The program then automatically renders intermittent frames of the ball moving across the screen. The successive positioning is evenly divided along the period of time that you predetermined on the time line. For example, if you want to create an animation for video tape, you set a frame rate of 30 frames per second.

If you want the ball to take 1 second to move across the screen for video, the program creates 28 successive frames between the first and last frames that you create. The distance that the ball travels in each frame is divided into 30 evenly spaced steps. This greatly reduces the amount of time that it takes to create animation; it also increases accuracy. All you need to do is set up keyframes, start the rendering, and leave your computer alone for a while. (See Figure 15.15.)

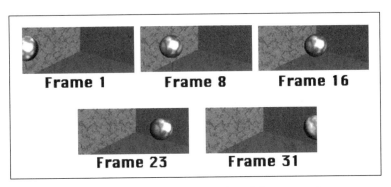

Frame 1   Frame 8   Frame 16

Frame 23   Frame 31

Figure 15.15 *A one-second animation of a ball flying across the screen*

Types of Three-Dimensional Animation

You can use several different forms of animation for your multimedia projects in three-dimensional programs. Two animate successive views of a scene, and one animates the objects within it. Combining these different methods can produce a dramatic and realistic effect. The three categories are fly-by, walk-through, and independent object animation.

Fly-By Animation

Fly-by animation occurs when you create keyframes by changing the positioning of your view of the scene. For example, if you position your view of a scene in one place and then create a later keyframe in which your view is different, the program creates all of the in-between frames that reflect the successive changes in your view. The effect is similar to flying by the object in the scene of the animation.

Walk-Through Animation

Walk-through animation is like fly-by animation, except that the animation path passes through the objects in a scene. For example, if you create an animation path that goes through a room, you have a virtual-reality effect of actually walking through your three-dimensional scene. This type of animation is commonly used in architecture to demonstrate the feel of being in a building that has not yet been built.

Independent Object Animation and Special Animation Effects

Independent object animation occurs when you animate the objects in a scene individually. For example, if you animate a car driving along a road, you make the car move through the scene as well as rotate the tires relative to the car's forward movement. This creates activity and "life" within a scene.

You can also render other object properties. For example, placing different textures on the same object at different points on its time line results in a gradual animated changing of the object's surface, which is similar to watching a chameleon's skin change. Some programs also allow you to change the geometry of an object along its time line, which results in a morphing effect such as having a car become a plane and then soar off into the sky.

You can also render the intensities, colors, positioning, and other effects of lights. If the relative positioning of a light alters shading and shadow effects in the scene, then those elements are edited as well. Consequently, if you animate a directional light, you can produce an effect similar to the sun passing overhead.

Rendering

Rendering is the process of creating the scene represented by your placed objects and lights. The different levels of rendering range from the finely detailed to the rough sketch that you use to preview your work while creating the scene. You cannot view your surfaces, reflections, shadows, and other lighting effects until you render the scene. This can be a time-consuming process depending upon the level of detail with which you choose to render your three-dimensional scenes.

Levels of Rendering

Wireframe

Wireframe is the default method of viewing your scene. The objects appear as framework that can be seen directly through. You can position and edit objects quickly while in this mode. (See Figure 15.16.)

NOTE

The example in Figures 15.16 through 15.22 use the same three-dimensional elements. The quality of the rendering brings out any details not previously visible.

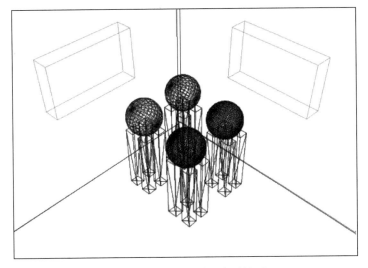

Figure 15.16 *Scene rendered in Wireframe*

Hidden Line Removed

The Hidden Line Removed method is similar to wireframe, except that you can no longer see through the objects. They appear solid, and their dimensional relationship is defined. This gives a clearer view of the true geometry of the objects that you are working with because it simplifies the information on-screen. This, too, is an editing mode but is a little slower than Wireframe to redraw on-screen. (See Figure 15.17.)

Quick Shading

Quick shading results in a solid rendering of the objects in the primary color of the surface applied. The objects are opaque, and there is no texture definition. No detail is visible, and the geometry of the objects are represented as facets instead of smooth surfaces. This method also calculates light intensity for the entire surface but does not show fine detail in shading. Using this method is the fastest way to create shaded scenes and still be able to edit your work. (See Figure 15.18.)

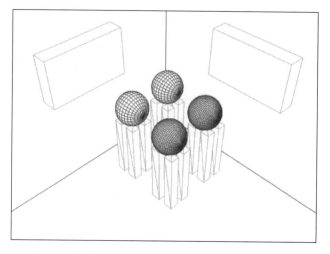

Figure 15.17 *Scene rendered with Hidden Line Removed*

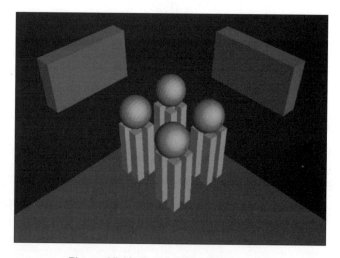

Figure 15.18 *Scene in Quick Shading mode*

Flat Shading

Flat shading is similar to quick shading, but it calculates light intensity and color for each facet separately. The geometry is smoother but still faceted. The resulting image is better, but it is still not well defined. This method is too slow to be used for preview purposes, and it does not have enough quality to be used as the final rendered image in your multimedia projects. It is almost always used for development and preview of animation. (See Figure 15.19.)

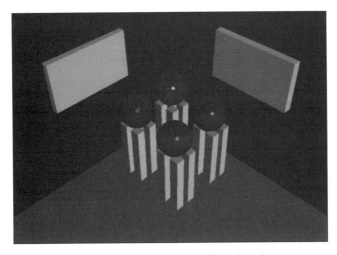

Figure 15.19 *Scene in Flat Shaded mode*

Gouraud Shading

Gouraud shading is the first level of rendering that shows a smooth surface. The facets are still there, but the way in which this method renders colors and light intensities makes them virtually invisible. This is good for quick rendering to check for geometry errors and to tweak shading detail and light effects. (See Figure 15.20.)

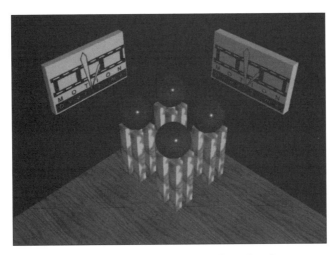

Figure 15.20 *Scene in Gouraud Shaded mode*

Phong Shading

Phong shading is one of the higher quality methods for rendering images. It calculates color and light information for every pixel in the image. Subtleties in lighting, color, shading, and texture are apparent. Shading and detail in surface and geometry are all now visible. Texture definition is visible in detail. For most applications this is adequate, but this method does not render special light effects such as reflectivity. (See Figure 15.21.)

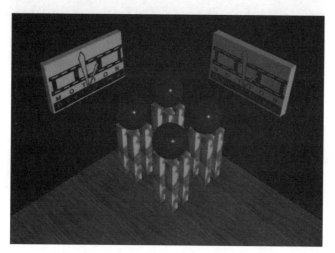

Figure 15.21 *Scene in Phong Shaded mode*

Ray Tracing

Ray tracing is an extremely slow but extremely high-quality rendering method. All detail and special effects are visible with reflections and lighting effects all visible. This is a particularly excellent way to render still images for extreme realism. This method is remarkably slow, so rendering for an animation can easily take days. Yes, days! Use this method judiciously, because it will tie up your machine for a long time. (See Figure 15.22.)

The actual length of time that ray-tracing requires is difficult to determine because the process is dependent upon the complexity of the images. Complexity involves the level of detail in surfaces, special effects such as transparency and reflectivity, the number of lights in the scene, and the calculation of shadows that are cast. The corporate logo used in *Chapter 4* was ray-traced in Specular International's Infini-D on a IIci with 8 megabytes of RAM at a resolution of 320×240, which is one quarter of an NTSC video screen. It took about 48 hours for all 30 frames of the 1 second animation to be completed. Of course, today's Macs are much faster, but you need to consider that even if the animation was 10 times faster it would still take about 5 hours. If you want to render that image for video tape you need to increase the size of the image by 4, which means that the image would take about 20 hours to render for video today. Also consider that most of the animation has a black background. Therefore, you would need to add some more time to the rendering if you want anything else to happen in the scene. This all adds up to a very busy Macintosh.

Figure 15.22 *Scene in Ray Tracing mode*

Proprietary Shading Techniques

Many programs offer a rendering option that is unique to its design. For example, Pixar has a rendering method called RenderMan (MacRenderMan for the Macintosh). This method is known for its high-quality rendering and surface detail. It does not provide much of the automatic detail that comes with ray tracing, but it still produces a very high-quality and realistic effect. Ray-tracing special effects can be achieved with some additional scene manipulation.

RenderMan also produces a text file that you can open in a word processing program. These files are called RenderMan Interface Bytestream (RIB) files and are similar to EPS files in that they can be edited in the word processor; the graphically rendered image reflects the changes. RIB files typically take a long time to render but are worth the wait. Pixar's ShowPlace and Typestry are the only programs that provide a GUI to this rendering method; a few others allow rendering through the proprietary RenderMan rendering engine, which is essential for rendering in this manner. MacroMedia's MacroMind 3D is an example of a program outside of Pixar's products that allows access to the RenderMan engine, but you must already own RenderMan to use this software.

Other programs also offer their own rendering methods. For example, Strata StudioPro offers a high quality rendering option called **Raydiosity** that is unique to Strata's products. Similar rules apply to these methods; the effects may be better, but they are still very slow. For the most part, sticking with the methods described above is most economical.

Rendering Special Effects

Many three-dimensional programs include special effects in rendering a scene, but the most common simulate special effects similar to that of a conventional camera. These effects are zoom, wide angle lens, fish-eyed lens, etc. They produce the same results as their real-world equivalents in the photography and cinema industries. If you think of your rendering view as actually being a camera, you will get a whole new perspective on creating graphics with these programs.

Using Text

Text can produce a powerful effect in any animation. It is the key tool used in creating most logos. The ability to use text in three-dimensional programs is a tremendous bonus. You simply select the text you want to use, edit it accordingly, and then extrude it into the third dimension. You can then treat it as any other three-dimensional object in your scene.

All three-dimensional programs offer a Text tool for creating three-dimensional text. A few products are designed to work with text alone, such as Pixar Typestry and StrataType 3D. These programs are cheaper than full-featured three-dimensional programs and are extremely useful. (See Figure 15.23.)

WARNING The Text tool in many three-dimensional programs works with any fonts installed in your system, but you may come across a few programs that work only with either TrueType or PostScript fonts. This limitation may affect the variety of fonts available for use with this tool. If you have a program with this limitation, then you can use a type conversion utility to convert any noncompatible fonts you have to the format that you need.

Figure 15.23 *Extruded text rendered in Pixar's Typestry using MacRenderMan*

Part V

Putting the "Multi" in Multimedia

Once you have captured your video, digitized your sound effects and music, recorded your voice-overs, created your graphics, and rendered your animations, you need to bring it all together. Multimedia composition software such as Adobe Premiere and DiVA VideoShop, along with interactive authoring programs, such as Macromedia Director, Authorware Professional, and Claris HyperCard come into play here. This software is the multimedia equivalent of page layout programs in desktop publishing. The elements are already created; you just work on the show now.

Multimedia Composition Software

You use this type of software to create a straightforward, linear presentation. The process is very similar to editing video or film: You bring all of your "footage" together in one place (video, sound, and graphics) and then combine them to create multisensory productions for output to video tape or for use in on-screen exhibits, or even interactive presentations that you prepare with different software. This topic is covered in *Chapter 16.*

QuickTime in Multimedia Composition Software

One of the most useful features of many multimedia composition software programs is the ability to export QuickTime files. QuickTime is the only file format on the Mac that effectively combines video and sound in one place, because it uses software compression methods that allow large video and audio files to be stored as smaller files. These compressed files are decompressed during playback in a method that optimizes playback. For example, only the information that changes in a frame is decompressed and displayed in the movie. There are several different compression methods called CODECs (compression/decompression) that are available as options in creating QuickTime movies. There are CODECS that are best for animation. Others that are designed for video. And the list goes on.

Besides video, multimedia composition software will bring in other elements such as still graphics, independent sound files, and animation. Multimedia composition software can also output single frames of a composition; the sound is lost, but you can create presentations that can be accurately output frame by frame to video tape.

Interactive Authoring Software

Chapter 17 covers interactive authoring software, which is used to create nonlinear, interactive presentations. In these presentations, the user can determine what happens next by pressing buttons on-screen or making some other form of selection, such as positioning objects relative to each other on screen, or entering text into a field. Interactive authoring software is used to create CD-ROM programming.

Essentially, this software is the true marriage of art and programming because it allows you to create graphics in programs designed for that purpose and then visually design how you will present them to the user. You then create interactivity by using scripting languages, which come with the authoring software, to write simple programs. Authoring program scripting languages, such as Macromedia Director's Lingo are constructed with highly intuitive techniques and language, and are very easy to learn.

Authoring software, such as Macromedia Director and Authorware Professional, is perfect for artists and other creative professionals because they do not need to know programming. Besides, an artist can learn how to program, but teaching someone how to be creative is impossible. Because of the emphasis on creativity, your programming already has the most important feature nailed down: It'll look good.

Sound-Editing Software

Sound is an all too important and often overlooked element of multimedia. Many multimedia and all interactive authoring programs have the ability to use sound, but few offer any editing features. If you want to work effectively with sound, you need to use a program designed specifically for that purpose.

Chapter 18 covers sound-editing software, which is the audio equivalent of image-editing software. You can bring in a sound in whatever format that you choose, even raw data that has been recorded directly to the hard drive, shorten it, expand it, clip it, and apply other filters and effects to it. In other words, you can create custom sounds at custom lengths that work best with your presentation. You can also create sound loops, which are sounds that immediately return to the beginning when they reach the end. This type of sound plays endlessly and is very useful in multimedia development, especially for hard disk space conservation.

Chapter 19 covers getting your multimedia projects out there to your audiences.

Multimedia Composition Software

Bringing It All Together

You use *multimedia software* to combine graphics, animation, video, music, voice-over, and sound effects. Once they are combined, you can use your compiled projects in other multimedia productions, output them to video tape, or incorporate then in your interactive projects or on-screen presentations. Essentially, multimedia begins here, because you incorporate elements of different media origin in the same digital environment at this point.

All multimedia software has common elements. They are capable of importing digitized files of various sorts. They allow you to edit and recompose them flexibly. Finally, they allow you to save and export your files in a format that is easily transferable and useful in other programs throughout the Macintosh environment.

Generally, you use graphics and other multimedia elements that were created outside of your multimedia editing program. For example, you use three-dimensional animation created in programs specifically designed for that purpose or video that was captured through a video capture card, saved in a digital file format, and then imported into your software. As a result, you put a tremendous amount of work into multimedia projects before you even begin to work with multimedia editing software.

This preliminary work is all part of the fun, but it requires a great deal of foresight and an understanding of the relationship between different types of software. You need to be aware of issues such as the dimensions of the graphics that you create in two-dimensional programs for import to multimedia software. You also need to keep frame rate, color depth, and other such issues in mind, especially if you intend to bring your multimedia projects out of the computer and onto video tape or CD-ROM. Multimedia production occurs in many stages, each increasingly dependent upon the prior stage.

As in most things, planning is key here. Begin with small projects. Use the software included on the CD-ROM, and, most of all, be patient. Once you become the least bit proficient with multimedia software, you will rapidly begin creating professional-quality work.

QuickTime

Multimedia composition software is the software that you will use to create QuickTime movies. As mentioned in *Chapter 11*, QuickTime is an extension of the Macintosh system software which allows animation, video, and audio information to be stored in a single document called a QuickTime file. QuickTime files allow multimedia projects to be transported between programs as easily as graphic files can be transported between programs. Also, because QuickTime is a system extension it is not dependent upon any software other than the system for playback. All multimedia composition software programs have the capability of producing QuickTime movies. QuickTime is also becoming a cross-platform file format with an increasing presence in the Microsoft Windows environment.

In multimedia composition software, you can customize the QuickTime window according to your intended use. For example, you can create an NTSC-sized window for use in video tape and a smaller window for CD-ROM. You can also use different frame rates in a QuickTime file that affect playback performance and file size. You may find, however, that slower frame rates do not negatively affect playback for many applications.

One other property of QuickTime are the compression methods. When you save a file as QuickTime, you are given several compression options that optimize playback according to the nature of the data. For example, there is a compression option for video and another for animation. These compression methods compress the QuickTime movie accordingly so that it uses less disk space and plays smoother and faster in your multimedia projects. The best way to determine which is best for your project is to simply experiment. (See Figure 16.1.) When you convert a multimedia composition into a QuickTime movie, it is translated into a single file. As a result, each multimedia element in your composition loses its identity as a separate file. This may not affect in-computer applications, but it does affect video applications in two ways:

✳ You will lose control of the file as individual frames, so it will be impossible for you to record to video frame accurately. As a result, you will need to rely upon your computer's ability to play video at NTSC screen size at 30 frames per second, which is quite demanding on any computer.

✳ The compression of a QuickTime movie diminishes quality in areas that may not be apparent in computer playback, but could be quite noticeable in video playback.

You will find more on QuickTime and how it is used with video in *Chapter 11.*

The Multimedia Composition and Editing Production Process

Preference Settings

At this time you need to determine the settings that apply throughout the project, such as frame rate and window size. Usually, this information is based upon what you ultimately intend to do with the finished composition. These settings work hand in hand with the type of files that you import for composition and the output setting that you choose for the completed work, such as QuickTime or numbered PICT files. Many programs now include preset preference settings making this process as simple as making a menu selection of **NTSC** settings or **CD-ROM Development** settings.

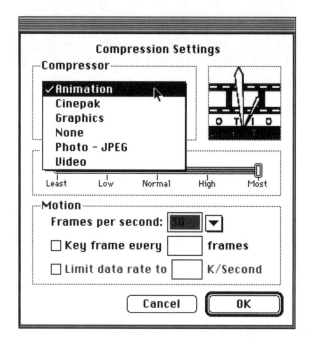

Figure 16.1 *A compression options dialog box*

Output for playback from a hard drive or a CD-ROM requires a relatively small window size and a frame rate around 10 FPS for eventual output as a QuickTime movie. You can follow these same settings for multimedia productions created in Macromedia Director to create files called Movies that will play independently of Director. These settings are necessary mainly because you cannot predict where your files will wind up, and conservative settings help ensure that your project has reasonably good playback on slower Macintosh computers. On the other hand, if you are creating for frame accurate recording to video tape, you need to be more concerned that your output image is large enough for a television's screen. Playback from the hard drive is unimportant, but maintaining that your project uses 30 frames to complete a second in video playback is. (See Figure 16.2.)

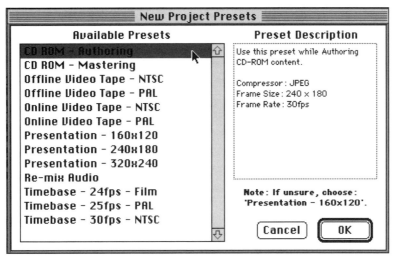

Figure 16.2 *The Adobe Premiere preferences dialog box*

WARNING

Remember that multimedia can play back on virtually all Macintosh computers, even though multimedia development is restricted to the machines that can power very demanding software. If you develop for only the fastest machines, you exclude a large percentage of your potential audience. There are ways to produce multiple versions of the same file that will work best based upon the playback machine. Your program, or other multimedia presentation, will use the appropriate version when it is opened. Selective playback is covered in *Chapter 17.*

Import

Compiling the files that you use in your multimedia production is similar to collecting all of the text and graphics that you would use in a page layout document. The files are imported but not immediately used in a composition. First they are stored until called upon to be incorporated into the composition. For example, Adobe Premiere has a window called the Project window where you can see all of the multimedia elements that have been imported into the program, as well as information that is pertinent to the clip. Imported files remain here until they are dragged into the Construction window where they become a part of the presentation. (See Figures 16.3 and 16.4.)

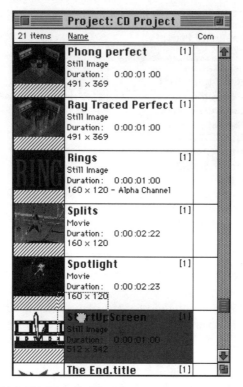

Figure 16.3 *The Adobe Premiere Project window with a selection being dragged to the construction window*

The major difference here, of course, is that the holding place in a multimedia program can store a large variety of files including graphics, video, audio, and animation. Typically, the holding place is a window, or palette, with some identifying information about the nature of the multimedia files within it. For example, the holding place may have the following information about an animation stored there: the type of animation that it is, its dimensions, its duration, a thumbnail graphic that consists of a single frame from the animation, and some other information that is pertinent to your work.

The preferences and output settings that you input for your project affect the incorporation of imported files. For example, imported files may simply differ in dimensions from your intended output window size. You may be able to correct this difference by resizing the imported file, but this option invariably results in distortion or loss of detail.

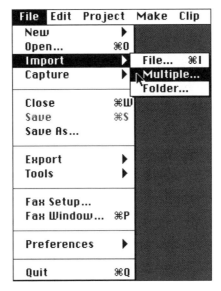

Figure 16.4 *An Import File pop-up menu*

The best way to avoid this type of problem is to create your multimedia files with all of the correct settings while they are still in their source programs. Make certain that color depth and frame rate are consistent, image size is correct, audio is properly prepared and of the appropriate length, and as many other fine-tuning elements as are necessary are accounted for. Any of these types of changes that can be altered within multimedia composition programs usually yield a lesser result, and you end up recreating the files in the original program anyway.

Proper preparation of your files allows you to use multimedia composition software for its specific intended purpose, which is combining multimedia elements from different sources. From experience you learn simple formulas that help you prepare files according to their intended use so that your multimedia projects come together smoothly. For example, you learn to make certain that the dimensions of images created for video are 640×480 pixels with a frame rate of 30 frames per second.

 If you need to change one of the multimedia elements within the composition program, you should downgrade the element rather than attempt an upgrade in quality. In other words, it is always better to

N O T E   decrease the size of an image, color depth, and so on, than to create higher settings or increase image sizes. You have more flexibility if you remove quality; because the information is already there, you are simply taking away what isn't needed.

On the other hand, you cannot add what is not already there. For greater flexibility with multimedia elements within the composition program, always produce your original files with higher quality than you may need. Of course, you get larger file sizes, which are entirely unnecessary if you are clear about what you want your end result to be from the start.

Composition

The time to position your multimedia elements within the Construction window is at hand. You arrange graphics, captured video, animation, audio, and other multimedia file types in the Construction window of your composition software according to where you want them to occur in your production. You can think of *composition* as being the general layout of your project, like an extremely detailed storyboard. (See Figure 16.5.)

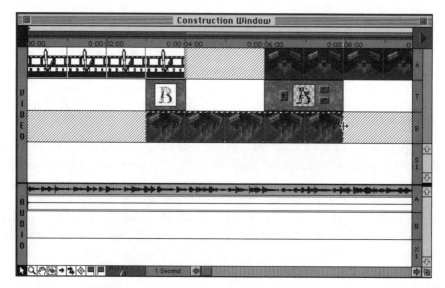

Figure 16.5 *The Adobe Premiere Construction window*

As you drag your multimedia elements from the storage window that they were imported to, you are actually dragging only a representation of that file. It does, however, carry the reference that the composition software will use to access the actual animation from the original file in the clip window. The image you drag into a Construction window is just a placemarker and visual reference for you. As a result, you can drag each multimedia element onto your construction window as frequently as you choose. The actual files are duplicated when you save your finished design as a file type that can be used in other programs.

The layout of the Construction window is a visual representation of a video-editing setup. In other words, there are tracks for visual elements, tracks for audio elements, and a separate track for effects and transitions, such as wipes and dissolves. The greater difference here is that you have much greater flexibility with the number and types of tracks available for your composition.

You place your multimedia elements on the Construction window timeline and then move them around to their correct positions in time. Next, you place audio (if the file doesn't already have audio attached to it, as may be the case with a QuickTime movie) and align it with the video elements. Finally, you edit the elements and apply filters and effects.

Many multimedia composition programs now offer the opportunity to customize the number of video and audio files that are available in the composition window. In this way, you can mix multiple tracks of audio in any portion of you project. You can also layer multiple video elements. This flexibility is a far cry from the previous limit of two audio tracks and two standard video tracks.

Adobe Premiere 3.0 (included on the CD-ROM) allows you to customize your window to include up to 99 tracks of video and 99 tracks of audio. You probably won't need that many tracks for most projects, especially in video, but for sound, numerous tracks can be extremely useful. You can add multiple sound effects over the standard voice-over and music that you use most frequently and that probably take up the first two tracks of audio available. (See Figure 16.6.)

Editing

At this point you need to use a nonlinear editing process (discussed later in this section) to change the length of the multimedia elements in you composition. Using the same technique as you use on the conventional video-editing process, you set *in-* and *out-points* that the program uses to determine what part of a multimedia element you actually want included in your composition. For example, say you have a bit of captured video that lasts for 10 seconds, but you want to use only a 5-second portion of it that begins 2 seconds into the clip. You can simply set an in-point 2 seconds into the clip and an out-point 7 seconds into the clip. These settings isolate the portion that you want to use. When you save the newly modified clip, the program creates a new multimedia element that you can call on from its own window. The original clip is usually unchanged so that all of the original information is available to you. (See Figure 16.7.)

Add/Delete Tracks

Total video tracks: 5

Total audio tracks: 16

Cancel   OK

Figure 16.6 *The custom track number dialog box*

Figure 16.7 *A video clip with in- and out-points*

You can also use this process to connect two portions of video or other elements that you want to happen consecutively, or occur within one another. This procedure is similar to creating insertions in video editing. For example, a movie may have two shots of an actor in the same scene, such as a close-up of her face and a shot of her in the same scene with her dog. By alternating the two shots and synchronizing the audio properly you can create a more visually interesting scene. Editing is as much a part of the process of production as is the actual creation of the original image. (See Figure 16.8.)

Figure 16.8 *A video clip inserted within another to create alternating clips*

When you place a still graphic on the composition line, the program displays an icon that represents an arbitrary unit of time depending upon the program you are using, usually 1 second because frame rates are based upon 1 second. You can change the length of time that a still graphic displays in an image, but the default setting of 1 second is only significant because it is a round figure that is already used by other standards. This graphic displays in your final composition for that 1 second unless you choose to do something else, such as stretch it farther along the timeline. Only this type of multimedia element can be edited in this manner, others last only the duration of the original file. You can, however, reduce the duration of other file types or, as mentioned, extract only a portion. (See Figure 16.9.)

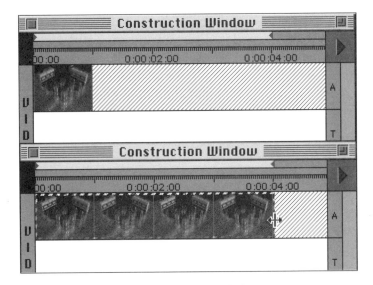

Figure 16.9 *A still graphic stretched out over time*

Nonlinear Editing

In the conventional method of video editing, you record only selected portions of an original (source) video tape to another (record) video tape. This process requires that each video tape be either fast-forwarded or rewound to the locations where the image and sound that you want to use is located. This process is called *linear editing*, because you must treat all of your video and audio production elements as if they were located along a string and must be accessed by moving backward and forward along that string.

Computer (digital) editing of the same materials is much more straightforward. All of the elements that you wish to use (video and audio) are digitized and stored on a hard drive. Here they can be randomly accessed. You need not move past other video and audio elements located on the same drive. This process is called *nonlinear editing*.

Video tape loses its quality each time it is recorded to a new generation or if it is played frequently enough to have the actual playback head wear the tape down. The professional editing industry is turning more and more toward using digital equipment, but there are setbacks such as the fact that nonlinear editing requires very fast computers and a great deal of hard disk space. The overall cost of conventional video editing equipment combined with the time that a digital non-linear editing system can save in post-production can very well justify the expense of a nonlinear editing system.

Transition Effects and Filters

The type of editing discussed so far results in *straight cuts*, video and audio that immediately switch to the next consecutive clip. Although using straight cuts gets the job done, you may want to make your multimedia projects more visually interesting by applying special effects to them. These types of effects are easy to apply; many of them use the same filters used in image-editing programs.

Transition Effects

Transition effects make the change from one portion of a video composition to another more interesting, as opposed to abrupt switching between scenes, which in editing terminology are referred to as *cuts*. An example is a *dissolve*, in which the original clip fades away while the next clip in sequence materializes, or a *wipe*, in which the next clip in sequence conceals the original clip in some direction, such as from the left or right side of the screen.

Most multimedia composition programs come with their own effects. Usually the program presents them in a floating window of their own and places them in the composition with the same method as the multimedia elements themselves are integrated. You actually drag the icon that represents the type of effect you want onto the composition window. By placing the transition icon between the clips that you want the transition to effect, you apply it. Then, you can make some adjustments to the effect such as specifying the duration of the effect and changing other settings that depend upon the type of effect you choose. (See Figures 16.10 and 16.11.)

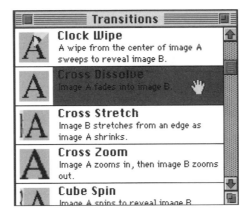

Figure 16.10 *The Adobe Premiere transition effects window*

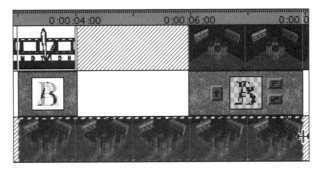

Figure 16.11 *A transition effect placed in the Construction window*

Strategic and artful use of transition effects can bring a cinematic quality to your productions that adds professionalism. Take advantage of them and learn their subtleties by testing them in different conditions. The fact that you can use

sophisticated transitions on a computer is a tremendous benefit; video professionals pay anything up to several thousands of dollars just for that functionality
in their editing setups.

Filters

Filters in multimedia composition programs function the same way as those found
in image-editing programs because the graphics in both programs are bitmap in
nature. In fact, many of the plug-in filters designed for image-editing programs
can also be used with multimedia composition programs. (See Figure 16.12.)

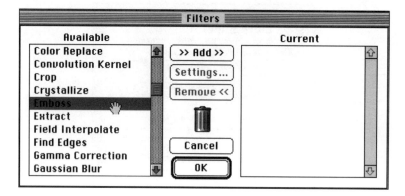

Figure 16.12 *A filters dialog box*

The major difference here is that filters in image-editing programs affect several
frames as opposed to only a single image in multimedia programs. This filtering
happens automatically when you determine the parts of the composition that
you want the filter to affect. Using this functionality can produce remarkable
results such as making captured video look as if it were created with mosaic
tiles and animated.

Many filters are designed to simply combine two images. These filters are
designed into the program's interface as opposed to being plug-ins that are
located external to the program and then linked to it. These types of filters are
used to create effects such as *superimposition*, masks to create an image within
a shape that is located within an image. You can even apply effects to transparencies so that one image is visible through another. For example, you could
create a composite image of horses running, while, visible through them, water
splashes down on a beach.

You could also animate one image over another. For example, in automobile commercials a car that has been driving along a road can gradually begin to move across the screen on a floating square while information is displayed below it. Remember that, because movement draws attention and generates greater visual interest, you should use it to your advantage whenever possible. Just be sure that you don't overdo the use of motion because it can distract the viewer and defeat the purpose of attracting attention to the important information in your composition.

Using Text

Most multimedia composition software includes the capability to create titles. This capability takes the form of most text utilities in bitmap programs: You have a dialog box in which you can enter the text and change its style, size, font, and alignment. You then are able to animate the text in your composition to produce effects such as scrolling text, which are shown at the end of a movie, or stationery titles that you can fade in and out at the beginning of your composition. (See Figure 16.13.)

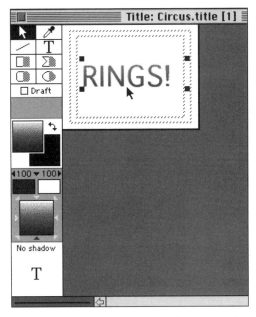

Figure 16.13 *The text dialog box for creating titles*

Sound

Sound has become rather sophisticated in multimedia composition programs. With multiple tracks, you can now layer as many sounds as you will ever find useful in a project. You can even save your composition as a sound that can be imported in another program or used within another composition. (See Figure 16.14.)

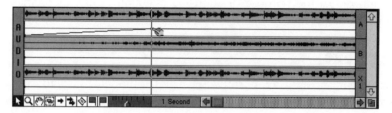

Figure 16.14 *Audio tracks in the Construction window*

Available in many multimedia composition programs now is the ability to capture audio from a playback device directly to the hard drive. With this technique, you can connect a microphone or other input device to your computer and record sounds directly into your composition. You can then determine where your new sound takes place in your composition. This capability allows you to use one program to serve all of your multimedia composition needs. (See Figures 16.15 and 16.16.)

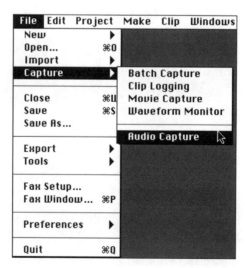

Figure 16.15 *The Audio Capture menu item (Adobe Premiere)*

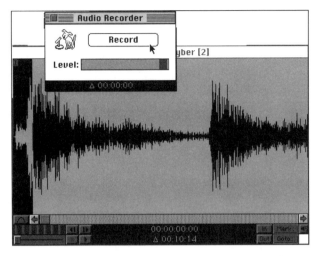

Figure 16.16 *Audio editing window (Adobe Premiere)*

Sound Editing Capability in Multimedia Composition Programs

Some multimedia composition programs, such as Adobe Premiere, can apply simple effects to audio, such as echo, fading a sound in or out, or using only a portion of a sequence of sounds. They do so by applying the same in and out-point technique used for video. Multimedia programs, however, do not provide the same level of editing capability over sound that specialized sound utility programs such as SoundEdit Pro can. Sound editing utilities can be used to apply effects to sounds, such as reversing the sound wave, adding reverb to the sound, or changing the pitch. Sound editing, and sound editing utilities are covered in greater detail in *Chapter 18*.

You may find that a specialized audio utility program creates a greater level of flexibility with sounds, but the audio manipulation capability of multimedia composition software may be all you truly need to start.

Previewing, Saving, and Exporting

While you are arranging, editing, and applying effects to your composition, you can preview it. Previewing the composition consists of telling the program to create a temporary composition based upon the information in the Construction window. In this way, you can survey your composition while you create it and determine whether you are getting the desired results. (See Figure 16.17.)

Figure 16.17 *The Preview window (Adobe Premiere)*

Once you have completed the composition process, you can save your file in any one of a number of file formats. You can even save and reimport a composition in another composition in the same program. You can also save the file in other popular file formats such as PICS files, which create a single image for each frame of the composition but retain a single file on the hard drive. You can also save the composition as a QuickTime movie that also retains audio information. The file format that you choose depends upon its final use. (See Figure 16.18.)

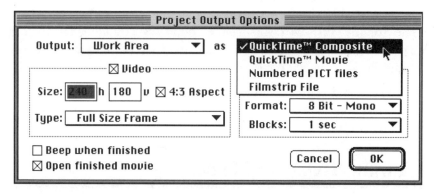

Figure 16.18 *The Multimedia Composition Output Options dialog box (Adobe Premiere)*

Filmstrip Files and Rotoscoping

Depending upon the program that you choose, you may have the option to export your compositions as *filmstrip* files. This special file type displays each frame of your composition in image-editing programs such as Adobe Photoshop. Here you can use a technique called *rotoscoping* to treat each frame. In this technique you paint each frame of your composition to create different animation style effects or to touch up a video file. The filmstrip composition can then be returned to the multimedia composition with the new information for export as a multimedia file that can be used in other programs. (See Figure 16.19.)

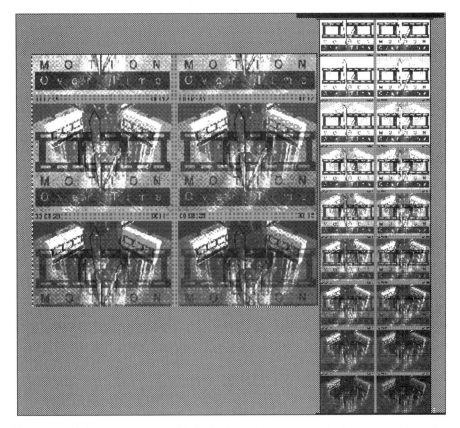

Figure 16.19 *A filmstrip file opened in Adobe Photoshop for rotoscoping (small and enlarged views)*

Chapter

17

Interactive Authoring Software

Multimedia brought sound and video to computer production, but it does so in a passive manner. In other words, it doesn't directly involve the user—just as television allows you to watch but not interact with the program. This peculiarity doesn't allow you to take full advantage of what can be accomplished with the computer, especially since most people will probably view your projects on a computer with a mouse and keyboard right in front of them. They could certainly interact with the computer if they had that option. Authoring software comes in here.

Interactive authoring software bridges the gap between graphic art and computer programming. You can integrate different multimedia elements, including graphics created in other programs, and use them in your program design. You can present them in as simple a format as a slideshow presentation or as detailed as a CD-ROM game.

Control in Multimedia

Authoring programs provide user control through the use of intuitive scripting languages that take the same structure as a programming language but are used more directly with the rest of the programs interface. For example, the scripting language for HyperCard is called HyperTalk, and the scripting language for Macromedia Director is called Lingo. Both can be used for similar results, but the syntax varies so that some terms are not the same in both programs. However, if you learn the structure of one scripting language, others are much easier to learn, and you can eventually learn complex dedicated programming languages such as C++ and Pascal, if that is in your plans.

Authoring programs are designed to be useful at whatever level of skill that you currently stand on. You can use them as an animation tool to create projects for video tape or other uncontrolled presentations, or you can use varying degrees of scripting to add little or great control or detail in your design. Authoring software is powerful, and can be used in as complex a manner as a dedicated programming language.

The recent tremendous increase in the popularity in the authoring area of multimedia can be attributed to CD-ROM. Authoring programs and projects created with them have been around for a long time, but they required large amounts of disk space and are difficult to distribute. Large-capacity hard disks are much less expensive now and are quickly becoming the norm in business as well as household computer systems. This change in status, coupled with the ability to distribute large amounts of data inexpensively on CD-ROM and the fact that CD-ROM readers are now common desktop equipment, has resulted in more people looking to authoring programs for program development. They are easier to use, can create much flashier results than any programming language could do alone, and allow graphic artists to use their greatest skills to their advantage without needing to be programmers. Authoring programs and CD-ROM have opened the doors of program and game development to virtually everyone.

The Authoring Process

The *authoring process* is similar to the multimedia composition process. First, you must determine what you want your project to accomplish. This end can be anything from a simple animation to a detailed interactive game that uses photorealistic graphics that you created in a three-dimensional graphics program. After you determine what your project is and what you want it to look like, you can begin composition.

The next step is to bring all of the elements that you plan to use in your authoring program together. They can be held either in a storage area built into the program's interface or in a common folder on the hard drive until you use them. Then, you need to create the composition by arranging your elements in a construction window in concert with a preview method of some sort. Finally, you need to integrate scripts that provide detail, interactivity, and user control in your program's design.

You then must package your program in a stand-alone application that does not require a copy of the authoring software to run. Most authoring programs provide a utility for accomplishing this task. Finally, you need to distribute your project in whatever manner you choose.

Interface Design

Interfaces can vary dramatically. Although the overall development process is similar in all cases, finding what works best for you is truly a matter of research and preference. Some interfaces provide a holding area for your multimedia elements, similar to the holding area found in multimedia composition programs. Others require that you import each element at the point when you intend to use it. For those programs that do not provide a holding area, it is good practice to create a special folder on your hard drive where you collect all of the multimedia elements that you intend to use in a project. (See Figure 17.1.)

The construction area of a program varies according to the focus of the program. For example, Authorware Professional, which is designed primarily for training applications and is used mostly by corporate users, is based upon a flowchart design in which the logic of the application is literally mapped out. Director, on the other hand, is based upon the concept of a music sheet, or score, creating a sort of visual symphony. The vertical cells represent a single frame containing graphics, audio, transitions, scripts, and other controls, and the

horizontal cells represent frames over time. This design reflects Director's primary users, who generally come from a variety of other artistic backgrounds
including music. (See Figures 17.2 and 17.3.)

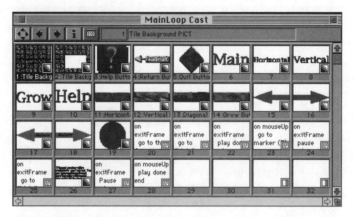

Figure 17.1 *The Main Loop Cast, the holding area in Macromedia Director*

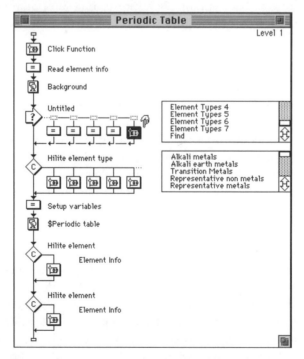

Figure 17.2 *The Authorware Professional construction window*

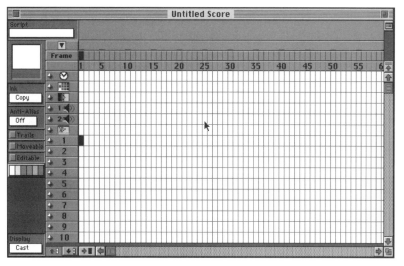

Figure 17.3 *The Macromedia Director score*

Composition

Importing Files

Authoring programs use the same multimedia elements that multimedia composition programs use—audio, video, animation, and still graphics. They can also import and use QuickTime movies and even files created in the same program. Using other files created in the same program allows you to nest your files and create very intricate designs while maintaining strong organization. (See Figure 17.4.)

Placing the Multimedia Elements

The next step is to place the graphic, sound, and other elements that you want included in your design. For example, if you are developing a simple presentation, you place the graphics that create the background and the buttons and other elements in their appropriate places on the screen. You also place transition effects between different slides, frames, animation, and so on, as well as integrate music into your composition here.

This is somewhat like the multimedia equivalent of document layout in a program like Aldus PageMaker, but the multimedia equivalent of pages are frames that are designed to be dynamic. You can place QuickTime movies in frames, buttons, text entry windows, or anything else that you would expect to find in a conventional program. The power here is that you can consider the design first and deal with the programming, if any, later. In this way, you can concentrate on content as opposed to the method.

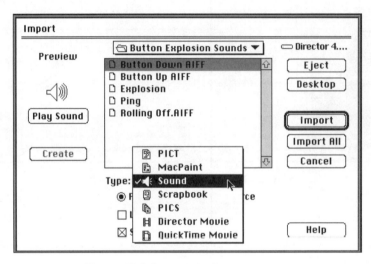

Figure 17.4 *Import dialog box pop-up menu*

Creating Simple Animation

With authoring programs you can create animation paralleling the traditional method of cell animation. You can create sequential images of some sort, such as images of a man walking, and then place them in consecutive frames of your program. You can control the speed of playback to get your desired result. This technique is really the only way to get two-dimensional animation out of the Macintosh computer, or any other computer for that matter. This function is the most elemental use for authoring software, but it is by no means the least important and can certainly enhance any interactive presentation. (See Figure 17.5.)

User Control and Scripting

When you use scripting, you determine how the user interacts with your program. If it is a simple slideshow presentation, then you write scripts for buttons that advance the program one frame at a time when they are pressed. If it is a game, then you write scripts that create game controls and methods for keeping score along with other gaming issues. This area of multimedia is very powerful. It is the fastest growing and most lucrative area to get involved with today.

Figure 17.5 *Sequential images for a two-dimensional animation*

Scripting languages in authoring programs are very similar in form to dedicated programming languages. You will be using If-Then-Else statements, repeat loops, tests, conditions, define methods and procedures, arguments, strings, variables, and just about anything else programming-like. If you have programming experience, then scripting languages in authoring software will be a breeze. If you have no programming experience, scripting languages in authoring software will be a terrific start and will greatly facilitate learning a dedicated programming language.

With scripts you can create all of the functionality of programs created strictly with code, including pull-down menus, dialog boxes, and alert windows. Programs created with the skillful use of scripting in authoring programs are indistinguishable from programs created with programming code alone.

Waiting for a Mouse Click

The design of an interaction can be as simple as what is found in programs like Microsoft PowerPoint or as complex as a complete programming language. The most basic form of interaction is the slideshow, in which the user can advance the program a frame at a time. Combined with transition effects, this form of interaction can create very impressive presentations.

Many programs, such as Macromedia Director and Authorware Professional, have a default setting that allows you to simply make a selection in a preferences dialog box such as a **Wait for Mouse Click** selection, in which you don't need to write a script but simply create the slides and place the transitions. Another form of slideshow presentation holds a slide on the screen for a predetermined period of time and then moves on to the next slide. (See Figure 17.6.)

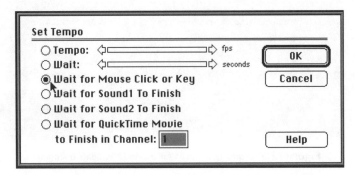

Figure 17.6 *The Set Tempo dialog box with Wait For Mouse Click or Key option selected*

Branching and Looping

Branching and looping is the next easiest form of authoring and requires some rudimentary understanding of scripting. In this type of presentation, the user controls what is next displayed on the screen by pressing buttons or some other type of authored selection device. The selection moves the program to that portion of the presentation.

For example, in an Automated Teller Machine the user determines what happens next in the presentation by making a selection from the menu window: withdrawal, deposit, transfer, savings, checking, and so on. The program branches to the next part of the presentation depending upon what the user selects. This selection method allows for a nonlinear presentation in which the users select what interests them most.

Looping consists of integrating an animation of some sort to generate a greater visual interest. For example, you can design a series of branches with buttons that control the progression of the presentation and then have the program present an animation or QuickTime movie while it is waiting for a selection to be made. This device makes the interaction dynamic, as well as controllable. (See Figure 17.7.)

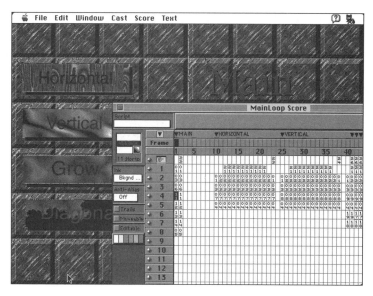

Figure 17.7 *To branch and loop in Director, you must select the buttons in the upper left corner. The program then branches to animation loops located in frames 10, 25, 40, and one other frame located in a different Director file that is branched to with special code*

Applying Greater Script Control

There is a great deal of power in simple branching and looping, and for many applications it is sufficient. However, many applications benefit from an element of randomness—something not provided for with branching and looping. CD-ROM gaming is a good example. (See Figure 17.8.)

In a game determining what the user wants to do is difficult, and anticipating every possible thing that can happen during the course of a game is impossible—especially if it is an arcade-style game in which things may need to be blown up on a random basis. This randomness is accomplished through authoring programs with more thorough and complex scripting.

This form of scripting is the most complex because it is so similar to scripting with a dedicated programming language. Although it is quite detailed, you can become very well versed in this type of authoring.

You can also use greater script control to accomplish other important presentation issues. For example, you can create a program that can be played on a wide variety of machines by creating a script that evaluates the capability of the machine that it is being played on and then displays the appropriate presentation. This type of program can take into account such issues as the amount of RAM available on the machine, the color depth of the monitor, and the size of the screen. You simply create several versions of the same presentation and include each with your program.

```
Movie Script 72                                             72

on Down whichChannel
  puppetSound "Button Down"
  set the castNum of sprite whichChannel to 3
  updatestage
  set silence = 0
  repeat while the mouseDown
    if rollover (whichChannel) = FALSE then
      if silence = 0 then
        puppetSound "Rolling Off"
      end if
      set silence = 1
      set the castNum of sprite whichChannel to 2
      updatestage
    else
      set the castNum of sprite whichChannel to 3
      updatestage
    end if
  end repeat
end

on Up  whichButton, where
  if rollover (whichButton) = FALSE then
    set the castNum of sprite whichButton to 2
    exit
  else
    puppetSound "Button Up"
    set the castNum of sprite whichButton to 2
    updatestage
    pupOn FALSE
    Wait 10
    puppetSound 0
    go to where
  end if
end
```

Figure 17.8 *A script that creates a realistic button.*
You can use similar structures to create more complex results

Controlling External Devices

Authoring programs allow you to control external devices for a number of important uses that enhance your presentation and more than likely economize production. For example, you could use scripts to access a laser disc player. You include whatever video that is part of your presentation on the laser disc. When the user makes a selection, they actually execute scripts that access the information on the laser disc. It's much cheaper to have video encoded on a laser disc than you may think, and it saves you the trouble of needing to have enough hard disk space to accommodate all of the video, not to mention the need for additional acceleration to display the video properly with a computer. Contact a local service bureau for current rates for video transfer to laser disc.

You can also use scripts, and other built-in control of external device features for music—MIDI instruments in particular. If you create MIDI music, you can import the MIDI code and have the program execute it automatically. You need to have the MIDI equipment connected to the computer; it provides the increased quality of having the audio produced on dedicated audio equipment played through any type of speakers you choose.

Using Other Programming Languages

On its highest level the scripting language of your program can be integrated with a dedicated programming language to connect your authoring program to virtually anything else in the computer. For example, you can use a dedicated programming language to create a bridge (called an *XObject* or *XCmd* for external object or external command) between the authoring program and an entirely different program. In this way, you can design a custom program interface that allows accessibility only to the elements of other programs that you want to have available to the user.

For example, you can connect your authoring program to a database program that stores the names and telephone numbers of the people who use your interactive program at a kiosk. You can create an interesting presentation and then have a portion of your program in which the users can put their information. The authoring program then places the information in the database program through the use of the extension that you created with the dedicated programming language.

The scripting possibilities are virtually limitless. The terrific thing here is that you can know nothing about scripting programs when you start working with these programs. As you learn more about them, it's as if you are discovering a whole new program. They are truly designed to grow with you. (See Figure 17.9.)

Export and Packaging for Distribution

You have several options available to you for creating a final product with authoring software. You could use this software to create the same files for which you would use a multimedia composition program: QuickTIme,

Sequential PICTs, and PICS. This choice allows you to use the animation benefits of these types of programs to create professional-quality animation. In fact,
programs like Director can be used to create broadcast commercials and other
special effects and graphics for television. (See Figure 17.10.)

```
Beeper.c

pascal void Beeper( XCmdPtr paramPtr )
{
  /*
   Check for the initial call to the XCMD, and create the window.
  */

 if (paramPtr->paramCount >= 0)
 {
   BeeperWindHndl  hWindRec;
   Rect      rWindow;
   Str255      strTitle, strInterval;
   long      interval;
   WindowPtr   window;

   if ((hWindRec = (BeeperWindHndl)NewHandle(sizeof(BeeperWindRec))) == 0)
   {
     paramPtr->returnValue = PasToZero(paramPtr, "\pCould not allocate memory.");
     return;
   }

   SetRect(&rWindow, 0, 0, 1, 1);

   HLock(paramPtr->params[0]);
   ZeroToPas(paramPtr, *paramPtr->params[0], strTitle);
   HUnlock(paramPtr->params[0]);
```

Figure 17.9 *An XCMD written in Pascal*

Another final step in the authoring process is creating a stand-alone application that can be distributed freely without requiring the original program. All
authoring programs either have the capability to directly output these stand-
alone applications, or the software companies provide a separate utility to
accomplish this task. For example, Macromedia Director has an output option
that creates a Projector file, which behaves, for all intents and purposes, just like
a program as complete as anything in the market. Projector files can also be distributed free of royalty payments to Macromedia.

You can then have the program encoded on CD-ROM in a variety of formats—everything from Macintosh and Windows operating systems to 3DO and the Philips interactive CD-I system. More and more companies are turning to authoring software programmers to create presentations, and electronic publishers are cropping up everywhere, including out of established print publishing houses. Learning how to use these programs is a very good idea. (See Figures 17.11 and 17.12.)

Export

Range of Frames:
- ⦿ Current frame: 6
- ○ Selected Frames: 6 to 6
- ○ All
- ○ From: [ ] To: [ ]

Within Range of Frames:
- ⦿ Every Frame
- ○ Every Nth Frame, N= [ ]
- ○ Frames With Markers
- ○ When Artwork Changes
  in Channel: [ ]

Destination:
File Type: ✓ PICT
           Scrapbook
           PICS
           QuickTime Movie   PICS

[Export] [Cancel] [Help]

Figure 17.10 *The Export dialog box*

Your CD-ROM

Figure 17.11 *A Macromedia Projector File created with Director*

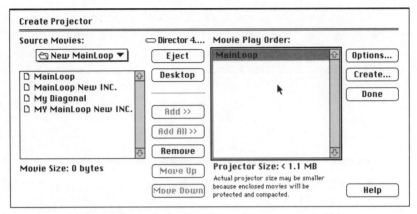

Figure 17.12 *The Macromedia Director Create Projector window*

Chapter

18

Sound-Editing Software

Many multimedia programs have only limited audio-editing capability, if any at all, so you may find including an audio-editing utility amongst your other development software useful. With this type of software you can use a microphone, CD-ROM reader using music CDs, or any other sound input device to digitize a sound. You can then edit and treat the sound to your liking. Finally, you can convert the sound to a format that your multimedia software can use.

Sound is easy to overlook in multimedia development because so much work is involved in creating the visuals. But once you begin to work with sound you will notice a distinct difference in the quality of presentations with sound. Just compare a presentation with no audio to a presentation that uses audio. I guarantee that you will agree that the one with sound is more interesting and professional. Most Macintosh computers already have sound input capability or have that upgrade path available to them, so that integrating this very important element into your productions is an easy process.

Capturing Audio

In this audio-capturing process you use a microphone or other sound-capturing device connected to your computer to record sound to your hard drive. Here the information is stored as raw data that can be edited and converted to a format your other programs can use. Sound from any audio source—a stereo receiver, a CD-ROM drive, a walkman, CD player, or anything else that outputs audio signals—can be captured. (See Figure 18.1.)

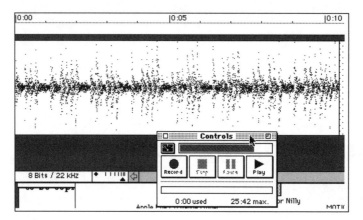

Figure 18.1 *The raw data sound wave in the editing window: SoundEdit Pro*

Editing Audio

You can edit the sound effects elements such as duration. Using the same cut, copy, and paste commands used in most programs you can select and manipulate portions of the audio clip. In this way, you can customize your sounds and eliminate the portions that you find unnecessary. (See Figure 18.2.)

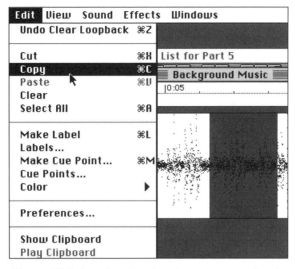

Figure 18.2 *A portion of a selected sound wave ready to be copied or cut and then pasted elsewhere*

Mixing Audio

You can add multiple tracks to a single sound document and then introduce sounds from different sources, thus creating a composite sound. For example, you may sample a drumbeat from a song that you like and mix it with a sound effect from a movie. This type of audio manipulation is used frequently in contemporary music, but there's no reason why you can't use it in your multimedia productions. The remixed sounds can lend a remarkable element of strength and creativity to your projects. (See Figure 18.3.)

Applying Effects and Filters

You can enhance existing audio or even create an entirely different sound by applying audio effects from your sound utility. First you need to select the portion of the wave that you want to apply the effect to. Then choose the effect along with your desired settings for the effect. This manipulation of sound can result in effects such as echo, reverb, increased amplification, and reversal of the sound wave. (See Figure 18.4.)

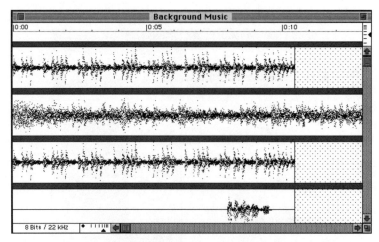

Figure 18.3 *Multiple tracks of raw audio*

Figure 18.4 *The Effects menu of SoundEdit Pro*

Looping

An important application of sound-editing programs is the creation of *sound loops*. These sounds play endlessly by looping back to the beginning each time the end is reached. To create a sound loop, you need to select the portion of the sound wave that you want to loop. Then use the appropriate loop setting from the program you're working with.

Sound loops are particularly useful in multimedia production for creating background music, especially in interactive applications. For example, you could design an interactive application for a kiosk and have music playing constantly in the background while the presentation waits for someone to step up and use it. Creating a very long sound is storage-intensive, so sound loops can serve a very practical and conservative purpose in the development of your projects. (See Figure 18.5.)

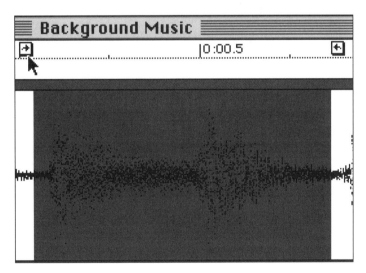

Figure 18.5 *A portion of a sound wave set to loop*

Saving and Exporting

Finally, sound-editing utilities serve as the audio equivalent of a conversion program. They can read sound files of many types, including the raw data type that cannot be read by much else, and allow you to convert the sound to a format that can be used elsewhere—such as AIFF files, which are the most common sound files on the Macintosh platform. They can also be used to create sounds for the Macintosh operating system so that you can customize the sounds your Macintosh computer makes. (See Figure 18.6.)

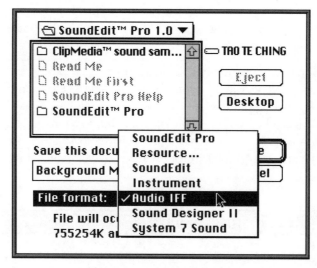

Figure 18.6 *The Save Options dialog box of SoundEdit Pro with all of the file types visible*

MIDI Software

MIDI can be integrated into your multimedia applications, but it is more a function of a dedicated audio application of the Macintosh computer. You do not actually capture sounds onto the hard drive with MIDI software, you control external audio devices with a software interface. If you want to integrate MIDI with your multimedia applications, you need to have a sound digitizer along with the rest of the necessary MIDI equipment. A second option is to use compatible multimedia applications to actually execute MIDI code in instruments that are connected to the computer through a MIDI device. Frankly, to write everything about MIDI requires another book's worth of information. Sounds that you capture on the hard drive are your best bet for beginning multimedia applications.

Chapter 19

Getting Your Multimedia Projects Out There

You have finished developing your multimedia project and want to bring it to your audience. The steps that you need to take at this point depend, of course, upon the nature of your project and your target audience. Generally, most multimedia projects fall under one of three broad categories: (1) those that end up on CD-ROM, (2) those that end up on video, and (3) those that playback directly from the computer's hard drive.

Multimedia projects that are designed to play directly from the computer's hard drive can be transferred from one computer to another through conventional media, such as a diskette, SyQuest cartridge, or other removable media, modem, or network. We will call this category of multimedia projects *simple presentations*.

No one output method is better than another, they each have their advantages and disadvantages. In fact, it isn't uncommon to discover that a project requires an incorporation of all three methods. Output considerations are academic. Follow them like a recipe, and you may never encounter a problem. The most complex issue that you need to deal with is whether to send your files out to a service bureau for output or to invest in the equipment that allows you to do it at your desktop.

CD-ROM

Advantages

Currently, CD-ROM is capable of containing about 650 megabytes of information. This capacity clearly lends itself to more extensive and sophisticated program designs than were ever possible with diskettes. Distributing a program on a single CD-ROM is cheaper than distributing it on several diskettes, not to mention that hundreds of megabytes of data would require hundreds of diskettes.

Since the data is available to the computer but not necessarily copied to the hard drive, CD-ROM programming helps end users to economize disk space. Also, files encoded to CD-ROM can be kept in their uncompressed state. This feature is virtually impossible to do with simple diskettes considering the average size of current multimedia applications.

Another tremendous benefit of CD-ROM's large capacity is that there is typically a large amount of space left on the disc even after a multimedia project has been recorded on it. As a result, you can be rather liberal in your designs and still have plenty of room on a single disc for other incentives, like bonus programs, tutorials, and clip media. Since all of it is available on the same disc and never needs to be moved to the hard drive, additional software will truly be useful and accessible, as opposed to forgotten and left in the box on a diskette because the program alone takes up a great deal of space.

Finally, multimedia projects can be formatted for several different platforms, even some noncomputer platforms such as CD video game systems and CD-ROM player systems such as Philips CD-I and the 3DO system. Currently you can only have Mac and IBM/Compatible software on a CD-ROM for computers—the other systems require a formatting procedure that allow them to only be read by their specific players. You can, however, have a CD-ROM that will operate on both a Macintosh and an IBM/Compatible. It's a matter of having both formats encoded on the same disc and, of course, having a program that is small enough to be encoded on the same disc twice.

Disadvantages

CD-ROM is a major key to the multimedia industry because it provides a way to conveniently mass produce and distribute large-sized files. The slow speed of CD-ROM drives is the only drawback. Currently CD-ROM players run at about 5 to 10 percent of the speed performance possible with hard drives. Nonetheless, CD-ROM is still the best media for distributing large multimedia project files. Any speed issues that exist now will undoubtedly change as the technology improves in both the computer's processor and the CD-ROM player.

Best CD-ROM Projects

CD-ROM is the best form of distribution for projects that contain very large files. Interactive games, 3D animation, video, and high quality sound are typically the type of projects distributed on CD-ROM. CD-ROMs are also useful for distributing clipmedia, or graphics for use in other projects.

Another specific project type best written to CD-ROM are complex interactive projects. An interactive project frequently uses many different files that reference one another, share aspects and features with one another, or depend upon each other in some other manner, such as to pass stored information from one part of a game to another, in order to operate properly. If one of those files became unavailable to the others, it could ruin the entire project. However, CD-ROM provides a single location for all of the files and, therefore, ensures that this type of mishap never happens.

Considerations in Developing for CD-ROM

Is Your Project Entertaining?

Often in developing a CD-ROM project you can become lost in the technical aspects of development and not the factors such as sound, animation, and ease of use that matter ultimately to the end user. Your audience won't pay attention to the technical aspects of your design unless they are developers themselves or something is wrong with your design.

Think of your CD-ROM projects as if they were a movie. There are a lot of technical concerns such as lighting, quality of film, and focus, but the audience is interested in aspects such as a good story, nice special effects, good acting, and the other "show" aspects of the final product. They won't notice something like the focus unless it fails. Make sure that the technical aspects of your program are in tact, but remember that the most important aspect is the show.

Does Your Project Play Well on a Hard Drive?

Information is read slower from a CD-ROM drive then it is from a hard drive, so a project that doesn't run well on a hard drive will certainly have problems on a CD-ROM. Making certain that your project meets this criterion is a process of trial, error, and correction.

Is Your Project Clear and Easy to Operate?

Your project should be as intuitive as possible. This means that anyone using your project should be able to get reasonably comfortable in operation without needing to use a manual or other form of instruction. If your project does require instruction, build it into the interface. You can still include instructional material on paper, but generally, people first start using software right away—before they even look at the documentation. In this way, people can concentrate on your game, educational program, or other program and not on how to start running the software.

You can offer many cues: buttons that are shaped to fit their function such as arrow shapes for navigational functions or a button labeled with a question mark for help functions. Other buttons, controls, and other design aspects can look like real-world objects and materials, like metal and marble.

Your program should also contain good feedback methods like button clicks and flashing lights to indicate that an action taken by the user has been registered. These aesthetic issues make your design slightly more complex to author but make it more successful in the long run. People like to have a button appear depressed when selected and offer other types of feedback such as a tone so it behaves more like what they would expect from an actual button.

Good feedback also helps to ensure that the program runs smoothly. For example, a button may trigger a function that takes time to actually occur. If there is no clear feedback when the user presses the button, most users will touch it again and possibly cause your program to repeat the same function several times. Even worse, users could become frustrated and not want to be bothered with your program.

Does Your Project Conform to the Macintosh Interface?

Most authoring programs are equipped with the capability of creating pull-down and pop-up menus, windows with title bars, icons that can be clicked and opened like ordinary finder icons, as well as many other Macintosh system features. If your project calls for going into some sort of directory, then the closer it is to a Mac program in design, the better, because it will already be familiar to the users. Users will feel comfortable with your program especially if you include the capability of saving files created in your program, such as partially completed games that can later be continued.

Can Your Project Be Played on a Variety of Macs?

A big mistake that many people make is designing programs only for one type of computer (the one on which they created the project) rather than accounting for the large variety of machines that your CD-ROM may encounter. You can create several versions of the same program taking different features into account, such as color depth, CPU model, RAM, and screen size. You can then write into your program scripts that register the capability of the Macintosh computer they are running on and load the version of your program that is best suited for that machine.

You can also work into your design alert signals that inform the users of issues such as low memory and instruction dialog boxes. These dialog boxes can also offer suggestions. For example, if your program requires a certain amount of RAM to run properly, then it could offer a dialog box that suggests the user close other applications or otherwise make more memory available, such as by turning off their system extensions and restarting. These scripts are actually far easier to write than you may realize. The following Macromedia Director Lingo script checks for available memory and presents an alert dialog box with an OK button if the memory is less than 8M.

```
If the freebytes/ 1000000 < 8 then

        alert "This game requires at least 8 megabytes to run.
        Please make more memory available and try again."

else

        open Game

End
```

Since the computer thinks in the fundamental terms of bytes and not megabytes, this script accommodates the computer and divides the number of bytes into the equivalent megabytes before continuing. If that number is less than 8, the program gives a system beep with a dialog box containing the statement within the quotations. This simple script ensures that the program does not even attempt to open without the correct amount of memory available. It also explains the problem, but you could offer more detailed information such as possible solutions to the problem.

By employing strategies such as multiple versions within the same disc and alert/solution dialog boxes, you can maximize your audience. Just remember that not all Macs are created equal but that all can run a CD-ROM drive. Ideally, those CD-ROM drives will be playing one of your CDs.

How and Where to Encode CD-ROMs

CD-ROMs must be sent to a service bureau with a CD-ROM press that can create the metal plate used to mass-produce discs. Contacting a general service bureau, like a print service bureau, is the best way to find a CD-ROM-equipped bureau in your area. Naturally, your project must be absolutely complete for this step to be cost-effective. Once your project is in a service bureau's hands, they create a preview for you before they produce the actual master disc, but they are not likely to preview the work for you. Besides, a service bureau may not know whether something is truly wrong if they came across it.

As with most work that involves a service bureau, it is your responsibility to provide complete work. If the project doesn't run well, you get a CD that doesn't run well. There are, however, ways to ensure that your work is truly complete and ready for a CD-ROM press.

CD-ROM Simulation Software

CD-ROM simulation software, such as MacTopix CD-ROM Simulator, alters the playback of your project on the computer to simulate the slower speed of a CD-ROM drive. In this way, you can determine whether your video, animation, and other presentation elements are actually running as you expected. CD-ROM simulation typically ships with CD-ROM development hardware such as a CD-ROM burner (discussed later), but you can also get the software separately from the same manufacturers.

Test Your Project on Several Machines

Machines have varying temperaments; the only way you can find out if a machine will play your program is to test it out on a bunch of models. Remeber that once the CD is pressed, any changes mean starting from scratch. There is no such thing as a simple upgrade.

Quality assurance for playback on different machines is the most difficult test for your project. The only way that you can be certain that your project will run on every Macintosh system is to run it to every conceivable Macintosh configuration. However, this is a tremendous task and is probably not cost-effective. You can, however, cover broad bases. For example, you can test your project on a Macintosh computer with an 030 processor, one with a 040 processor, an 040AV machine and a Power Macintosh. You can also test on other general machines, such as an IBM PC running Windows. You don't need to test on every machine. You can use a good cross section.

You can usually find a good variety of Macs in computer rental centers where you rent a machine in a stall for a time. Call the centers to find one with the selection of machines you need. Also, find out if the machines have removable media drives available. If not, find out if the facility has any objection to you attaching your own drive.

Burn a WORM

A *CD-ROM burner* is a drive that writes to a CD-ROM disc. These drives are also called *WORM drives* (Write Once Read Many). They are used for database generation and for development of software to be distributed on CD-ROM. They can create a CD-ROM that can be used on its own or sent to a service bureau for the generation of a master disc that can be used for mass production.

The discs these machines generate is also called a *one-off*, because they are typically used to create one disc that is sent to the service bureau instead of raw data on a removable drive. If you send your files to a service bureau in raw data form, they usually send back a one-off for you to preview before going to press. You can save this time by having the drive at your immediate disposal. (See Figure 19.1.)

Figure 19.1 *A WORM drive: JVC's Personal RomMaker*

Developing for Noncomputer Platforms

This area of development is still quite small, for the simple reason that it is extremely new. Proprietary systems for developing programs for specific systems such as the Philips CD-I system exist. Inexpensive conversion methods for Macintosh multimedia software to noncomputer system's, such as CD-I and 3DO, are now under development and promise to convert Mac files easily. If you develop programs on the Macintosh using tools such as Adobe Premiere and Macromedia Director, you should be able to convert your files to the noncomputer system conventions with little problem. You will be able to do this either through software, such as OptImage for CD-I emulation and development, at home or through service bureaus with the proprietary systems available. Contact Philips and 3DO for current information about developing for their systems.

Multimedia for Video

Advantages of Video

Video is the most common type of playback media currently on the market. Many people may not have a computer, but they more than likely own a VCR. As a result, video is the safest media to distribute projects that do not require interactivity to be effective.

Video also offers good and reliable playback performance. Computers cannot offer this guarantee, because so many different configurations are possible. Besides, only the most sophisticated (and enhanced) Macs are capable of handling full-frame video over an extended length of time. All VCRs are built to similar specs so that you can always be certain that 30 frames in your presentation will play as 30 frames on the screen.

A tremendous advantage of developing for video is that your projects can be output to professional-grade tape. Your projects can then be used for professional broadcast applications. With the current quality of software available for the Macintosh, you can produce a commercial right at your desktop.

Disadvantages of Video

The major disadvantage to video is that it cannot contain interactivity. It can be linked to a program, such as Macromedia Director, that provides interactivity in playback, but the video itself can never have the same type of nonlinear interactivity that a CD-ROM or other digital format can have. Essentially, projects for video can be presented to your audience, but they do not allow for user control over the presentation.

The other disadvantage is that video is an analog medium. In other words, video requires special equipment in order to be used in a computer. This also means that, once you have transferred your projects to video tape, you have only two options for modifications: edit the projects using conventional video equipment, or make your changes in the computer files and re-output to video tape. The former alternative means having a video-editing suite, or a Macintosh computer specially modified for video editing, at your disposal, which spells additional expense.

Best Projects for Video

The best projects for video are those that are very dynamic and do not require interaction on the part of the viewer. Video is good for these types of projects because playback is superior to the capability of the average computer. Animation, television graphics, and other linear presentation methods are best suited for video.

Concerns in Developing for Video

Aspect Ratio

Aspect ratio refers to the overall dimensions of each image that becomes a video frame. These dimensions are standard, so that conforming to a frame size that uses the same aspect ratio throughout a project is all you need to do. You must be aware of three standards: NTSC (used in the United States), PAL and SECAM (used in other locations throughout the world).

You need to be concerned with PAL and SECAM only if you intend to have your video viewed outside of the United States. Standard video equipment elsewhere may not be able to display your video work. In these instances you need to either recreate your project with the new aspect ratio and proper conversion equipment or convert your project already on video tape to another standard using video equipment designed for that purpose. (See Table 19.1.)

Table 19.1 *Aspect Ratios and Frame Rates Table*

STANDARD	PIXEL × RATIO	FRAME RATE
NTSC (National Television Standards Committee)	640×480	30
PAL (Phase Alternating Line)	768×576	25
SECAM (Sequential Color and Memory)	768×576	25
Film	(Dependent upon selected stock)	24

NOTE

The differences between PAL and SECAM are in the treatment of color, not in the preparation of files for output. Countries with an electrical current standard of 60Hz, such as the United States, use NTSC. Countries with an electrical current standard of 50Hz, such as European countries, use PAL or SECAM.

Frame Rate

Frame rate refers to the number of images you create for each second in your project. Video runs at 30 FPS, so you need to create 30 images for every second of your project. Film runs at 24 FPS. Frame rate is not important to your projects when they are still within the computer, but it is crucial when you output them to tape. Just be certain that you design your animation and other projects around this convention. (See Table 19.1.)

Field Frames

Each frame of video is actually divided into two separate frames (called fields) that consist of alternating even and odd lines. There are two fields per frame, so the field frame-rate is double the conventional frame-rate: 60 fields per second for NTSC, 50 fields per second for PAL and SECAM. This division is necessary because of the way in which the image is projected onto the back of a video screen. When you develop for video, you must take this into account, otherwise your image will flicker when played from video tape. Computer images can be split into separate fields through a digital/analog transfer device, most of which have the **Field** option.

Although most video output equipment automatically accounts for the field frame division, video capture may present a problem because images do not need to be split into fields in order to be displayed on a computer monitor. You will need to use a field interlace interpolation filter, which is a software plug-in found in multimedia composition programs such as Adobe Premiere and CoSA After Effects. These filters fill in any information that was missed from a field during capture.

Video and Audio Synchronization

Video and audio synchronization refers to having directly related sound and video elements occur at the same time. For example, if your project has a close-up of a person talking, the movement of the mouth must match the words said.

Having your video and audio "synch up," coupled with the large size of a video frame within the computer can make for a challenging endeavor in getting your project successfully onto tape.

In order to get your project onto video tape, with the original audio, you need a Mac computer that is capable of playing your project, in full-frame size, in real time. This means that you can play your project directly from you hard drive onto your computer's screen with the same quality in playback that you would expect from video tape. The only Macintosh computers that are capable of this are higher-end machines such as the Power Macintosh and the Quadra 840 AV. Other systems will require accelerators in order to play full-frame size video in real-time.

The amount of RAM that you have installed in your computer, along with the complexity of your project, will play a role in how well the project plays from your computer, even on the higher-end machines. If a project is playing well on a computer, then begins to *stutter* (or pause at frames before continuing) then you are probably experiencing a RAM problem. Upgrading the amount of RAM installed in your Mac will likely stop the stutter.

There is an alternative for getting your projects onto tape from lower-performance machines. You could generate your visual elements as separate images on the computer, as opposed to a QuickTime movie. Any audio in the file is lost, but you can add the audio with the video portion later by editing the video tape with video-production equipment.

This technique allows you to use an analog/digital output card to frame your graphics onto video tape accurately. Essentially, you would be using video-editing equipment for your multimedia compositions, as opposed to multimedia composition software. You would still be creating all of your graphics with the computer, but they would first be output to video tape before being incorporated into the rest of the composition. Naturally, you leave anything that was created originally on video tape in its video form. Using this frame-by-frame transfer method is the best way to get multimedia projects such as three-dimensional animation onto video tape.

NTSC Color

The displays of computer monitors and television sets are different; as a result, they may show certain elements differently. For example, color on a television's screen may change dramatically. Filters in some image enhancement programs, such as Adobe Photoshop, and multimedia composition programs, such as

COSA After Effects, Adobe Premiere and Macromedia Director, convert the colors used in a project to those found in an NTSC palette.

The only way to be certain that the image is entirely accurate is to preview it on a television's screen. You need to connect a television monitor to your computer via whatever video expansion card is necessary. Then, you can simply drag your project's window onto the television screen from your computer monitor screen. If you preview on a television screen, you know if the image is correct before you even go to tape.

Making Certain You're Getting What You Want on Tape

Consider a Good Desktop Video Previewing System

Ultimately, the true test of whether your project is perfect is when you have a video tape that can be popped into a VCR and played. If the image is what you want, you did it right. If it isn't what you want, something needs to change.

If you plan to do a great deal of developing for video, then it may be cost effective for you to invest in your own video previewing equipment. If you own an AV Mac, or a Power Macintosh, then all you will need to buy is a good VCR, and perhaps some additional RAM. Currently this will cost about $2,000 in addition to the cost of the computer. If you do not have an AV or Power Macintosh, then you will also need to buy a digital/analog transfer card and probably an accelerator card, which adds about $2-4,000 more to the price tag.

This may be a large initial cash outlay, but you will be able to make presentations and output them to video tape right at your desktop. You will also save time not having to wait for preview tapes to be made by a service bureau. This way you will be able to turn the money that you would have spent on previews into your own equipment. However, if you intend to develop for broadcast video you will still need to send your files to a service bureau for output to professional grade tape. See *Chapter 11* for more information about video equipment.

Computer-Based Presentations

Computer-based multimedia projects do not require any special processing to be completed. That is, they are distributed on conventional media such as diskettes and SyQuest cartridges. These projects are much easier to get to your audience, but creating multimedia projects that are truly small enough to be contained on just one or two diskettes is extremely difficult.

The only media that is practical for distributing these types of projects are diskettes, because larger media are more expensive and require special drives. However, a simple presentation is the best way to make a small business presentation, like an interactive letter, in which you combine text with graphics and simple animation. You can also add some level of interactivity, such as page turning. If you can somehow keep your designs to a size smaller than a diskette's capacity, then you will have a very easy time getting it to your audience.

Your only true concern in developing a computer-based presentation is that it play well from a hard drive, and that it be compatible with a wide range of Macintosh configurations. As in CD-ROM development, you can test playback of your project on a large cross section of Mac systems. If it plays well on different systems during these tests then it will play well in distribution, as well.

Effective On-Screen Presentations

The best way to give an on-screen presentation is to have a second screen available to the audience, like an overhead video projector. A second option is a large-screen television connected to your computer via an NTSC video NuBus expansion card, which allows the computer to display to a video monitor as well as a computer monitor. The built-in video capability of the AV Macs does not suffice, because these machines can not run RGB and NTSC monitors simultaneously. You must choose between the two. Furthermore, the built-in video in AV systems does not allow more than one monitor to share the computer's display. As a result, you need to incorporate an NTSC video card, or an analog/digital transfer card into your AV systems.

An interesting twist on this method of presentation is to have one thing occurring on your screen, while another is occurring on theirs. For example, you could drag the display window of your presentation onto the television screen facing the audience, while you have a teleprompter program or word processing document open on your monitor with notes for your presentation. If your screen is large enough, you could even have both occurring at once.

Using a Service Bureau to Output Files to CD-ROM or Video Tape

Provide a Finished Product (or Close to it)

Service bureaus are usually equipped to receive and process your multimedia files on whatever digital transfer media you choose. Using a method that allows you to transfer your data in its most complete form is best. This means that if you are developing a CD-ROM, it is better to give the service bureau a One-Off than it is to give them a series of SyQuest cartridges and instructions about what goes where. This method can also save you money as service bureaus charge you for all of the time involved in working with your project. If you streamline the work, you reduce the time.

Never Refuse a Preview

Service bureaus usually give you a preview of your project for a fee. The preview may take the form of a video transfer to VHS tape or a test print of a CD-ROM. It usually can be played on an ordinary VCR or CD-ROM player. In this way you can check to be certain that you are getting your desired results before the service bureau transfers the project to professional-grade video tape or creates the CD-ROM master. If you don't have equipment that will allow you to create a preview yourself (equipment that will allow you to output to video or a CD-ROM burner), then accepting a preview is absolutely essential for the successful development of your project. On the other hand, even if you do have previewing equipment at home, allowing the service bureau to send you at least one preview is still a good idea. In this way, you can be certain that the settings on the machines at the bureau are in synch with your own.

Consider a Tape Back-Up System

The least expensive method of data transfer to a service bureau is tape storage media. The cartridges are currently about 2 Gigabytes large, and the cost of each is very low. If you send off a SyQuest cartridge or an optical disk, that media is unavailable to you for all of the time that it is at the bureau, not to mention the fact that you need an inexpensive method for storing the original files.

Therefore, tape back-up system is a good idea if you plan to use a service bureau. (See *Chapter 6* for an example of a tape back-up system.)

Stick to the Specs

Sticking to the specs really only affects projects for video tape where a specific frame size is essential for proper transfer to tape. As long as you adhere to the aspect ratios, your project will be fine. Projects for CD-ROM can always be saved to the disc, but you determine issues such as image size. You should still be certain that your playback is smooth and that you follow the other guidelines listed above with any other considerations that are specific to your project.

WARNING
Not all service bureaus are created equal. Equipment such as CD-ROM mastering equipment is costly, so you may find that there aren't any local alternatives. The service bureaus near you may be able to let you know where you can go for high-end video and CD-ROM services.

Appendix

A

Apple Computers for Multimedia

This appendix lists all the multimedia capable Macintosh computers that are being and have been manufactured that can be used for multimedia development. All the information you need for choosing your Mac is here: RAM configurations, NuBus slots, clock speed, processor type, and a variety of other details, including information on the Power Macintosh line.

Use the following key for a guide to abbreviations in this appendix:

Maximum RAM: The maximum megabytes of RAM the computer will recognize and run.

Motherboard RAM: The megabytes of RAM soldered into the computer when it leaves the factory.

Clock Speed (MHz): The speed at which the computer runs.

TBD: To be determined. These facts were unavailable at the time of printing.

POWERBOOKS

	Maximum RAM (Megabytes)
Mac PowerBook 145B 4/80	8
Mac PowerBook 145B 4/120	8
Mac PowerBook 165 4/80	14
Mac PowerBook 165 4/160	14
Mac PowerBook 165 4/160 w/Express Modem	14
Mac PowerBook 180 4/80	14
Mac PowerBook 180 4/120	14
Mac PowerBook 180 4/120 w/Express Modem	14
Mac PowerBook 180c 4/80 (discontinued)	14
Mac PowerBook 180c 4/160 (discontinued)	14
Mac PowerBook 180c 4/160 w/Express Modem (discontinued)	14

POWERBOOK DUO

DUO 230 4/120	24
DUO 230 4/80 w/Floppy Adapter & External Floppy Drive	24
DUO 230 4/160 w/Modem & Duo Dock	24
DUO 250 4/200	24
DUO 250 4/200 w/Express Modem	24
DUO 270c 4/240	32
DUO 270c MB Hard Disk 240	32
MINI DOCK	
DUO DOCK	
DUO DOCK HD230 W/FPU	

DESKTOP MACINTOSH SYSTEMS

Discontinued Macintosh Systems	
Macintosh II	8
Macintosh IIcx	8
Macintosh IIci	32
Macinstosh IIfx	32
Quadra 800	136
Quadra 700	68

Standard RAM (Megabytes)	Clock Speed (MHz)	Number of NuBus slots	Audio
4	25	N/A	N/A
4	25	N/A	N/A
4	33	N/A	N/A
4	33	N/A	N/A
4	33	N/A	N/A
4	33	N/A	Mono In/Stereo Out
4	33	N/A	Mono In/Stereo Out
4	33	N/A	Mono In/Stereo Out
4	33	N/A	Mono In/Stereo Out
4	33	N/A	Mono In/Stereo Out
4	33	N/A	Mono In/Stereo Out
4	33	N/A	N/A
4	33	N/A	N/A
4	33	N/A	N/A
4	33	N/A	N/A
4	33	N/A	N/A
4	33	N/A	N/A
4	33	N/A	N/A
1	15.6672	6	Stereo Out
1	16	6	Stereo Out
1	25	3	Mono Out
1	40	6	Stereo Out
8	33	3	Mono In/Stereo Out
4	25	3	Mono In/Stereo Out

(continued)

CURRENT MODELS	Maximum RAM (Megabytes)
Quadra 605 (512 VRAM) 4/80	36
Quadra 605 (512 VRAM) 8/160	36
Quadra 610 (512 VRAM) 8/160	64
Quadra 610 (512 VRAM) 8/160 DOS Compatible	64
Quadra 610 (512 VRAM) 8/230	64
Quadra 610 (512 VRAM) 8/230 w/CD-ROM	64
Quadra 650 (512 VRAM) 8/230	132
Quadra 650 (512 VRAM) 8/230 w/CD-ROM	132
Quadra 650 (512 VRAM) 8/500 w/CD-ROM	132
Quadra 660AV 8/230	128
Quadra 660AV 8/230 w/CD-ROM	128
Quadra 660AV 8/500 w/CD-ROM	128
Quadra 840AV 8/230	128
Quadra 840AV 8/230 w/CD-ROM	128
Quadra 840AV 16/500 w/CD-ROM	128
Quadra 840AV 16/1000 w/CD-ROM	128
Quadra 950 8/0	256
Quadra 950 8/230	256
Quadra 950 8/500	256
Quadra 950 16/1000	256
Apple PowerMacintosh	
6100/60 8/160	72
6100/60 8/250 w/CD-ROM	72
6100/60 16/250 w/SoftWindows	72
6100/60AV (2MB VRAM) 8/250 w/CD-ROM	72
7100/66 (1MB VRAM) 8/250	136
7100/66 (1MB VRAM) 8/250 w/CD-ROM	136
7100/66 (1MB VRAM) 16/250 w/SoftWindows	136
7100/66AV (2MB VRAM) 8/500 w/CD-ROM	136
8100/80 8/250	264
8100/80 8/250 w/CD-ROM	264
8100/80 8/250 w/SoftWindows	264
8100/80 16/500 w/CD-ROM	264
8100/80 16/1000 w/CD-ROM	264

Standard RAM (Megabytes)	Clock Speed (MHz)	Number of NuBus slots	Audio
4	25	0	Mono In/Stereo Out
8	25	0	Mono In/Stereo Out
8	25	1	Mono In/Stereo Out
8	25	1	Mono In/Stereo Out
8	25	1	Mono In/Stereo Out
8	25	1	Mono In/Stereo Out
8	33	3	Mono In/Stereo Out
8	33	3	Mono In/Stereo Out
8	33	3	Mono In/Stereo Out
8	33	1	Stereo In/Out
8	33	1	Stereo In/Out
8	33	1	Stereo In/Out
8	40	3	Stereo In/Out
8	40	3	Stereo In/Out
8	40	3	Stereo In/Out
8	40	3	Stereo In/Out
8	33	5	Stereo In/Out
8	33	5	Stereo In/Out
8	33	5	Stereo In/Out
8	33	5	Stereo In/Out
8	60	(1) Optional 7"	Stereo In/Out 16
8	60	(1) Optional 7"	Stereo In/Out 16
16	60	(1) Optional 7"	Stereo In/Out 16
8	60	(1) Optional 7"	Stereo In/Out 16
8	66	3	Stereo In/Out 16
8	66	3	Stereo In/Out 16
16	66	3	Stereo In/Out 16
8	66	3	Stereo In/Out 16
8	80	3	Stereo In/Out 16
8	80	3	Stereo In/Out 16
8	80	3	Stereo In/Out 16
16	80	3	Stereo In/Out 16
16	80	3	Stereo In/Out 16

(continued)

POWERBOOKS	Video (VRAM)
Mac PowerBook 145B 4/80	N/A
Mac PowerBook 145B 4/120	N/A
Mac PowerBook 165 4/80	N/A
Mac PowerBook 165 4/160	N/A
Mac PowerBook 165 4/160 w/Express Modem	N/A
Mac PowerBook 180 4/80	N/A
Mac PowerBook 180 4/120	N/A
Mac PowerBook 180 4/120 w/Express Modem	N/A
Mac PowerBook 180c 4/80 (discontinued)	N/A
Mac PowerBook 180c 4/160 (discontinued)	N/A
Mac PowerBook 180c 4/160 w/Express Modem (discontinued)	N/A

POWERBOOK DUO	
DUO 230 4/120	N/A
DUO 230 4/80 w/Floppy Adapter & External Floppy Drive	N/A
DUO 230 4/160 w/Modem & Duo Dock	N/A
DUO 250 4/200	N/A
DUO 250 4/200 w/Express Modem	N/A
DUO 270c 4/240	N/A
DUO 270c MB Hard Disk 240	N/A
MINI DOCK	
DUO DOCK	
DUO DOCK HD230 W/FPU	

DESKTOP MACINTOSH SYSTEMS	
Discontinued Macintosh Systems	
Macintosh II	N/A
Macintosh IIcx	N/A
Macintosh IIci	N/A
Macinstosh IIfx	N/A
Quadra 800	512K exp. to 1M
Quadra 700	512K exp. to 2M

PDS Slot	Upgrade Path	Built-in Video Capture	Built-in NTSC Video Output	Central Processing Unit (CPU)
No	No	No	No	68030
No	No	No	No	68030
No	No	No	No	68030
No	No	No	No	68030
No	No	No	No	68030
No	No	No	No	68030
No	No	No	No	68030
No	No	No	No	68030
No	No	No	No	68030
No	No	No	No	68030
No	No	No	No	68030
No	No	No	No	68030
No	No	No	No	68030
No	No	No	No	68030
No	No	No	No	68030
No	No	No	No	68030
No	No	No	No	68030
No	No	No	No	68030
No	No	No	No	68020
No	No	No	No	68030
Yes	No	No	No	68030
Yes	No	No	No	68030
Yes	PPC Upgrade Card	No	No	68040
Yes	No	No	No	68040

(continued)

CURRENT MODELS	Video (VRAM)
Quadra 605 (512 VRAM) 4/80	512K exp. to 1M
Quadra 605 (512 VRAM) 8/160	512K exp. to 1M
Quadra 610 (512 VRAM) 8/160	512K exp. to 1M
Quadra 610 (512 VRAM) 8/160 DOS Compatible	512K exp. to 1M
Quadra 610 (512 VRAM) 8/230	512K exp. to 1M
Quadra 610 (512 VRAM) 8/230 w/CD-ROM	512K exp. to 1M
Quadra 650 (512 VRAM) 8/230	512K exp. to 1M
Quadra 650 (512 VRAM) 8/230 w/CD-ROM	512K exp. to 1M
Quadra 650 (512 VRAM) 8/500 w/CD-ROM	512K exp. to 1M
Quadra 660AV 8/230	1M exp. to 1M
Quadra 660AV 8/230 w/CD-ROM	1M exp. to 1M
Quadra 660AV 8/500 w/CD-ROM	1M exp. to 1M
Quadra 840AV 8/230	1M exp. to 2M
Quadra 840AV 8/230 w/CD-ROM	1M exp. to 2M
Quadra 840AV 16/500 w/CD-ROM	1M exp. to 2M
Quadra 840AV 16/1000 w/CD-ROM	1M exp. to 2M
Quadra 950 8/0	1M exp. to 2M
Quadra 950 8/230	1M exp. to 2M
Quadra 950 8/500	1M exp. to 2M
Quadra 950 16/1000	1M exp. to 2M

Apple PowerMacintosh

6100/60 8/160
6100/60 8/250 w/CD-ROM
6100/60 16/250 w/SoftWindows
6100/60AV (2MB VRAM) 8/250 w/CD-ROM
7100/66 (1MB VRAM) 8/250
7100/66 (1MB VRAM) 8/250 w/CD-ROM
7100/66 (1MB VRAM) 16/250 w/SoftWindows
7100/66AV (2MB VRAM) 8/500 w/CD-ROM
8100/80 8/250
8100/80 8/250 w/CD-ROM
8100/80 8/250 w/SoftWindows
8100/80 16/500 w/CD-ROM
8100/80 16/1000 w/CD-ROM

PDS Slot	Upgrade Path	Built-in Video Capture	Built-in NTSC Video Output	Central Processing Unit (CPU)
Yes	PPC Upgrade Card	No	No	68040
Yes	PPC Upgrade Card	No	No	68040
Yes	6100/60 LogicBoard	No	No	68040
Yes	6100/60 LogicBoard	No	No	68040
Yes	6100/60 LogicBoard	No	No	68040
Yes	6100/60 LogicBoard	No	No	68040
Yes	7100/66 LogicBoard	No	No	68040
Yes	7100/66 LogicBoard	No	No	68040
Yes	7100/66 LogicBoard	No	No	68040
Yes	6100/60 LogicBoard	Yes	Yes	68040/AV
Yes	6100/60 LogicBoard	Yes	Yes	68040/AV
Yes	6100/60 LogicBoard	Yes	Yes	68040/AV
Yes	8100/80 LogicBoard	Yes	Yes	68040/AV
Yes	8100/80 LogicBoard	Yes	Yes	68040/AV
Yes	8100/80 LogicBoard	Yes	Yes	68040/AV
Yes	8100/80 LogicBoard	Yes	Yes	68040/AV
Yes	PPC Upgrade Card	No	No	68040
Yes	PPC Upgrade Card	No	No	68040
Yes	PPC Upgrade Card	No	No	68040
Yes	PPC Upgrade Card	No	No	68040
Yes	TBD*	Yes	Yes	PowerPC 601
Yes	TBD	Yes	Yes	PowerPC 601
Yes	TBD	Yes	Yes	PowerPC 601
Yes	TBD	Yes	Yes	PowerPC 601
Yes	TBD	Yes	Yes	PowerPC 601
Yes	TBD	Yes	Yes	PowerPC 601
Yes	TBD	Yes	Yes	PowerPC 601
Yes	TBD	Yes	Yes	PowerPC 601
Yes	TBD	Yes	Yes	PowerPC 601
Yes	TBD	Yes	Yes	PowerPC 601
Yes	TBD	Yes	Yes	PowerPC 601
Yes	TBD	Yes	Yes	PowerPC 601
Yes	TBD	Yes	Yes	PowerPC 601

Computer and Multimedia Hardware and Peripherals

Accelerator Card Manufacturers

Andromedia Systems, Inc.
9000 Eton Ave.
Canoga Park, CA 91304
818-709-7600

Applied Engineering
3210 Beltline Rd.
Dallas, TX 75234
800-554-6227

Arroyo Technologies, Inc.
42808 Christy St., Ste. 220
Fremont, CA 94538
510-651-6714

ATTO Technology, Inc.
Baird Research Park
1576 Sweet Home Rd.
Amherst, NY 14228
716-688-4259

Brainstorm Products
1145 Terra Bella Ave.
Mountain View, CA 94043
415-964-2131

CTA, Inc.
25 Science Park
New Haven, CT 06511
800-252-1442

DayStar Digital, Inc.
5556 Atlanta Hwy.
Flowery Branch, GA 30542
800-962-2077

Digital Eclipse Software, Inc.
5515 Doyle St., Ste. 1
Emeryville, CA 94608
800-289-3374

ETC Peripherals, Inc.
5414 Beaumont Center Blvd.
Tampa, FL 33634
800-995-2334

Extreme Systems
1050 Industry Dr.
Tukwila, WA 98188
800-995-2334

Fusion Data Systems
8920 Business Park Dr.,
Ste. 350
Austin, TX 78759
800-285-8313

Harris International Limited
400 Commerce Ct.
Badnais Heights, MN 55127
612-482-0570

Hash Tech, Inc.
3140 Alfred St.
Santa Clara, CA 95054
408-988-2646

Impulse Technology
210 Dahlonega St., #205
Cumming, GA 30130
404-889-8294

Logica Research Inc.
8760 Research Blvd., Ste. 313
Austin, TX 78758
800-880-0988

Memory Technologies
3009 N. Lamar
Austin, TX 78705
800-950-8411

MicroMac Technology, Inc.
27111 Aliso Creek Rd., Ste. 145
Aliso Viejo, CA 92656
714-362-1000

Mobius Technologies, Inc.
5835 Doyle St.
Emeryville, CA 94608
800-523-7933

Monotype, Inc.
2100 Golf Rd.
Rolling Meadows, IL 60008
708-427-8800

Newer Technology
7803 E. Osie, Ste. 105
Wichita, KS 67207
800-678-3726

Novy Systems, Inc.
107 E. Palm Way, #14
Edgewater, FL 32132
800-553-2038

Pacific Parallel
Sales Office
15875 Highland Ct.
Solana Beach, CA 92075
619-481-8427

Perceptics Corp.
725 Pellissippi Pkwy.
Knoxville, TN 37932
615-966-9200

Perspect Systems, Inc.
630 Venice Blvd.
Venice, CA 90291
310-821-7884

Quantum Leap Systems
15875 Highland Ct.
Solana Beach, CA 92075
619-481-8427

Quesse Computer Co., Inc.
PO Box 922
Issaquah, WA 98027
206-854-9714

Radius, Inc.
1710 Fortune Dr.
San Jose, CA 95131
800-227-2795

RasterOps Corp.
2500 Walsh Ave.
Santa Clara, CA 95051
408-562-4200

Second Wave, Inc.
9430 Research Blvd.,
Bldg. II, #260
Austin, TX 78759
512-343-9661

Spectral Innovations, Inc.
1885 Lundy Ave., Ste. 208
San Jose, CA 95131
408-955-0366

StarTech
26243 Shauna Way
Valley Center, CA 92082
619-749-4383

SuperMac Technology
215 Moffett Park Dr.
Sunnyvale, CA 94089
800-541-7680

System Technology Corp.; a
Division of Noby Systems, Inc.
107 E. Palm Way, #14
Edgewater, FL 32132
800-638-4784

TechWorks
4030 Branker Ln. W., Ste. 350
Austin, TX 78759
800-688-7466

Visual Information
Development, Inc.
16309 Doublegrove St.
LaPuente, CA 91744
818-918-8834

Wavetracer, Inc.
289 Great Rd.
Acton, MA 01720
800-533-9283

YARC Systems Corp.
975 Business Center Cir.
Newbury Park, CA 91320
800-275-9272

Hard Drives, CD-ROM, and Mass Storage Devices

Key

Hard Drives=**HD**
Removable Disk=**RD**
Tape Back-up Systems=**TBS**
Magneto-Optical Drives=**MOD**
CD-ROM Drives=**CDR**
CD-ROM WORM Drives=**CDRW**
Laserdisc Recorder=**LDR**
Laserdisc Player=**LDP**

Alphatronix, Inc.
MOD
PO Box 13687
Research Triangle Park, NC
27709
919-544-0001

Amambyte
HD, TBS
2672 Bayshore Pkwy., Ste.
1045
Mountain View, CA 94043
415-988-1415

Apple Computer, Inc.
HD, CDR
20525 Mariani Ave.
Cupertino, CA 95014
408-996-1010

ATTO Technology, Inc.
HD
Baird Research Park
1576 Sweet Home Rd.
Amherst, NY 14228
716-688-4259

Blackhole Technology, Inc.
TBS
225 East St.
Winchester, MA 01890
800-227-1688

CharisMac Engineering, Inc.
HD, MOD
66 "D" P&S Lane
Newcastle, CA 95658
800-487-4420

CMS Enhancements
HD, TBS, RD
2722 Michelson Dr.
Irvine, CA 92714
714-837-6033

Computer Modules, Inc.
HD
2350A Walsh Ave.
Santa Clara, CA 95051
408-496-1881

Contemporary Cybernetics
Group
TBS
Rock Landing Corporate
Center
11846 Rock Landing
Newport News, VA 23606
804-873-9000

Core International, Inc.
HD
7171 N. Federal Hwy.
Boca Raton, FL 33487
800-688-9910

Corel Corp
MOD

1600 Carling Ave.
Ottowa, Ontario, Canada K1Z
8R7
800-836-7274

Corporate Center
MOD
11846 Rock Landing
Newport News, VA 23606
804-873-9000

Deltaic Systems
HD, MOD, RD
1701 Junction Ct., Ste. 302
San Jose, CA 95112
800-745-1240

DGR Technologies
MOD, CDR
1219 W. 6th St., Ste. 205
Austin, TX 78703
512-476-9855

DynaTek Automation
Systems, Inc.
HD, TBS, RD
15 Tangiers Rd.
Toronto, Ontario, Canada
M3J 2B1
416-636-3000

ETC Peripherals, Inc.
HD, MOD, RD
5414 Beaumont Center Blvd.
Tampa, FL 33634
800-876-4382

Exabyte
TBS
1685 38th St.
Boulder, CO 80301
303-442-4333

FWB, Inc.
HD, MOD, TBS
2040 Polk St., Ste. 215
San Francisco, CA 94109
415-474-8055

GCC Technologies, Inc.
HD, MOD
209 Burlington St.
Bedford, MA 01730
800-422-7777

Hard Drives International
HD
1912 W. 4th St.
Tempe, AZ 85281
800-488-0001

HeyerTech, Inc.
MOD
726 Marion Ave.
Palo Alto, CA 94303
415-325-8522

Hitachi America, Ltd.
HD
Computer Division
2000 Sierra Point Pkwy.
Brisbane, CA 94005
415-589-8300

Infotek, Inc.
HD, MOD, RD
56 Camille
East Patchogue, NY 11772
516-289-9682

Introl Corp.
MOD
2817 Anthony Ln. S.
Minneapolis, MN 55418
612-788-9391

Iomega Corp.
HD, MOD, Bernoulli remov-
able cartridge
1821 W. 4000 South
Roy, UT 84067
800-456-5522

Irwin Magnetic Systems, Inc.
TBS
2101 Commonwealth Blvd.
Ann Arbor, MI 48105
313-930-9000

JVC Information Products
17811 Mitchell Ave.
Irvine, CA 92714
714-261-1292

La Cie, Ltd.
HD, MOD, TBS, RD
8700 SW Creekside Pl.
Beaverton, OR 97005
800-999-0143

Laser Magnetic Storage Intl. Co.
MOD, TBS
4425 Arrows West Dr.
Colorado Springs, CO 80907
800-777-5674

Liberty Systems, Inc.
HD, MOD, TBS, RD,CDR
160 Saratoga Ave., Ste. 38
Santa Clara, CA 95051
408-983-1127

Mass Microsystems
HD, MOD, RD
810 W. Maude Ave.
Sunnyvale, CA 94086
800-522-7979

Maximum Storage, Inc.
MOD
5025 Centennial Blvd.
Colorado Springs, CO 80919
800-843-6299

Maynard Electronics, Inc.
TBS
36 Skyline Dr.
Lake Mary, FL 32746
800-821-8782

Mega Drive Systems
HD, RD
489 S. Robertson Blvd.
Beverly Hills, CA 90211
310-247-0006

Memorybank, Inc.
HD, TBS
2223 Packard Rd., Ste. 12
Ann Arbor, MI 48104
800-562-7593

Memory Technologies
HD
3009 N. Lamar
Austin, TX 78705
800-950-8411

Micronet Technology, Inc.
HD, TBS, MOD, RD, CDR
20 Mason
Irvine, CA 92718
714-837-6033

Micropolis Corp.
HD
21211 Nordhoff St.
Chatsworth, CA 91311
818-718-7777

Microtech International, Inc.
HD, MOD, TBS
158 Commerce St.
East Haven, CT 06512
800-626-4276

Mirror Technologies, Inc.
HD, MOD, TBS, RD
2644 Patton Rd.
Roseville, MN 55113
800-654-5294

NEC Technologies, Inc.
MOD, CDR
1255 Michael Dr.
Wood Dale, IL 60191
708-860-9500

Neutral Ltd.
HD
633 High Rd.
Seven Kings, Ilford
Essex, England 1G3 8RA
081-590-3422

Newer Technology
HD
7803 E. Osie, Ste. 105
Wichita, KS 67207
800-678-3726

Novastor Corp.
HD, TBS
30961 Agoura Rd., Ste. 109
Westlake Village, CA 91361
818-707-9900

O.C.E.A.N. Microsystems, Inc.
MOD
246 E. Hacienda Ave.
Campbell, CA 95008
408-374-8300

Optical Access
International, Inc
MOD, CDR
800 W. Cummings Park,

Ste. 2050
Woburn, MA 01801
800-433-5133

Optical Media International
MOD, CDRW
180 Knowles Dr.
Los Gatos, CA 95030
800-347-2664

Optima Technology Corp.
HD, MOD, TBS, RD
17526 Von Karman
Irvine, CA 92714
714-476-0515

Panasonic Communications
& Systems Co.
MOD, CDR, CDRW, LDR, LDP
2 Panasonic Way.
Secaucus, NJ 07094
201-348-7155

Peripheral Land, Inc.
HD, MOD, TBS, RD, CDR
47421 Bayside Pkwy.
Fremont, CA 94538
800-288-9754

Personal Computer Peripherals
HD, MOD, TBS
4 Daniels Farm Rd., Ste. 326
Trumbull, CT 06611
800-622-2888

Pinnacle Micro
MOD, CDRW
19 Technology
Irvine, CA 92718
800-553-7070

Pioneer Communications
of America, Inc.
MOD, CDR, CDRW
3255-1 Scott Blvd., Ste. 103
Santa Clara, CA 95954
800-527-3766

PLEXTOR
CDR
4255 Burton Dr.
Santa Clara, CA 95054
800-886-3935

Procom Technology, Inc.
HD, MOD, TBS, RD, CDR
2181 Dupont Dr.
Irvine, CA 92715
800-800-8600

Qualstar Corp.
TBS
9621 Irondale Ave.
Chatsworth, CA 91311

Quantum Corp.
HD, RD
500 McCarthy Blvd.
Milpitas, CA 95035
408-894-4000

Relax Technology, Inc.
HD, MOD, TBS
3101 Whipple Rd.
Union City, CA 94587
510-471-6112

Ricoh Corp.
MOD
File Products Division
5150 El Camino Real, Ste. C20
Los Altos, CA 94022
415-962-0443

Rodime Systems, Inc.
HD, MOD, RD
7700 W. Camino Real
Boca Raton, FL 33433
407-391-7333

Sankyo Seiki
TBS
2649 Campus Dr.
Irvine, CA 92715
714-724-1505

Sharp Electronics Corp.
MOD
Sharp Plaza
Box F
Mahwah, NJ 07430
201-529-9594

Sony Corp. of America
MOD, LDP
Computer Peripheral
Products Co.

655 River Oaks Pkwy.
San Jose, CA 95134
800-352-7669

Sparrow Corp.
TBS
PO Box 6102
Mississippi State, MS 39762
601-324-0982

Spectra Logic
TBS
1700 N. 55th St.
Boulder, CO 80301
800-833-1132

Storage Dimensions
HD, MOD, TBS
1656 McCarthy Blvd.
Milpitas, CA 95035
408-954-0710

Sumo Systems
HD, MOD, RD
1580 Old Oakland Rd.,
Ste. C103
San Jose, CA 95131
408-453-5744

Tandburg Data, Inc.
TBS
2649 Townsgate Rd.
Westlake Village, CA 91361
805-495-8384

Tass Optical World
MOD
6730 Mesa Ridge Rd.,
Bldg. B
San Diego, CA 92121
619-558-8882

Tecmar, Inc.
TBS
6225 Cochran Rd.
Solon, OH 44139
800-624-8560

Transitional Technology, Inc.
TBS
5401 E. La Palma Ave.
Anaheim, CA 92807
714-693-1133

Transoft Corp.
HD
31 Parker Way
Santa Barbara, CA 93101
800-949-6463

Tulin Technology
HD, MOD, TBS, RD
2156H O'Toole Ave.
San Jose, CA 95131
408-432-9057

Unbound, Inc.
MOD
17951 Lyons Cir.
Huntington Beach, CA 92647
800-862-6863

Vineyard Software Inc.
TBS
2318-A S. Vineyard Ave.
Ontario, CA 91761
714-930-1724

Vision Logic
HD
283 E. Brokaw
San Jose, CA 95112
408-437-1000

XYXIS Corp.
MOD
8084 Wallace Rd.
Eden Prairie, MN 55344
612-949-2388

Z Microsystems, Inc.
HD, RD
2382 Faraday Ave., Ste. 150
Carlsbad, CA 92008
619-431-5290

Input Devices

Advanced Gravis Computer
Technology, Ltd.
Optical joystick
101-3750 N. Frasier Way
Burnaby, BC, Canada V5J 5E9
800-663-8558

AirMouse Remote Controls
Infrared mouse
PO Box 100
Williston, VT 05495
802-655-9600

Altec Lansing Multimedia
Communications headset and microphone
PO Box 277
Milford, PA 18337
800-548-0620

Altra
Optical pointing device
520 W. Cedar St.
Rawlins, WY 82301
800-726-6153

Apple Computer, Inc.
Keyboards
20525 Mariani Ave.
Cupertino, CA 95014
800-776-2333

Applied Technologies
Adaptor box
Niedstrasse 22, D-12159
Berin, Germany
+49-30-8592958

Appoint, Inc.
Pen input device
4473 Willow Rd., Ste. 110
Pleasanton, CA 94588
800-448-1184

Articulate Systems, Inc.
Voice recognition input
600 W. Cummings Park,
Ste. 4500
Woburn, MA 01801
800-443-7077

Business Technology Mfg., Inc.
Input device
42-20-235th St.
Douglaston, NY 11363
718-229-8080

CalComp Digitizer Division
Remote digitizer tablet
14555 N. 82nd St.

Scottsdale, AZ 85260
800-932-1212

Canto Software, Inc.
Atari/Commodore adaptor
800 Duboce Ave.
San Francisco, CA 94117
800-332-2686

Carroll Touch
Touch frame
PO Box 1309
Round Rock, TX 78680
512-388-5613

Communication Intelligence
Corp.
Handwriting recognition device
275 Shoreline Dr., 6th floor
Redwood Shores, CA 94065
415-802-7888

ComputAbility Corp.
Keyboard with mouse emulator
40000 Grand River, #109
Novi, MI 48375
800-433-8872

Computer Support Corp.
Remote control input device
15926 Midway Rd.
Dallas, TX 75244

CoStar Corp.
Trackball
100 Field Point Rd.
Greenwich, CT 06830
800-426-7827

CTI Electronics Corp
Touch-screen, joystick
110 Old Middlefield Way
Mountain View, CA 94943
800-526-5920

Curtis Manufacturing Co., Inc.
Mouse
30 Fitzgerald Dr.
Jaffrey, NH 03452
800-955-5544

DataDesigns
Bar-code reader
8269 Fredericksburg Rd.

San Antonio, TX 78229
210-697-0780

Datadesk International
Keyboard
9524 SW Tualatin-Sherwood Rd.
Tualatin, OR 97062
800-477-3473

Datalogic, Inc.
Bar-code reader
104 Whispering Pines Dr.
Scotts Valley, CA 95066
408-438-7000

Discus Data Systems, Inc.
Optical mark reader
31 Fairview Blvd., #108
St. Albert, Alberta,
Canada T8N 3M5
403-458-0303

Don Johnston, Inc.
Computer access package
1000 N. Rand Rd., Bldg. 115
PO Box 639
Wauconda, IL 60084
800-999-4660

DualTouch Technology
Touch screen
38917 20th St. E., Ste. 701-G
Palmdale, CA 93550
805-274-9678

Edmark Corp.
Touch window
6727 185th Ave., NE
PO Box 3218
Redmond, WA 98073
206-556-8484

Elographics, Inc.
Touch screen
105 Randolph Rd
Oak Ridge, TN 37830
615-482-4100

FTG Data Systems
Digitizer tablet
8381 Katella Ave., Ste. J
Stanton, CA 90680
800-962-3900

Gyration, Inc.
Pointing device
12930 Saratoga Ave., Bldg. C
Saratoga, CA 95070
408-255-3016

Info Products
Mouse
541 Division St.
Campbell, CA 95008
800-755-7576

Infogrip, Inc.
Keyboards
1145 Eugenia Pl., Ste. 201
Carpinteria, CA 93013
800-397-0921

IntelliTools, Inc.
Input devices for the disabled
5221 Central Ave., Ste. 205
Richmond, CA 94804
800-899-6687

Interex Computer Products
*Mouse; keyboard; numeric
keypad*
2971 S. Madison
Wichita, KS 67216
316-524-4747

Kensington Microware, Ltd.
*Mouse/trackball device;
numeric keypad*
2855 Campus Dr.
San Mateo, CA 94403
800-535-4242

Key Tronic Corp.
*Four-button trackball; online
keypad; keyboard*
PO Box 14687
Spokane, WA 99214
800-262-6006

Kraft Systems, Inc.
Joystick/mouse
450 W. California Ave.
Vista, CA 92083
619-724-7146

Logitech, Inc.
Mouse

6505 Kaiser Dr.
Fremont, CA 94555
510-795-8500

MacSema
Voice recognition
29383 Lamb Dr.
Albany, OR 97321
800-344-7228

Memory Technologies
3007 N. Lamar
Austin, TX 78705
800-950-8411

MicroSpeed, Inc.
*Pointing device; keyboard;
mouse*
5005 Brandin Ct.
Fremont, CA 94538
510-490-1403

MicroTouch Systems, Inc.
Touch screen
300 Griffin Park
Methuen, MA 01844
508-659-9000

Mouse Systems Corp.
Mouse
4755 Seabridge Dr.
Fremont, CA 94538
510-656-1117

Percon, Inc.
Bar-code reader
1720 Willow Creek Cir.,
Ste. 530
Eugene, OR 97402
800-873-7266

Plusware Inc.
Keyboard
7305 Woodbine Ave., Dept. 562
Markham, Ontario, Canada
L3R 3V7
800-268-7587

Pointer Systems
*Optical pointer mouse for the
severely disabled*
1 Mill St.
Burlington, VT 05401
800-537-1562

Presentation Electronics, Inc.
*Device for remote keyboard
and mouse*
4320 Anthony Ct., Ste. 1
Rocklin, CA 95877
800-888-9281

Proxima Corp.
Presentation pointer
6610 Nancy Ridge Dr.
San Diego, CA 92121
800-447-7694

Sayett
Infrared remote
17 Tobey Village Office Park
Pittsford, NY 14534
800-678-7469

Silicon Valley Bus Co.
Bar-code reader
475 Brown Rd.
San Juan, Bautista, CA 95045
408-623-2300

Sophisticated Circuits, Inc.
Keypad for PowerBooks
19017 120th Ave., NE, Ste. 106
Bothell, WA 98011
800-827-4669

Spark International, Inc.
Mouse
PO Box 314
Glenview, IL 60025
708-998-6640

Summagraphics Corp.
Digitizer tablet
60 Silvermine Rd.
Seymour, CT 06483
203-881-5400

SuperMac Technology
Touch screen
215 Moffett Park Dr.
Sunnyvale, CA 94089
800-541-7680

Synex
Bar-code reader
692 10th St.
Brooklyn, NY 11215
800-447-9639

TimeKeeping Systems, Inc.
Bar-code reader
1306 E 55th St.
Cleveland, OH 44103
216-361-9995

TPS Electronics
Bar-code reader
2495 Old Middlefield Way
Mountain View, CA 94943
800-526-5920

Troll Technology Corp.
Touch-screen systems
25020 W. Avenue Stanford
Valencia, CA 91355
805-295-0770

Videx, Inc.
Portable bar-code reader
1105 NE Circle Blvd.
Corvallis, OR 97330

VPL Research
Input device
3977 E. Bayshore Rd.
Palo Alto, CA 94303
415-988-2550

Wacom Technology, Corp.
Digitizer tablet
501 SE Columbia Shores Blvd.,
Ste. 300
Vancouver, WA 98661
800-922-6613

Weingarten Gallery
Mouse
625 Congress Park Dr.
Dayton, OH 45459
513-435-0134

Monitors and Color Expansion Cards

All companies listed produce
monitors. Companies that also
produce color expansion
cards are indicated with the
initials **CEC**.

Amdek
3471 N. First St.
San Jose, CA 95134
800-722-6335

Apple Computer, Inc.
CEC
20525 Mariani Ave.
Cupertino, CA 95014
800-776-2333

Applied Engineering
3210 Beltline Rd.
Dallas, TX 75234
800-554-6227

Aydin Controls
414 Commerce Dr.
Ft. Washington, PA 19034
215-542-7800

BARCO, Inc.
Monitor Division
1000 Cobb Place Blvd.
Kennesaw, GA 30144
404-590-7900

Business Technology Mftg., Inc.
42-20 235th St.
Douglaston, NY 11363
718-229-8080

Computer Care, Inc.
CEC only
Ford Centre
420 N. 5th St., Ste. 1180
Minneapolis, MN 55401
800-950-2273

Digital Equipment Corporation
6 Technology Park Dr.
Westford, MA 01886
508-635-8238

Dome Imaging Systems, Inc.
400 Fifth Ave.
Waltham, MA 02154
617-895-1155

E-Machines, Inc.
CEC
215 Moffett Park Drive
Sunnyvale, CA 94089
800-344-7274

Electrohome Ltd.
Monitor Division
809 Wellington St. N.
Kitchener, Ontario,
Canada N2G 4J6
519-744-7111

Hitachi America, Ltd.
Office Animation Systems Div.
110 Summit Ave.
Montvale, NJ 97645
800-25-1370

Ikegami Electronics (USA), Inc.
37 Brook Ave.
Maywood, NJ 07607
201-368-9171

Infotek, Inc.
56 Camille
E. Patchogue, NY 11772
516-289-9682

Intelligent Resources
Integrated Systems, Inc.
CEC only
3030 Salt Creek Lane,
Ste. 100
Arlington Heights, IL 60005
708-670-9388

Intercolor
2150 Boggs Rd.
Duluth, GA 30136
404-623-9145

Lapis Technologies, Inc.
CEC
1100 Marina Village Pkwy.,
Ste. 100
Alameda, CA 94501
800-435-2747

Lifetime Memory Products
CEC only
305 17th St.
Huntington Beach, CA 92648
800-742-8324

Mass Microsystems
810 W. Maude Ave.
Sunnyvale, CA 94086
800-522-7979

Mitsubishi Electronics
America, Inc.
Professional Electronics Div.
800 Cottontail Lane
Somerset, NJ 08873
800-733-8439

Mobius Technologies, Inc.
5835 Doyle St.
Emeryville, CA 94608
800-523-7933

Nanao USA Corp.
23535 Telo Ave.
Torrance, CA 90505
800-800-5202

NEC Technologies, Inc.
CEC
1255 Michael Dr.
Wood Dale, IL 60191
708-860-9500

Neutral Ltd.
CEC only
633 High Rd.
Seven Kings, Ilford
Essex, England 1G3 8RA
081-590-3422

NovaCorp International, Inc.
2260 Lake Ave., Ste. 330
Rochester, NY 14612
716-647-6510

Nutmeg Systems
CEC
25 South Ave.
New Canaan, CT 06840
800-777-8439

Panasonic Communications &
Systems Co.
2 Panasonic Way
Secaucus, NJ 07094
201-348-7155

PDS Video Technology, Inc.
7700 NE 8th Ct.
Boca Raton, FL 33487
407-994-9588

Personal Computer
Peripherals

CEC only
4 Daniels Farm Rd., Ste. 326
Trumbull, CT 06611
800-622-2888

Philips Consumer
Electronics Co.
One Philips Dr.
Knoxville, TN 37914
615-521-4316

Radius, Inc.
CEC
1710 Fortune Dr.
San Jose, CA 95131
800-227-2795

RasterOps Corp.
CEC
2500 Walsh Ave.
Santa Clara, CA 95051
408-562-4200

Relax Technology, Inc.
CEC only
3101 Whipple Rd.
Union City, CA 94587
510-471-6112

Relisys
320 S. Milpitas Blvd.
Milpitas, CA 05035
408-945-9000

Sampo America
5550 Peachtree Industrial Blvd.
Norcross, GA 30071
404-449-6220

Scion Corp.
152 W. Patrick St.
Fredrick, MD 21701
301-695-7870

Seiko Instruments USA, Inc.
1130 Ringwood Ct.
San Jose, CA 95131
800-533-5312

Sharp Electronics Corp.
LCD Products Group
Sharp Plaza
Mail Stop One

Mahwah, NJ 07430
201-529-8731

Sigma Designs
CEC
47900 Bayside Pkwy.
Fremont, CA 94538
800-845-8086

Sony Electronics, Inc.
Computer Peripheral
Products Co.
3300 Zanker Rd.
San Jose, CA 95134
800-352-7669

SuperMac Technology
CEC
215 Moffett Park Dr.
Sunnyvale, CA 94089
800-541-6100

ViewSonic
20480 E. Business Pkwy.
Walnut, CA 91789
800-888-8583

Scanners

Key

Flatbed Scanners=**FB**
Handheld Scanners=**HH**
Slide Scanners=**S**

Advanced Gateway
Solutions, Inc.
FB
670 N. Commercial St.
Manchester, NH 03101
800-247-0722

Agfa Division, Miles Inc.,
Graphic Systems
FB
100 Challenger Rd.
Ridgefield Park, NJ 07660
800-685-4271

Animas Technologies, Inc.
HH

47505 Seabridge Dr.
Freemont, CA 94538
510-656-4479

Apple Computer, Inc.
FB
20525 Mariani Ave.
Cupertino, CA 95014
408-996-1010

AVR Technology, Inc.
FB
71 E. Daggett Dr.
San Jose, CA 95134
800-544-6243

Caere Corp.
HH
100 Cooper Ct.
Los Gatos, CA 95030
800-395-7226

Chinon America, Inc.
FB
Information Equipment Div.
615 Hawaii Ave.
Torrance, CA 90503
800-441-0222

The Complete PC
HH
1983 Concourse Dr.
San Jose, CA 95131
800-229-1753

Computer Friends, Inc.
FB
14250 NW Science Park Dr.
Portland, OR 97229
503-626-2291

Dangraf North America, Inc.
FB
3456 Lindell Blvd.
St. Louis, MO 63103
800-535-7689

DPI Electronic Imaging
Systems
FB
7932 Blackthorn Ave.
Cincinnati, OH 45255
800-597-3837

DuPont Printing & Publishing
FB
Barley Mill Plaza
PO Box 80018
Wilmington, DE 19880
800-538-7668

Eastman Kodak Co.
FB
Professional Imaging
343 State St.
Rochester, NY 14650
800-242-2424

ECRM
FB
554 Clark Rd.
Tewksbury, MA 01876
508-851-0207

Ektron Applied Imaging, Inc.
FB
23 Crosby Dr.
Bedford, MA 01730
800-922-8911

Epson America, Inc.
FB
20770 Madrona Ave.
Torrance, CA 90503
800-922-8911

Hardware That Fits
FB
610 S. Frazier
Conroe, TX 77301
800-364-3487

Hewlett-Packard
FB
Inquiries
PO Box 58059
Santa Clara, CA 95051
800-752-0900

Howtek, Inc.
FB
21 Park Ave.
Hudson, NH 03051
603-882-5200

HSD Microcomputer U.S., Inc.
FB

1350 Pear Ave., Ste. C
Mountain View, CA 94043
415-964-1400

La Cie, Ltd.
FB
8700 SW Creekside Pl.
Beaverton, OR 97005
800-999-0143

Leaf Systems
FB
250 Turnpike Rd.
Southboro, MA 01772
800-685-9462

Logitech, Inc.
HH
6505 Kaiser Dr.
Fremont CA 94555
510-795-8500

Microtek Lab, Inc.
S, FB
680 Knox St.
Torrance, CA 90502
213-321-2121

Mirror Technologies, Inc,
FB
2644 Patton Rd.
Roseville, MN 55113
800-654-5294

Mouse Systems Corp.
HH
47505 Seabridge Dr.
Fremont, CA 94538
510-656-1117

Mustek, Inc.
HH
15225 Alton Pkwy
Irvine, CA 92718
800-468-7835

Nikon Electronic Imaging
FB
1300 Walt Whitman Rd.
Melville, NY 11747
516-547-4355

NISCA, Inc.
FB

1919 Old Denton Rd., Ste. 104
Carrollton, TX 75006
800-466-9096

Percon, Inc.
HH
1720 Willow Creek Cir.,
Ste. 530
Eugene, OR 97402
800-873-7266

Polaroid Corp.
FB
575 Technology Sq.
Cambridge, MA 02139
800-225-1618

Relisys
FB
320 S. Milpitas Blvd.
Milpitas, CA 95035
408-945-9000

Ricoh Corp.
FB
Peripheral Products Div.
3001 Orchard Pkwy.
San Jose, CA 95134
408-944-3318

Spark Int'l, Inc.
FB
PO Box 314
Glenview, IL 60025
708-998-6640

Thunderware, Inc.
HH
21 Orinda Way
Orinda, CA 94563
510-254-6581

Truvel
FB
520 Herndon Pkwy.
Herndon, VA 22070
703-742-9500

Oce Graphics
FB
385 Ravendale Dr.
Mountain View, CA 94043
800-545-5445

Optronics, An Intergraph Div.
FB
7 Stuart Rd.
Chelmsford, MA 01824
510-562-2480

Panasonic Communications
& Systems Co.
FB
2 Panasonic Way
Secaucus, NJ 07094
201-348-7155

Pentax Technologies Corp.
FB
100 Technology Dr.
Broomfield, CO 80021
303-460-1600

PixelCraft, A Xerox Co.
FB
130 Doolittle Dr., #19
San Leandro, CA 94577
510-562-2480

RastorOps Corp.
2500 Walsh Ave.
Santa Clara, CA 95051
408-562-4200

Sharp Electronics Corp.
FB
Sharp Plaza
Box F
Mahwah, NJ 07430
201-529-9594

Santos Technology, Inc.
FB
383 Van Ness Ave.,
Ste. 1604
Torrance, CA 90501
800-966-9960

Truvel
FB
520 Herndon Pkwy.
Herndon, VA 22070
703-742-9500

UMAX Technologies, Inc.
FN
3170 Coronado Dr.

Santa Clara, CA 95054
800-562-0311

Varityper, Inc.
FB
11 Mt. Pleasant Ave.
E. Hanover, NJ 07936
201-887-8000, ext. 999

XRS
FB
4030 Spencer St., Ste. 101
Torrance, CA 90503
310-214-1900

Video and Audio Digitizing Devices and System Manufacturers

Abbate Video, Inc.
83 Main Street
Norfolk, MA 02056-1416
508-520-0199

Advanced Digital Imaging
1250 N. Lakeview, Unit 0
Anaheim, CA 92807
714-779-7772

Advent Computer
Products, Inc.
449 Santa Fe Dr., Ste. 213
Encinitas, CA 92024
619-942-8456

Avid Technologies, Inc.
Metropolitan Technology Park
One Park West
Tewksbury, MA 01876
800-949-2843

Canon USA, Inc.
One Canon Plaza
Lake Success, NY 11042
516-488-6700

Computer Friends, Inc.
14250 NW Science Park Dr.
Portland, OR 97229
503-626-2291

Computer Sciences Corp.
102 Executive Dr., Ste. 5
Moorestown, NJ 08057
609-234-1166

Data Translation, Inc.
100 Locke Dr.
Marlboro, MA 01752
508-460-1600, ext. 100

Digital Vision, Inc.
270 Bridge St.
Dedham, MA 02026
800-346-0090

Fast Electronics Sales Inc.
805 W. Orchard Dr., #4
Bellingham, WA 98225
800-248-3278

Koala Acquisitions, Inc.
P.O. Box 1924
Morgan Hill, CA 95038
408-776-8181

Kurta Corp.
3007 E. Chambers St.
Phoenix, AZ 85040
602-276-5533

Macromedia, Inc.
600 Townsend St.
San Francisco, CA 94103
415-252-2000

Mass Microsystems
810 W. Maude Ave.
Sunnyvale, CA 94086
800-522-7979

Media Vision, Inc.
47300 Bayside Pkwy.
Fremont, CA 94538
800-348-7116

Mutoh America Inc.
500 W. Algonquin Rd.
Mt. Prospect, IL 60056
708-952-8880

New Video Corp.
1526 Cloverfield Blvd.
Santa Monica, CA 90404
310-449-7000

Numonics Corp.
101 Commerce Dr.
Montgomeryville, PA 18936
800-247-4517

Perceptics Corp.
725 Pellissippi Pkwy.
Knoxville, TN 37932
615-966-9200

Radius, Inc.
1710 Fortune Dr.
San Jose, CA 95131
800-227-2795

RasterOps Corp.
2500 Walsh Ave.
Santa Clara, CA 95051
408-562-4200

Rebo Research
530 W. 25th St.
New York, NY 10001
212-989-9466

Scion Corp.
152 W., Patrick St.
Frederick, MD 21701
301-695-7870

Sigma Designs
47900 Bayside Pkwy.
Fremont, CA 94538
800-845-8086

SuperMac Technology
215 Moffet Park Dr.
Sunnyvale, CA 94089
800-541-7680

TrueVision, Inc.
7340 Shadeland Station
Indianapolis, IN 46256
800-933-8865

VideoLogic, Inc.
245 First St.
Cambridge, MA 02142
617-494-0530

Workstation Technology, Inc.
18010 Sky Park Cir., Ste. 155
Irvine, CA 92714
714-250-8983

Video Production and Post-Production Manufacturers

Ambico, Inc.
50 Maple Street
Norwood, NJ 07648
800-621-1106

Canon
1 Canon, Inc.
Lake Success, NY 11041
516-488-6700

JVC
41 Slater Dr.
Elmwood Park, NJ 07407
201-523-2077

Mitsubishi
800-Cottontail Ln.
Somerset, NJ 08873
800-733-8439

Nikon
1300 Walt Whitman Rd.
Melville, NY 11747
516-547-4355

Panasonic
1 Panasonic Way
Secaucus, NJ 07094
800-524-0864

Pioneer Electronics, Inc.
2265 E.220th Street
Long Beach, CA 90801-1720
213-PIONEER

Sharp
Sharp Plaza, Box F
Mahwah, NJ 07430
201-529-9594

Sony Corporation
One Sony Drive
Park Ridge, NJ 07656
201-930-1000

Videonics
1370 Dell Avenue
Campbell, CA 95008
800-338-EDIT

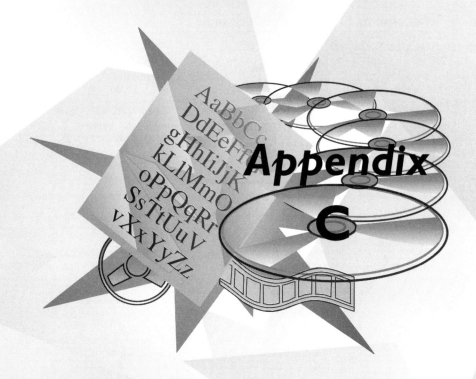

Multimedia Software

Animation and Interactive Authoring Software

ADDmotion
Animation software
Motion Works
International, Inc.
1020 Mainland St., Ste. 130
Vancouver, BC, Canada
V6B 2T4
604-685-9975

The Animation Stand
Animation software
Linker Systems, Inc.
13612 Onkayha Cir.

Irvine, CA 92720
714-552-1904

Animation Works
Animation software
Gold Disk
3350 Scott Blvd., Bldg. 14
Santa Clara, CA 95054
800-465-3375

ArchiMovie
Animation software
Unic, Inc.
1330 Beacon St., Ste. 320
Brookline, MA 02146
617-731-1766

Authorware Professional
Interactive authoring
Macromedia
600 Townsend St.

San Francisco, CA 94103
415-252-2000

Auto-PICT QT
Animation software
Videomedia, Inc.
175 Lewis Rd., Unit 23
San Jose, CA 95111
408-227-9977

Body Electric
Real-time animator
VPL Research Inc.
3977 E. Bayshore Rd.
Palo Alto, CA 94303
415-988-2550

Cinemation and
Cinemation CD
*Interactive presentation
software*

Vividus Corp.
378 Cambridge Ave., Ste. I
Palo Alto, CA 94306
415-321-2221

Frame By Frame
Graphic animation system
Image Management
Systems, Inc.
239 W. 15th St.
New York, NY 10011
212-741-8765

HyperCard
Interactive authoring software
Claris Corp.
5201 Patrick Henry Dr.
P.O. Box 58168
Santa Clara, CA. 95052
408-727-8227

MacAnimator Pro
Animation to video tape
Videomedia, Inc.
175 Lewis Rd., Unit 23
San Jose, CA 95111
408-227-9977

Macromedia Director
Interactive authoring software
Macromedia
600 Townsend St.
San Francisco, CA 94103
415-252-2000

PACo Producer
Compression and playback
The Company of Science
& Art (CoSA)
14 Imperial Pl., Ste. 203
Providence, RI 02903
401-831-2672

PROmotion
Animation software
Motion Works
International, Inc.
1020 Mainland St.,
Ste. 130
Vancouver, BC, Canada V6B 2T4
604-685-6105

Multimedia Composition, Desktop Presentation, and Special Effects Software

1000 Of The World's Greatest
Sound Effects/250 Of The
World's Greatest Music Clips
Sound clips
Interactive Publishing Corp.
300 Airport Executive Park
Spring Valley, NY 10977
914-426-0400

3D Models
Clip media
Sound/Image
One Kendall Sq.,
Bldg.. 300, 2nd Fl.
Cambridge, MA 02139
617-354-4189

3-D Object Library
Clip media
Viewpoint Data Labs
870 West Center St.
Orem, UT 84057
800-328-2738

A Zillion Sounds
Sound clips
BeachWare
5234 Via Valarta
San Diego, CA 92124
619-735-8945

Action!
Animation software
Macromedia
600 Townsend St.
San Francisco, CA 94103
415-252-2000

AdClips Volume One
Video clips
Mediacom, Inc.

PO Box 36173
Richmond, VA 23235
804-794-0700

Adobe Audition/Premiere
Multimedia software
Adobe Systems, Inc.
1585 Charleston Rd.
P.O. Box 7900
Montain View, CA 94039
800-833-6687

Aldus Fetch
Database for digital media
Aldus Corp.
411 First Ave. S, Ste. 200
Seattle, WA 98104
206-622-5500

Aldus Gallery Effects
Transforms images into art
Aldus Corp.
411 First Ave. S, Ste. 200
Seattle, WA 98104
206-622-5500

Aldus Persuasion
Desktop presentations
Aldus Corp.
411 First Ave. S, Ste. 200
Seattle, WA 98104
206-622-5500

Amazing Moves/America
In Motion
Clip art
Jasmine Multimedia
Publishing
6746 Valjean Ave., Ste. 100
Van Nuys, CA 91406
800-798-7535

Animation Clips
Clip media
Media In Motion
PO Box 170130
San Francisco, CA 94117
415-621-0707

AniMedia
Clip media
Animatics

126 York St., Ste. 207
Ottowa, Ontario, Canada
K1N 5T5
800-665-3898

The Archives Of History
Clip media
MPI Multimedia
5525 W. 159th St.
Oak Forest, IL 60452
800-777-2223

Aris Entertainment Medialips
Clip media, sound clips
Aris Multimedia
Entertainment, Inc.
310 Washington Blvd., Ste. 100
Marina del Rey, CA 92092
800-228-2747

Astound
Presentation software.
Gold Disk
3350 Scott Blvd., Bldg.. 14
Santa Clara, CA 95054
800-465-3375

Atmospheres Background
Systems
Clip media
TechPool Studios
1463 Warrensville Center Rd.
Cleveland, OH 44121
800-777-8930

Avid Videoshop
Avid Technology, Inc.
Metropolitan Technology Park
One Park West
Tewksbury, MA 01876
800-949-2843

Aware Speed-Of-Sound,
Vol. I: SFX
Sound clips
Aware, Inc.
1 Memorial Dr.
Cambridge, MA 02142
800-292-7346

Behind The Scenes
Clip media

Northwest Multimedia
4061 Winema Pl., NE
Salem, OR 97305
503-399-8390

The Best of Sound Bytes
Sound clips
Metatec Corp./Nautilus
7001 Discovery Blvd.
Dublin, OH 43017
800-637-3472

The Best Of Stock Video
Clip media
Jasmine Multimedia
Publishing
6746 Valjean Ave., Ste. 100
Van Nuys, CA 91406
800-798-7535

Blockbuster Sound F/X
Sound clips
The Music Bank
1821 Saratoga Ave., Ste. 204
Saratoga, CA 95070
800-995-1645

Bogas Sound Effects Disk
Sound clips
Bogas Productions
751 Laurel St., #213
San Carlos, CA 94070
415-592-5129

Business In Motion
Clip media
Jasmine Multimedia
Publishing
6746 Valjean Ave., Ste. 100
Van Nuys, CA 91406
800-798-7535

CA-Cricket Presents
Presentation software
Computer Associates
International, Inc.
One Computer Associates Plaza
Islandia, NY 11788
800-225-5224

Calculated Beauty: A Journey
Through Mandelbrot Space

Clip media
Rocky Mountain Digital Peeks
PO Box 1576
Nederland, CO 80466
800-266-7637

CameraMan
Movie capture software
Motion Works USA
524 Second St.
San Francisco, CA 94107
800-800-8476

Canyon Clipz
QuickTime movies
The San Francisco Canyon Co.
150 Post St., Ste. 620
San Francisco, CA 94108
415-398-9957

Cars! Cars! Cars!
Clip media
MPI Multimedia
5525 W. 159th St.
Oak Forest, IL 60452
800-777-2223

CineMedia
Clip media
Vividus Corp.
378 Cambridge Ave., Ste. I
Palo Alto, CA 94306
415-321-2221

Clip Audio
Sound clips
The Publishing Factory
310 Dover Rd.
Charlottesville, VA 22901
800-835-5546

Clip Tunes
Sound clips
Digidesign, Inc.
1360 Willow Rd. Ste. 101
Menlo Park, CA 94025
415-688-0600

Clip Video
Clip media
The Publishing Factory
310 Dover Rd.

Charlottesville, VA 22901
800-835-5546

Clip* Video* Art "Animation
Effects" V2c/"Presentation
Animation"
Clip media
Freemyers Design
575 Nelson Ave.
Oroville, CA 95965
916-533-9365

ClipMedia
Clip media
Macromedia
600 Townsend St.
San Francisco, CA 94103
415-252-2000

ClipTime
Clip media
ATG, Inc.
6921 Cable Dr., Ste. 100
Marriottsville, MD 21104
800-952-9073

ClipTime Volume II
"American Media"
Clip media
ATG, Inc.
6921 Cable Dr.,
Ste. 100
Marriottsville, MD 21104
800-952-9073

ColorUp
Color enhancement software
Pantone, Inc.
Commerce Blvd.
Carlstadt, NJ 07072
800-222-1149

CompassPoint
Image management system
Northpoint Software
2200 W. Eleven Mile Rd.
Berkley, MI 48072
810-543-1770

CoSA After Effects
Multimedia software
The Company of Science and
Art
14 Imperial Pl., Ste. 203

Providence, RI 02903
401-831-2672

Creative Backgrounds &
Textures
Clip media
Educorp
7434 Trade St.
San Diego, CA 92121
800-843-9497

Cumulus
Image database
Cantos Software, Inc.
800 Duboce Ave.
San Francisco, CA 94117
800-332-2686

DeltaGraph Pro
Charting and graphing
DeltaPoint, Inc.
2 Harris Court, Ste. B-1
Monterey, CA 93940
800-446-6955

DeskTop Sounds
Sound clips
Optical Media International
180 Knowles Dr.
Los Gatos, CA 95030
800-347-2664

The Digital Directory
Showcase of digital graphic
The Digital Directory, Inc.
301 W. 110th St., 2n
New York, NY 10026
212-864-8872

Digital Video LIbrary
Clip media
Educorp
7434 Trade St.
San Diego, CA 92121
800-843-9497

ElasticReality
Warping and morphing
ASDG, Inc.
925 Stewart St.
Madison, WI 53713
608-273-6585

Electronic Preview
Clip media

Studio Productions
18000 East 400 South
Elizabethtown, IN 47232
812-579-5063

Electronic Preview
Multimedia
Clip media
Studio Productions
18000 East 400 South
Elizabethtown, IN 47232
812-579-5063

Essential Backgrounds and
Textures
Clip media
Educorp
7434 Trade St.
San Diego, CA 92121
800-843-9497

Famous Faces/Famous Places
Clip media
Jasmine Multimedia
Publishing
6746 Valjean Ave., Ste. 100
Van Nuys, CA 91406
800-798-7535

Fast Pitch Pro
*Converts HyperCard stacks
into presentation slide shows.*
Objectic Systems, Inc.
P.O. Box 161
Carmel, IN 46032
800-859-9543

Frame Up
Multimedia tool
The Voyager Co.
578 Broadway, Ste. 406
New York, NY 10012
800-446-2001

Flo'
Free-form plasticity software
The Valis Group
PO Box 422
Point Richmond, CA 94807
510-236-4124

Folio 1
Clip media
D'pix, Inc.

414 W. 4th Ave.
Columbus, OH 43201
800-238-3749

Fontek Backgrounds &
Borders
Clip media
Letraset USA
40 Eisenhower Dr.
Paramus, NJ 07653
800-343-8973

Fountain View
Clip media
Isis Imaging Corp.
3400 Inverness St.
Vancouver, BC, Canada
V5V 4V5
604-873-8878

Fractal Terrain Modeler
Modeler
Strata Inc.
2 W. Saint George Blvd.,
Ste. 2100
St. George, UT 84770
800-869-6855

Gallery Of Dreams
Clip media
Wayzata Technology, Inc.
PO Box 807
Grand Rapids, MN 55744
800-735-7321

Grooves
Sound clips
Media Design Interactive
The Old Hop Kiln
1 Long Garden Walk
Farnham, Surrey GU9 7HP
U.K.
011-44-252-737630

Gryphon Dynamic Effects
/Gryphon's Morph
Clip media; Morphing
Gryphon Software Corp.
7220 Trade St., Ste. 120
San Diego, CA 92121
619-536-8815

Hi Rez Audio Vol. 1
Sound clips

Presto Studios, Inc.
PO Box 262535
San Diego, CA 92196
619-689-4895

The Hollywood Film Music
Library
Sound clips
The Hollywood Film Music
Library
11684 Ventura Blvd., Ste. 850
Studio City, CA 91604
818-985-9997

IllusionArt
Clip media
IllusionArt
PO Box 21398
Oakland, CA 94611
510-839-9580

ImageAccess
Image database software
Nikon Electronic Imaging
1300 Walt Whitman Rd.
Melville, NY 11747
516-547-4355

ImageAXS
Catalogs pictures
AXS
1301 Marina Village Pkwy.
Alameda, CA 94501
510-814-7200

ImageCELs CD-ROM
Clip media
IMAGETECTS
7200 Bollinger Rd., #802
San Jose, CA 95129
408-252-5487

InfoLynx
Interactive presentations
InfoTOuch Marketing Corp.
445 Hawley Ave.
Syracuse, NY 13203
800-966-5969

Instant Buttons & Controls
CD-ROM
Clip media
stat media
21151 Via Canon

Yorba Linda, CA 92687
714-779-8176

Interactive Video Design
Toolkit
Interactive presentations
Electronic Vision, Inc.
5 South Depot
Athens, OH 45701
614-592-2433

Intelligent System Controller
Video and audio distribution
RGB Technology, Inc.
11440 Isaac Newton Sq., Ste.
200
Reston, VA 22090
703-834-1500

IntelliKeys Overlay Maker
Overlay drawing program
IntelliTools, Inc.
5221 Central Ave., Ste. 205
Richmond, CA 94804
800-899-6687

The Interactive Brainwave
Visual Analyzer
Input tool
Psychic Lab, Inc.
249 E. 48th St., #15D
New York, NY 10017
212-754-4282

Kaleidoscope
Fractal art generator
Abbott Systems, Inc.
62 Mountain Rd.
Pleasantville, NY 10570
800-552-9157

Killern Tracks Multi Media
Music Library
Sound clips
6534 Sunset Blvd.
Hollywood, CA 90028
800-877-0078

Kodak Shoebox Photo CD
Image Manager
Clip media
Eastman Kodak Co.
CD Imaging
343 State St.

Rochester, NY 14650
800-242-2424

Kroy Sign Studio II
Sign-making software
Kroy Sign Systems
14555 N. Hayden Rd.
Scottsdale, AZ 85260
800-773-5769

Kudo Image Browser
Mixed-media cataloging
Imspace Systems Corp.
4747 Morena Blvd., Ste. 360
San Diego, CA 92117
619-272-2600

Laptop Sales Systems
Multimedia presentations
Galileo, Inc.
680 14th St. NW, Ste. A
Atlanta, GA 30318
404-425-4536

Laser Award Maker
Awards and certificates
Education Library or Border
Library
Baudville, Inc.
5380 52nd. St. SE
Grand Rapids, MI 49512
616-698-0888

ListMaster
Transforms names into graphics
Nikrom Technical Products, Inc.
176 Ft. Pond Rd.
Shirley, MA 01464
508-537-9970

Loops: Music For Multimedia
Sound clips
Educorp
7434 Trade St.
San Diego, CA 92121
800-843-9497

Mac-A-Mug
Human face composition
Shaherazam
PO Box 26731
Milwaukee, WI 53226
414-367-8683

MacPresents—Multimedia
Presentation Manager
Presentation software
Educational Multimedia
Concepts, Ltd.
1313 Fifth St. SE, Ste. 202E
Minneapolis, MN 55414
800-356-6826

MacSignMaker
Sign manufacturing
Sign Equipment
Engineering, Inc.
PO Box 6188
Bellevue, WA 98008
206-747-0693

Magiclips Music
Sound clips
Wolfetone Publishing
1010 Huntcliff, Ste. 1350
Atlanta, GA 30350
800-949-8663

Media Cataloger
*Manages graphic, movie, and
sound files*
Interactive Media Corp.
PO Box 0089
Los Altos, CA 94023
415-948-0745

MediaMaker
Desktop video publishing
Macromedia
600 Townsend St.
San Francisco, CA 94103
415-252-2000

Media-Pedia Video Clips
Clip media
Media-Pedia Video Clips, Inc.
22 Fisher Ave.
Wellesley, MA 02181
617-235-5617

Media Scheduler
*Runs multimedia in
continuous loop*
Galileo, Inc.
680 14th St. NW, Ste. A
Atlanta, GA 30318
404-425-4536

Mediasource: Gen 2 Sampler
/Mediasource: National
Sciences Library
Clip media; sound clips
Applied Optical Media Corp.
1450 Boot Rd., Bldg.. 400
West Chester, PA 19380
800-321-7259

Media Suite Pro
Desktop video system
Avid Technology, Inc.
Metropolitan Technology Park
One Park West
Tewksbury, MA 01876
800-949-2843

Media Tree
Media organazation tool
Tulip Software
PO Box 3046
Andover, MA 01810
800-972-9659

Medior Renaissance
Multimedia software
Medior, Inc.
371 Princeton Ave.
P.O. Box 1205
El Granada, CA 94018
415-728-5100

Metrics
Measures conversion
Expert Systems, Inc.
2616 Quebec Ave.
Melbourne, FL 32935
407-242-0140

Microsoft Movie PIM
QuickTime plug-in module
Microsoft Corp.
One Microsoft Way
Redmond, WA 98052-6399
206-882-8080

Microsoft PowerPoint
Presentation software
Microsoft Corp.
One Microsoft Way
Redmond, WA 98052-6399
206-882-8080

Mindmap
Interactive presentations
Full Circle Media
25 Valley View Ave.
San Rafael, CA 94901
415-453-9989

Motion Works Multimedia
Utilities
Multimedia production tools
Motion Works USA
524 Second St.
San Francisco, CA 94107
800-800-8476

MovieProducer
QuickTime movies
Computer Friends, Inc.
14250 NW Science Park Dr.
Portland, OR 97229
503-626-2291

MovieWorks
Interactive multimedia
Interactive Solutions, Inc.
1710 S. Amphlett Blvd., Ste. 107
San Mateo, CA 94402
415-377-0136

Multi-Ad Search
Image cataloging and retrieval
Multi-Ad Services, Inc.
1720 W. Detweiller Dr.
Peoria, IL 61615
800-447-1950

The Multimedia Library CD-
ROM Royalty Free Series
Clip media; sound clips
The Multimedia Library
37 Washington Sq. W., Ste. 4-D
New York, NY 10011
800-362-4978

Multiple Media Tour
Clip media, sound clips
Audio Visual Group
398 Columbus Ave., Ste. 355
Boston, MA 02116
800-676-7284

MultiWare
Clip media

BeachWare
5234 Via Valarta
San Diego, CA 92124
619-492-9529

The Music Bakery
Sound clips
The Music Bakery
7134-A Campbell Rd., #1
Dallas, TX 75248
800-229-0313

Music Madness I CD-ROM
/II CD-ROM
Sound clips
AMUG
4131 N. 24th St. #A-120
Phoenix, AZ 85016
602-553-8966

Musical Instruments & Sound
Effects Resources Libraries
Sound clips
B&B Soundworks
PO Box 7828
San Jose, CA 95150
408-241-7986

MusicBytes
Sound clips
Prosonus 2820 Honolulu
Ave., #268
Verdugo City, CA 91046
818-766-5221

Nature In Motion
Clip media
Jasmine Multimedia
Publishing
6746 Valjean Ave., Ste. 100
Van Nuys, CA 91406
800-798-7535

On The Air
Presentation software
Meyer Software
616 Continental Rd.
Hatboro, PA 19040
800-643-2286

Passport Producer Pro
Interactive presentations
Passport Designs, Inc.

100 Stone Pine Rd.
Half Moon Bay, CA 94019
415-726-0280

Philmont Symposium Systems
Interactive software
the Philmont Software Mill
14 Maple Ave.
Philmont, NY 12565
800-527-9199

Pixar One Twenty Eight
Clip media
Pixar
1001 W. Cutting Blvd.
Richmond, CA 94804
800-888-9856

Pixar Typestry
Create dimensional type
Pixar
1001 W. Cutting Blvd.
Richmond, CA 94804
800-888-9856

PolyTechnics
Special effects
Shaman Exchange, Inc.
12708 Foxton Rd.
Foxton, CO 80441
800-624-8597

Popcorn
QuickTime viewer and editor
Aladdin Systems, Inc.
165 Westridge Dr.
Watsonville, CA 95076
408-761-6200

Portfolio
Database for PICT graphics
SoftShell International Ltd.
715 Horizon Dr.,
Ste. 390
Grand Junction, CO 81506
303-242-7502

PosterWorks
Create posters
S.H. Pierce & Co.
One Kendall Sq., Ste. 323,
Bldg.. 600
Cambridge, MA 02139

Power Backgrounds
Clip media
California Clip Art
1750 California St., #114
Corona, CA 92719
909-272-1747

PROclaim!
Clip media, sound clips
Compact Designs, Inc.
PO Box 8535
Gaithersburg, MD 20898
301-869-3919

ProGraphix
Clip media
East*West Communications, Inc.
1631 Woods Dr.
Los Angeles, CA 90069
800-833-8339

Pyromania! (Playing With Fire
On CD-ROM)
QuickTime movies
VCE, Inc.
13300 Ralston Ave.
Sylmar, CA 91342
800-242-9627

QuickColor
Color HyperCard stacks
Bliss Interactive Technologies
6034 W. Courtyard Dr., Ste. 305
Austin, TX 78730
512-338-2458

QuickFlix!
Movie-making software
VideoFusion, Inc.
1722 Indian Wood Cir., Ste. H
Maumee, OH 43537
800-638-5253

QuickLaffs Volumes 1 & 2
QuickTime classic movies
Educorp
7434 Trade St.
San Diego, CA 92121
800-843-9497

Resource Library Vol. 1
/Resource Navigator II

*Color pictures and QuickTime
movies / Multimedia in
Hypercard stacks*
Bliss Interactive Technologies
6034 W. Courtyard Dr., Ste. 305
Austin, TX 78730
512-338-2458

Scenic Stills
Clip media
Jasmine Multimedia
Publishing
6746 Valjean Ave., Ste. 100
Van Nuys, CA 91406
800-798-7535

Smart Art
Clip media
Adobe Systems, Inc.
1585 Charleston Rd.
P.O. Box 7900
Montain View, CA 94039
800-833-6687

Sound Bytes Developer's Kit
Speech synthesis software
Emerson & Stern
Associates, Inc.
10150 Sorrento Valley Rd.,
Ste. 210
San Diego, CA 92121
619-457-2526

Sound Clips
Sound clips
Olduvai Corp.
9200 S. Dadeland Blvd.
Ste. 725
Miami, FL 33156
800-548-5151

Sound Creative
Sound clips
CDR Informatique
BP32
Limours 91470 France
33-1-64-91-26-76

SoundEdit 16
Sound editing utility
Macromedia
600 Townsend St.

San Francisco, CA 94103
415-252-2000

Sound F/X C
Sound clips
Educorp
7434 Trade St.
San Diego, CA 92121
800-843-9497

Sound Library 2000
Sound clips
Wayzata Technology, Inc.
PO Box 807
Grand Rapids, MN 55744
800-735-7321

Sound Machine
Sound clips
Educorp
7434 Trade St.
San Diego, CA 92121
800-843-9497

Special Delivery
Presentation software
Interactive Media Corp.
P.O. Box 0089
Los Altos, CA 94023
415-948-0745

StandOut!
Presentation software
Manhattan Graphics
Software Corp.
250 E. Hartsdale, NY 10530
914-725-2048

Stingers
Sound clips
The Music Bank
1821 Saratoga Ave., Ste. 204
Saratoga, CA 95070
800-995-1645

StrataShapes
Clip media
Strata, Inc.
2 W. Saint George Blvd., Ste.
2100
St. George, UT 84770
800-869-6855

StrataTextures
Clip media
Strata, Inc.
2 W. Saint George Blvd.,
Ste. 2100
St. George, UT 84770
800-869-6855

SwivelArt Collections
Clip media
Macromedia
600 Townsend St.
San Francisco, CA 94103
415-252-2000

Take This Down
Text speech recognition
Electrohouse VR Publishers
1507 E. Franklin St., Ste. 545
Chapel Hill, NC 27514
919-933-9830

Ted Does Sound Effects
Sound clips
Ted Productions
14567 Big Basin Way, #4B
Saratoga, CA 95070
408-741-4770

Texture City Pro 100 #1
Clip media
Texture City
3203 Overland Ave., #6157
Los Angeles, CA 90034
310-836-9224

Thumbs Up
Image database
Graphic Detail, Inc.
4020 Westchase Blvd., Ste. 500
Raleigh, NC 27607
800-234-8635

Trick Of Light
Clip media
Educorp
7434 Trade St.
San Diego, CA 92121
800-843-9497

TypeStyler
Display-type special effects

Broderbund Software, Inc.
500 Redwood Blvd.
P.O. Box 6121
Novato, CA 94948
800-521-6263

VideoFusion
QuickTime video editing
VideoFusion, Inc.
1722 Indian Wood Cir., Ste. H
Maumee, OH 43537
800-638-5253

VideoScript
Video transition software
Truevision, Inc.
7340 Shadeland Station
Indianapolis, IN 46256
800-933-8865

VideoShow
Presentation software
General Parametrics Corp.
1250 9th St.
Berkeley, CA 94710
800-223-0999

Video Special Effects
Clip media
Jasmine Multimedia
Publishing
6746 Valjean Ave., Ste. 100
Van Nuys, CA 91406
800-798-7535

Virtus Voyager
*WalkThrough files become
self-running documents*
Virtus Corp.
117 Edinburgh S, Ste. 204
Cary, NC 27511
800-847-8871

Virtus VR
Virtual reality for the desktop
Virtus Corp.
117 Edinburgh S, Ste. 204
Cary, NC 27511
800-847-8871

Visuals
Clip media

N-Depth
50 Clarkson Center, Ste. 477
Chesterfield, MO 63017
314-458-6526

Voice Navigator SW
Voice recognition software
Articulate Systems, Inc.
600 W. Cummings Park,
Ste. 4500
Woburn, MA 01801
800-443-7077

Voice Record
Voice and sound recording
Articulate Systems, Inc.
600 W. Cummings Park,
Ste. 4500
Woburn, MA 01801
800-443-7077

Wild, Weird & Wacky
Clip media
MPI Multimedia
5525 W. 159th St.
Oak Forest, IL 60452
800-777-2223

Wilderness Stills /Working Stills
Clip media
Jasmine Multimedia
Publishing
6746 Valjean Ave., Ste. 100
Van Nuys, CA 91406
800-798-7535

The WPA Multimedia Sampler
Clip media, sound clips
MPI Multimedia
5525 W. 159th St.
Oak Forest, IL 60452
800-777-2223

WraptureReels One
Clip media
Educorp
7434 Trade St.
San Diego, CA 92121
800-843-9497

Wraptures One
Clip media

Educorp
7434 Trade St.
San Diego, CA 92121
800-843-9497

Zounds
Sound clips
Digital Eclipse Software, Inc.
5515 Doyle St., Ste. 1
Emeryville, CA 94608
800-289-3374

Drawing Software

addDepth
Adds depth and perspective
Ray Dream, Inc.
1804 N. Shoreline Blvd..
Mountain View, CA. 94043
415-960-0765

Adobe Illustrator and
Streamline
Object-oriented drawing
Adobe Systems, Inc.
1585 Charleston Rd.
PO Box 7900
Montain View, CA 94039
800-833-6687

Aldus Freehand
Object-oriented drawing
Aldus Corp.
411 1st Ave. S, Ste. 200
Seattle, WA 98104
206-622-5500

Aldus Intellidraw
Automatic drawing software
Aldus Corp.
Consumer Division
5120 Shoreham Pl.
San Diego, CA. 92122
619-558-6000

ArtBeat Professional
Low-cost drawing software
Pie Practical Solutions, Inc.
PO Box 788
Union City, NJ 07087
800-333-2328

CA-Cricket Draw III
Object-oriented drawing
Computer Associates
International, Inc.
One Computer Associates
Plaza
Islandia, NY 11788
800-225-5224

Canvas
Drawing software
Deneba Software
7400 SW 87th Ave.
Miami, FL 33173
305-596-5644

Canvas Add-On Tools
Three extension packages
Deneba Software
7400 SW 87th Ave.
Miami, FL 33173
305-596-5644

ClarisDraw
Drawing software
Claris Corp.
5201 Patrick Henry Dr.
PO Box 58168
Santa Clara, CA 95052
408-727-8227

Deneba artWorks
Drawing software
Deneba Software
7400 SW 87th Ave.
Miami, FL 33173
305-596-5644

Expert Draw
Low-cost drawing software
Expert Software, Inc.
800 Douglas Rd.
North Tower, Ste. 355
Coral Gables, FL 33134
800-759-2562

IsoMetrix
Technical drawing software
Airo Design and Manufacturing
PO Box 427
Port Washington, WI 53074
414-284-7169

MacDraw II/MacDraw Pro
Drawing software
Claris Corp.
5201 Patrick Henry Dr.
PO Box 58168
Santa Clara, CA 95052
408-727-8227

Michaels Draw
Low-cost drawing software
Event One
222 Del Norte Ave.
Sunnyvale, CA 94086
408-734-4773

Mighty Draw
Low-cost drawing software
Abracadata, Ltd.
PO Box 2440
Eugene, OR 97402
800-451-4871

Image Editing and Paint Software

Adobe Photoshop
Image-editing software
Adobe Systems, Inc.
1585 Charleston Rd.
PO Box 7900
Montain View, CA 94039
800-833-6687

Aldus SuperPaint
Painting software
Aldus Corp.
Consumer Division
5120 Shoreham Pl.
San Diego, CA. 92122
619-558-6000

Amazing Paint
*Black-and-white paint
program*
PrairieSoft, Inc.
PO Box 65820
West Des Moines, IA 50265
515-225-3720

Andromeda Filters
Plug-in filters for Photoshop
Andomeda Software, Inc.
849 Old Farm Road
Thousand Oaks, CA 91360
800-547-0055

AXA WaterColor
Paint program
AXA Corp.
17752 Mitchell, #C
Irvine, CA 92714
714-757-1500

AXS PhotoProcessor
Prepares images
AXS
1301 Marina Village Pkwy.
Alameda, CA 94501
510-814-7200

Bliss Paint
Animated color painting
PO Box 6386
Albany, CA 94706
800-294-6252

BrushStrokes
Image-editing software
Claris Clear Choice
5201 Patrick Henry Dr.
PO Box 58168
Santa Clara, CA 95052
800-325-2747

Charger Suites
Image processing acceleration
DayStar Digital, Inc.
5556 Atlanta Hwy.
Flowery Branch, GA 30542
800-962-2077

Chromassage
Color palette manipulation
Second glance Software
25381-G Alicia Pkwy., Ste.
357
Laguna Hills, CA 92653
714-855-2331

Color It!
Image-editing software
MicroFrontier, Inc.

3401 101st St., Ste. E
Des Moines, IA 50322
515-270-8109

Color MacCheese
Paint program
Baseline Publishing, Inc.
1770 Moriah Woods Blvd.,
Ste. 14
Memphis, TN 38117
901-682-9676

Colorize
Image-processing software
DS Design
2440 SW Cary Pkwy., Ste. 210
Cary, NC 27513
800-745-4037

DAfx
Paint desk accessory
Mi Concepts
PO Box 8822
Kentwood, MI 49508
616-765-3312 ext. 14

DeBabelizer / DeBabelizer Lite
Graphics translation.
Equilibrium
475 Gate Five Rd., Ste. 225
Sausalito, CA 94965
800-524-8651

DeskPaint & DeskDraw
Paint and drawing software
Zedcor, Inc.
4500 E. Speedway, Ste. 22
Tucson, AZ 85712
800-482-4567

Easy Color Paint
8-bit paint program
MECC
6160 Summit Dr. N
Minneapolis, MN 55430
800-685-6322 ext. 549

EfiColor For Adobe Photoshop
Color seperation software
Electronics for Imaging, Inc.
2855 Campus Dr.
San Mateo, CA 94403
800-285-4565

Enhance
Image enhancement
MicroFrontier, Inc.
3401 101st St.,
Ste. E
Des Moines, IA 50322
515-270-8109

Expert Color Paint
Paint program
Expert Software, Inc.
800 Douglas Rd.
North Tower, Ste. 355
Coral Gables, FL 33134
800-759-2562

Exposure Pro
Screen manipulation
Baseline Publishing, Inc.
1770 Moriah Woods Blvd.,
Ste. 14
Memphis, TN 38117
901-682-9676

Fast Eddie
24-bit color compression
LizardTech
PO Box 2129
Sante Fe, NM 87504
505-989-7117

Fastedit/CT
Photoshop plug-in
Total Integration, Inc.
334 E. Colfax St., Ste. A-1
Palatine, IL 60067
708-776-2377

Fractal Design Color Studio
With Shapes
Image-editing software
Fractal Design Corp.
335 Spreckels Dr.
Aptos, CA 95003
408-688-8800

Fractal Design Painter
Paint program
Fractal Design Corp.
335 Spreckels Dr.
Aptos, CA 95003
408-688-8800

Fractal Design Painter X2
Extension
Fractal Design Corp.
335 Spreckels Dr.
Aptos, CA 95003
408-688-8800

Fractal Design Sketcher
Grayscale paint software
Fractal Design Corp.
335 Spreckels Dr.
Aptos, CA 95003
408-688-8800

Handshake/LW
Photoshop plug-in
Total Integration, Inc.
334 E. Colfax St., Ste. A-1
Palatine, IL 60067
708-776-2377

Image Assistant
Image-editing software
Caere Corp.
100 Cooper Ct.
Los Gatos, CA 95030
800-535-7226

JAG II—Jaggies Are Gone
Anti-aliasing software
Ray Dream, Inc.
1804 N. Shoreline Blvd.
Mountain View, CA 94043
415-960-0765

Kai's Power Tools
*Image-editing and enhance-
ment plug-in software*
HSC Software
1661 Lincoln Blvd., Ste. 101
Santa Monica, CA 90404
310-392-6015

Kid Pix
Paint program for children
Broderbund Software, Inc.
500 Redwood Blvd.
PO Box 6121
Novato, CA 94948
800-521-6263

Kid Pix Companion
Extension for Kid Pix

Broderbund Software, Inc.
500 Redwood Blvd.
PO Box 6121
Novato, CA 94948
800-521-6263

Kodak Colorsqueeze
Image compression software
Eastman Kodak Co.
CD Imaging
343 State St.
Rochester, NY 14650
800-242-2424

Lightning Effects
Image-processing software
Spectral Innovations, Inc.
1885 Lundy Ave., Ste. 208
San Jose, CA 95131
408-955-0366

MacPaint
Paint program
Claris Corp.
5201 Patrick Henry Dr.
P.O. Box 58168
Santa Clara, CA 95052
800-544-8554

Oasis
Graphics for video
Time Arts, Inc.
1425 Corporate Center Pkwy.
Santa Rosa, CA 95407
800-959-0509

Optix ImagePak
Image compression
Blueridge Technologies, Inc.
P.O. Box 430
Flint Hill Sq.
Flint Hill, VA 22627
703-675-3015

Paint Alchemy
Photoshop plug-ins
Xaos Tools, Inc.
600 Townsend Street
San Francisco, CA 94103
800-289-XAOS

Paint It!
Low-cost paint program

MicroFrontier, Inc.
3401 101st St., Ste. E
Des Moines, IA 50322
515-270-8109

PhotoFlash
Add images to documents
Apple Computer, Inc.
20525 Mariani Ave.
Cupertino, CA 95014
800-776-2333

PhotoFusion
Image compositing
Ultimatte Corp.
20554 Plummer St.
Chatsworth, CA 91311
818-993-8007

Photon Paint
Paint program
Hollyware Entertainment
13464 Washington Blvd.
Marina Del Rey, CA 90291
310-822-9200

PhotoSpot/PaintThinner
Photoshop plug-in
Second Glance Software
25381-G Alicia Pkwy., Ste. 357
Laguna Hills, CA 92653
714-855-2331

PicturePress
Image-handling tools
Storm Technology
1861 Landings Dr.
Mountain View, CA 94043
800-275-5734

PixelPaint Pro3
Image enhancement
Pixel Resources, Inc.
PO Box 921848
Norcross, GA 30092
404-449-4947

Planet Color
Image compression software
LizardTech
P.O. Box 2129
Sante Fe, NM 87504
505-989-7117

ScanMatch
Color calibration software
Savitar, Inc.
139 Townsend St., Ste. M100
San Francisco, CA 94107
415-243-3080

ScanTastic ps
Photoshop plug-in
Second Glance Software
25381-G Alicia Pkwy., Ste. 357
Laguna Hills, CA 92653
714-855-2331

Smoothie
Anti-aliasing software
Peirce Software
719 Hibiscus Pl., Ste. 301
San Jose, CA 95117
800-828-6554

Specular Collage
Image composition software.
Specular International
479 West St.
Amherst, MA 01002
800-433-7732

Studio/1, Studio/8, and
Studio/32.
Paint and graphics software
Electronic Arts
1450 Fashion Island Blvd.
San Mateo, CA 94404
800-245-4525

ThunderWorks for the Apple
Scanner
Image-editing software
Thunderware, Inc.
21 Orinda Way
Orinda, CA 94563
800-628-069

UltraPaint
Paint and drawing software
Deneba Software
7400 SW 87th Ave.
Miami, FL 33173
305-596-5644

VideoPaint
Paint and editing software

Olduvai Corp.
9200 S. Dadeland Blvd., Ste. 725
Miami, FL 33156
800-548-5151

Three-Dimensional Rendering and Animation Software

Acuris Clipmodel Libraries
Three-dimensional clipmodels
Acuris Inc.
931 Hamilton
Menlo Park, CA 94025
800-652-2874

Alias Sketch!
Three-dimensional rendering
Alias Research, Inc.
110 Richmond St. E.
Toronto, Ontario, Canada
M5C 1P1
800-447-2542

Atlantis Render
Rendering Software
Graphisoft
400 Oyster Point Blvd., Ste. 429
So. San Francisco, CA 94080
800-344-3468

BackBurner
Network rendering system
Specular International
479 West Street
Amherst, MA 01002
800-433-7732

Electric Image Animation
System
Three-dimensional rendering
Electric Image, Inc.
117 E. Colorado Blvd., Ste. 300
Pasadena, CA 91105
818-577-1627

form•Z
Modeling and rendering

auto•des•sys, Inc.
2011 Riverside Drive
Columbus, OH 43221
614-488-8838

Infini-D
Rendering and animation
Specular International
479 West Street
Amherst, MA 01002
800-433-7732

Life Forms
Human figure animation
Macromedia
600 Townsend St.
San Francisco, CA 94103
415-252-2000

MacroModel
Modeling software
Macromedia
600 Townsend St.
San Francisco, CA 94103
415-252-2000

ModelPro
Modeling software
Visual Information
Development, Inc.
136 W. Olive Ave.
Monrovia, CA. 91016
818-358-3936

ModelShop II
Three-dimensional design
600 Townsend St.
San Francisco, CA 94103
415-252-2000

Pixar ShowPlace
Pixar
1001 W. Cutting Blvd.
Richmond, CA 94804
800-888-9856

Presenter Professional
*Modeling, rendering, and
animation software*
Visual Information Dvpmt. Inc.
136 W. Olive Ave.
Monrovia, CA 91016
818-358-3936

Ray Dream Designer
Modeling and rendering software
Ray Dream, Inc.
1804 N. Shoreline Blvd.
Mountainview, CA 94043
415-960-0765

RB2Swivel
Modeling and rendering
VPL Research, Inc.
3977 E. Bayshore Rd.
Palo Alto, CA 94303
415-988-2550

RenderPro 2
Rendering accelerator
Strata, Inc.
2 W. Saint George Blvd.,
Ste. 2100
St. George, UT 84770
800-869-6855

Rend-X
File converter for StrataVision
Strata, Inc.
2 W. Saint George Blvd., Ste.
2100
St. George, UT 84770
800-869-6855

Sculpt 3D, and 3D RISC
Modeling and rendering
Byte by Byte Corp.
9442-A Capital of Texas Hwy.
N, Ste. 650
Austin, TX 78759
512-795-0150

Sculpt 4D, and 4D RISC
Rendering, and animation
Byte by Byte Corp.
9442-A Capital of Texas Hwy. N,
Ste. 650
Austin, TX 78759
512-795-0150

Sculptor
Modeling and rendering
Byte by Byte Corp.
9442-A Capital of Texas Hwy.
N, Ste. 650

Austin, TX 78759
512-795-0150

Strata StudioPro
Rendering, and animation
Strata Inc.
2 W. Saint George Blvd.,
Ste. 2100
St. George UT 84770
800-869-6855

StrataVision 3D
Rendering, and animation
Strata Inc.
2 W. Saint George Blvd.,
Ste. 2100
St. George UT 84770
800-869-6855

Swivel 3D Professional
Modeling software
600 Townsend St.
San Francisco, CA 94103
415-252-2000

Three-D
Rendering and animation
Macromedia
600 Townsend St.
San Francisco, CA 94103
415-252-2000

TREE
Tree modeling and rendering
Onyx Computing, Inc.
10 Avon St.
Cambridge, MA 02138
617-876-3876

VG Shaders and VG Looks
Surfaces for RenderMan
The Valis Group
PO Box 422
Point Richmond, CA 94807
510-236-4124

Virtus WalkThrough
/WalkThrough Pro
Walkthrough software
Virtus Corp.
117 Edinburgh S, Ste. 204
Cary, NC 27511

800-847-8871

Will Vintons's Playmation
Rendering and animation
Anjon & Associates
714 E. Angeleno St., Unit C
Burbank, CA 91501
800-377-8287

Zoom and Focus
Rendering software
Graphisoft
400 Oyster Point Blvd., Ste. 429
So. San Francisco, CA 94080
800-344-3468

Mail Order Houses

KEY

Accelerator Cards=**AC**
CD-ROM Drives=**CDRD**
CD-ROM Games=**CDRG**
CD-ROM Software, Clip
   Media, Clip Art=**CDRS**
Display Card=**DC**
Hard Disk Drives=**HD**
Input Devices=**ID**
Magneto Optical
   Drives=**MO**
Monitors=**MTRS**
Removable Media=**RM**
Scanners=**SCNRS**
Software=**STWR**
Tape Backup Systems=**TBS**

Advance Business Center
SCNRS, MNTRS, RM, ID, HD
23510 Telo Ave., #5
Terrance, CA 90505
800-723-8262

APS Technologies
CDRD, HD, MO, TBS, RM
6131 Deramus
Kansas City, MO 64120
800-235-3707

Bottom Line Distribution
MTRS, ID, SCNRS, RM,
TBS, STWR, MO, AC
1219 W. 6th St.
Austin, TX 78703
512-472-4956

ClubMac
HD, RM
7 Hammond
Irvine, CA 92718
800-258-2622

Computer Discount
Warehouse
MTRS, STWR, ID, HD, RM,
CDRD, RAM
No available address
800-291-4CDW

DGR Technologies
HD, MO, STWR
1219 West Sixth, Ste. 205
Austin, TX 78703
800-235-9748

Digital Axis International
HD, ID
5000 Plaza On The Lake,
Ste. 250
Austin, TX 78746
800-622-4473

Direct Connections
HD, MO, CDRD, TBS, CDRS
7668 Executive Drive
Eden Prairie, MN 55344
800-572-4305

Dr. Mac
STWR, CDRS
No available address
800-825-6227

Express Direct
MTRS, CDRD, SCNRS
No available address
800-765-0040

First Source International
RAM
7 Journey
Aliso Viejo, CA 92656
800-304-9866

The LLB Company
RAM, SCNRS, CDRD, CDRS,
HD, RM, AC
300 120th Ave., NE, Bldg. 1,
Ste. 120
Bellevue, WA 98005
800-304-9866

MacCenter
CDRD, MTRS, RM, HD, MO,
RAM
4930 South Congress, Ste. 303
Austin, TX 78745
800-950-3726

MacConnection
STWR, CDRS, HD, RM
14 Mill Street
Marlow, NH 03456
800-800-4444

MacLand
RM, SCNRS,
4685 S. Ash Ave., Ste. H-5

Tempe, AZ 85282
800-333-3353

MacMail
MTRS, RAM, ID, CDRD, CDRS, AC
2645 Maricopa St.
Torrance, CA 90503
800-222-2808

MacNews/Relisys
SCNRS
1555 Sherman Ave., Ste. 361
Evanston, IL 60201
800-723-7755

MacProducts, USA
RAM, AC, HD, RM, CDRD, ID,
STWR, SCNRS
608 W. 22nd St.
Austin, TX 78705
800-622-3475

MacWarehouse
CDRS, SCNRS, STWR, MNTRS,
ID, AC, RAM, RHD
1720 Oak St., PO Box 3031
Lakewood, NJ 08701
800-255-6227

The MacZone
STWR, AC
17411 N.E. Union Hill Rd.
Redmond, WA 98052-6716
800-436-8000

MegaHaus
CDRD, RM, HD, TBS, MO
1110 NASA Rd. 1, #306
Houston, TX 77058
800-786-1191

Syex Express
RM, MTRS, SCNRS, AC, ID
1030 Wirt Rd., #400
Houston, TX 77055
800-876-3467

Third Wave Computing
RAM, AC, HD, RM, CDRD, ID,
STWR, SCNRS
608 W. 22nd St.
Austin, TX 78705
800-622-3475

USA Flex
SNRS, MTRS, CDRD, RM, DC
471 Brighton Dr.
Bloomington, IL 60103
800-950-0354

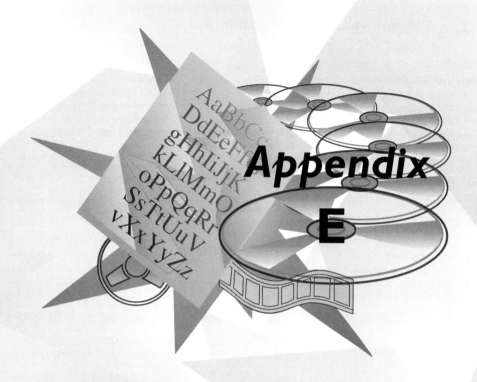

Appendix E

Utility, Back-Up, and Development Software

1-Anubis
Formatter/driver/utility
CharisMac Engineering, Inc.
66 "D" P&S Ln.
Newcastle, CA 95658
800-487-4420

3d Graphic Tools
Three-dimensional data
Micro Systems Options
PO Box 95167
Seattle, WA 98145
206-868-5418

Alki Seek
Fast file retrieval utility
Alki Software Corp.
300 Queen Anne Ave. N.,
Ste. 410

Seattle, WA 98109
800-669-9673

All Of MacTech Magazine
CD-ROM
Mac Tech Magazine
PO Box 250055
Los Angeles, CA 90025
310-575-4343

Anubis Multifunction Utility
CharisMac Engineering, Inc.
66 "D" P&S Ln.
Newcastle, CA 95658
800-487-4420

Anibus Optical Jukebox
Utility
CharisMac Engineering, Inc.

66 "D" P&S Ln.
Newcastle, CA 95658
800-487-4420

Anibus WORM Time Stamp
Manager
Formats and supports
CharisMac Engineering, Inc.
66 "D" P&S Ln.
Newcastle, CA 95658
800-487-4420

AppleScript Scripter's Kit
*Integrate applications across
desktops and networks*
Apple Computer, Inc.
20525 Mariani Ave.
Cupertino, CA 95014
800-776-2333

ARTI Developer's Kit
Advanced Remote video and
multimedia devices
Technologies, Inc. (ARTI)
307 Orchard City Dr., Ste. 204
Campbell, CA 95008
408-374-9044

BB Progression
Computer language
Basis International, Ltd.
5901 Jefferson St. NE
Albuquerque, NM 87109
505-345-5232

Besearch PostScript Examples
PostScript as a programming
language
Besearch Information Services
26160 Edelweiss Cir.
Evergreen, CO 80439
800-851-0289

BRU Pro
Backup/restore utility
Millennium Computer Corp.
640 Kreag Rd.
Pittsford, NY 14534
716-248-0510

Cat*Back
Cataloging program
Enterprise Software
12943 Andy Dr.
Cerritos, CA 90701
310-809-7184

CD AllCache
Increase speed of CD-ROM
players
CharisMac Engineering, Inc.
66 "D" P&S Ln.
Newcastle, CA 95658
800-487-4420

CD Author
CD-ROM development tools
Dataware Technologies, Inc.
222 Third St.
Cambridge, MA 02142
617-621-0820

CD-i Animation Stack
Convert QuickTime to CD-i
MediaMogul
OptImage Interactive
Services Co.
1501 50th St., Ste. 100
West Des Moines, IA 50266
800-254-5484

CD-IT!
Multimedia printing
OptImage Interactive
Services Co.
1501 50th St., Ste. 100
West Des Moines, IA 50266
800-254-5484

CD-Record
CD-ROM development tools
Dataware Technologies, Inc.
222 Third St.
Cambridge, MA 02142
617-621-0821

The CD-ROM Developer's Lab
Multimedia production
Software Mart, Inc.
3933 Steck Ave., Ste. B-115
Austin, TX 78759
512-346-7887

CLImate
Command line interface
Orchard Software, Inc.
PO Box 380814
Cambridge, MA 02238
617-876-4608

CommControl
Communications control
FaceWare
1310 N. Broadway
Urbana, IL 61801
217-328-5842

The Debugger & MacNosy
Symbolic debugger
Jasik Designs
343 Trenton Way
Menlo Park, CA 94025
415-322-1386

Design/CPN
Analyze concurrent systems
Meta Software Corp.
125 Cambridge Park Dr.
Cambridge, MA 02140
800-227-4106

Design/OA
C-language developer's kit
Meta Software Corp.
125 Cambridge Park Dr.
Cambridge, MA 02140
800-227-4106

Development Solutions
For C and C++
Port to GUI without rewriting
XVT Software, Inc.
4900 Pearl East Cir.
Boulder, Co 80301
800-678-7988

DeX Algorithm
Intellectual property security
Expert Systems, Inc.
2616 Quebec Ave.
Melbourne, FL 32935
407-242-0140

Disk Cafe
SCSI drive utility
Bering Technology, Inc.
1357 Dell Ave.
Campbell, CA 95008
800-237-4641

DiscFit Direct
Personal backup
Dantz Development Corp.
4 Orinda Way, Bldg. C
Orinda, CA 94563
510-253-3000

DiskFit Pro
Backup application
Dantz Development Corp.
4 Orinda Way, Bldg. C
Orinda, CA 94563
510-253-3000

Disc To The Future:
Source code and utilities

Wayzata Technology, Inc.
PO Box 807
Grand Rapids, MN 55744
800-735-7321

DiskExpress II
Disk optimizer utility
ALSoft Inc.
PO Box 927
Spring, TX 77383
713-353-4090

DiskMaker
Universal SCSI formatter
Golden Triangle
Computers, Inc.
11175 Flintkote Ave.
San Diego, CA 92121
619-587-0110

Disk Manager Mac
Disk installation utility
Ontrack Computer Systems, Inc.
6321 Bury Dr., Ste. 15-21
Eden Prairie, MN 55346
800-752-1333

DiskQuick
Catalogs hard drives and disks
Ideaform Inc.
PO Box 1540
Fairfield, IA 52556
515-472-7256

DiskTwin
Disk duplexing system
Golden Triangle
Computers, Inc.
11175 Flintkote Ave.
San Diego, CA 92121
619-587-0110

DocuBase
Document/database manager
FaceWare
1310 N. Broadway
Urbana, IL 61801
217-328-5842

Double-XX
Build applications
Heizer Software

PO Box 232019
Pleasant Hill, CA 94523
800-888-7667

DrawIt
QuickDraw extensions
FaceWare
1310 N. Broadway
Urbana, IL 61801
217-328-5842

Drive7
Drive management utility
Casa Blanca Works, Inc.
148 Bon Air Center
Greenbrae, CA 94904
415-461-2227

DriveShare
Share devices over a network
Casa Blanca Works, Inc.
148 Bon Air Center
Greenbrae, CA 94904
415-461-2227

DSP3210/ARTA Developer
Toolkit
Development environment
Spectral Innovations, Inc.
1885 Lundy Ave.,
Ste. 208
San Jose, CA 95131
408-955-0366

eDisk
Hard disk performance
Alysis Software Corp.
1331 Columbus Ave., 3rd Flr.
San Francisco, CA 94133
800-825-9747

EditControls
Advanced controls for ViewIt
FaceWare
1310 N. Broadway
Urbana, IL 61801
217-328-5842

EHelp
Multimedia documentation
Foudation Solutions, Inc.

2000 Regency Pkwy., Ste. 345
Cary, NC 27511
919-481-3517

E.T.O.: Essentials-Tools-Objects
Software development system
APDA—Apple Computer, Inc.
PO Box 319
Buffalo, NY 14207
800-282-2732

ExpressMirror
Disk mirroring/array software
ATTO Technology, Inc.
Audubon Technology Park
40 Hazelwood #106
Amherst, NY 14228
716-691-1999

FileDuo
Personal backup utility
ASD Software, Inc.
4650 Arrow Hwy., Ste. E-6
Montclair, CA 91763
909-624-2594

File Safe
Backup program
Enterprise Software
12943 Andy Dr.
Cerritos, CA 90701
310-809-7184

FindAll
Find the files you need
Abbott Systems, Inc.
62 Mountain Rd.
Pleasantville, NY 10570
800-552-9157

FlowChart Express
Creates flowcharts
Kaetron Software Corp.
25211 Grogans Mill Rd.
Ste. 260
The Woodlands, TX 77380
800-938-8900

FormatterOne
SCSI driver and utility
Software Architects, Inc.

19102 N. Creek Pkwy., Ste. 101
Bothell, WA 98011
206-487-0122

FormatterTwo
SCSI drive and utility software
Software Architects, Inc.
19102 N. Creek Pkwy., Ste. 101
Bothell, WA 98011
206-487-0122

FormsProgrammer
Programming utility
OHM Software
98 Long Pasture Way
Tiverton, RI 02878
800-346-9034

FreeForm/U*DB*os
Database operating system
Dimension Software
1717 Walnut Hill Ln., Ste. 104
Las Colinas, TX 75038
214-580-1045

Fulcrum SearchTools
Build text-retrieval products
Fulcrum Technologies Inc.
785 Carling Ave.
Ottawa, Ontario, Canada
K1S 5H4
613-238-1761

GCS Compressor/Installer
Compress files
Glen Canyon Software
3921 Shasta View
Eugene, OR 97405
800-477-6947

GKSBx and GPHIGS
Graphics library
G5G
Parc D'Activities Chateau
Rouquey
PO Box 168
Merignac Cedex, France
33708
33-566-34-82-48

Grafpak-CGM and
Grafpak-GKS

*Library and graphics
development*
Advanced Technology Center
22982 Mill Creek Dr.
Laguna Hills, CA 92653
714-583-9119

Great Plains Dexterity
*Graphical, cross-platform
development*
Great Plains Software
1701 SW 38th St.
Fargo, ND 58103
800-456-0025

Green Hills C++ Cross And
Native Compiler From Oasys
C++ compiler
Oasys, Inc.
One Cranberry Hill
Lexington, MA 02173
617-862-2002

Halo Advanced Imaging
Library
Imaging toolkit
Media Cybernetics, Inc.
8484 Georgia Ave., Ste. 200
Silver Spring, MD 20910
800-992-4256

Halo Imaging Library
Multiplatform toolkit
Media Cybernetics, Inc.
8484 Georgia Ave.,
Ste. 200
Silver Spring, MD 20910
800-992-4256

Hard Disk ToolKit
Hard disk utility
2040 Polk St., Ste. 215
San Francisco, CA 94109
415-474-8055

Hard Drive TuneUp
Tunes up System 7
Software Architects, Inc.
19102 N. Creek Pkwy.,
Ste. 101
Bothell, WA 98011
206-487-0122

HFS Backup
Archive and restore utility
Personal Computer
Peripherals Corp.
34 Jerome Ave., Ste. 214
Bloomfield, CT 06002
813-530-0123

HOOPS A.I.R./Graphic
*Photorealistic rendering and
3D graphics*
Ithaca Software
1301 Marina Village Pkwy.
Alameda, CA 94501
510-523-5900

HyperFace
HyperCard interface
FaceWare
1310 N. Broadway
Urbana, IL 61801
217-328-5842

Lasertalk
*PostScript language
environment*
Adobe Systems, Inc.
1585 Charleston Rd.
Montain View, CA 94043
800-833-6687

Late Night Attendant
Automatic backup utility
Broad Ripple Systems, Inc.
2902 N. Meridian St.
Indianapolis, IN 46208
317-923-2194

Lido 7
Initialize any disk storage
Surf City Software
1095 N. Main St. #M1
Orange, CA 92667
714-289-8543

Linear And Non-Linear
Programming
Mathematical programming
Lionheart Press, Inc.
PO Box 20756
Mesa, AZ 85277
514-526-7877

Logo Plus For The Macintosh
Programming language
Terrapin Software, Inc.
400 Riverside St.
Portland, ME 04103
800-972-8200

LusterPIC
Converts color PixMap
DataPak Software
9317 NE Hwy. 99, Ste. G
Vancouver, WA 98665
206-573-9155

MacApp
Object-oriented application
APDA—Apple Computer, Inc.
PO Box 319
Buffalo, NY 14207
800-282-2732

MacExpress
Interface manager
ALSoft, Inc.
PO Box 927
Spring, TX 77383
713-353-4090

MacFlow
Flowchart design
Mainstay
591-A Constitution Ave.
Camarillo, CA 93012
805-484-9400

MachTen X Software
X Client, Motif and X Server
Tenon Intersystems
1123 Chapala St.
Santa Barabara, CA 93101
805-963-6983

Macintosh Programmer's
Workshop
Development system
APDA—Apple Computer, Inc.
PO Box 319
Buffalo, NY 14207
800-282-2732

MacIRMA API
Interface for the MacIRMA

Digital Communications
Associates, Inc. (DCA)
1000 Alderman Dr.
Alpharetta, GA 30202
800-348-3221

MacMumps
Mumps language
MGlobal
2900 Weslayan, Ste. 415
Houston, TX 77027
713-960-0205

MacParlog
Parallel logic programming
Parallel Logic Programming Ltd.
PO Box 49
Twickenham, London, UK
TW2 5PH
0454-201652

MacsBug
Machine language debugger
APDA—Apple Computer, Inc.
PO Box 319
Buffalo, NY 14207
800-282-2732

MacTools
Hard disk utilities
Central Point Software, Inc.
15220 NW Greenbrier
Pkwy., #200
Beaverton, OR 97006
503-690-8090

MacTopix CD-ROM Simulator
CD-ROM simulation system
Optical Media International
180 Knowles Dr.
Los Gatos, CA 95030
800-347-2664

MacYACC
Generates ANSI C source code
Abraxas Software, Inc.
5530 SW Kelly Ave.
Portland, OR 97201
503-244-5253

Marksman
Graphical program tool

IT Makers
PO Box 730152
San Jose, CA 95173
408-274-8669

MARS Shuttle
Application program interface
Micro Dynamics, Ltd.
8555 16th St., 7th Fl.
Silver Springs, MD 20910
301-589-6300

MasterFinder
Disk management utility
Olduvai Corp.
9200 S. Dadeland Blvd.,
Ste. 725
Miami, FL 33156
800-548-5151

Matrix Engine
Macintosh List Manager
DataPak Software
9317 NE Hwy. 99, Ste. G
Vancouver, WA 98665
206-573-9155

MaxSPITBOL
SNOBOL4 programming
Catspaw, Inc.
PO Box 1123
Salida, CO 81201
719-539-3884

MediaMogul Mac Pak
CD-i development software
OptImage Interactive
Services Co.
1501 50th St., Ste. 100
West Des Moines, IA 50266
800-254-5484

MemManager
Prevent crashes
DataPak Software
9317 NE Hwy. 99, Ste. G
Vancouver, WA 98665
206-573-9155

Metacheck And Metacals
Conformance analyzers
Advanced Technology Center

22982 Mill Creek Dr.
Laguna Hills, CA 92653
714-583-9119

Mini IDL
Data management tool
Persistent Data Systems, Inc.
PO Box 38415
Pittsburg, PA 15238
412-963-1843

Moby Language
Word lists world languages
Grady Ward
3449 Martha Ct.
Arcata, CA 95521
707-826-7715

More Disk Space
Hard disk performance
Alysis Software Corp.
1331 Columbus Ave., 3rd Fl.
San Francisco, CA 94133
800-825-9747

Mr. File
Finder alternative utility
Softways
5066 El Roble
San Jose, CA 95118
408-978-9167

Mug Shot III
Expandable system profile
Mi Concepts
PO Box 8822
Kentwood, MI 49508
616-765-3312

MultiDisk
Hard disk partitioning
ALSoft Inc.
PO Box 927
Spring, TX 77383
713-353-4090

Net Check
Anti-piracy network library
Famous Engineer Brand
Software
4855 Finlay St.
Richmond, VA 23231
804-222-2215

NetStream
Network backup
Personal Computer
Peripherals Corp.
34 Jerome Ave., Ste. 214
Bloomfield, CT 06002
813-530-0123

Norton Utilities For Macintosh
Data recovery backup
Symantec Corp.
10201 Torre Ave.
Cupertino, CA 95014
800-3441-7234

Oasys 68000/10/20/30/40 +
68881/851/332 Macro
Assembler/Linker System
Oasys, Inc.
One Cranberry Hill
Lexington, MA 02173
617-862-2002

Oasys 680x0 Optimizing
Native And Cross Compilers
Optimizing compilers
Oasys, Inc.
One Cranberry Hill
Lexington, MA 02173
617-862-2002

Oasys 88000 Macro
Assembler/Linker System
Oasys, Inc.
One Cranberry Hill
Lexington, MA 02173
617-862-2002

Oasys 88000 Optimizing
Cross Compilers
Compilers
Oasys, Inc.
One Cranberry Hill
Lexington, MA 02173
617-862-2002

Oasys 88000 Simulator
*88000 RISC runtime
environment*
Oasys, Inc.
One Cranberry Hill
Lexington, MA 02173
617-862-2002

Object Logo
Object-oriented Logo
Paradigm Software, Inc.
PO Box 2995
Cambridge, MA 02238
617-576-7675

Object Logo Student Edition
Programming; ages 11 and up
Paradigm Software, Inc.
PO Box 2995
Cambridge, MA 02238
617-576-7675

Object Master Universal
Object-oriented progamming
ACI US, Inc.
20883 Stevens Creek Blvd.
Cupertino, CA 95014
800-759-7272

Objectworks Smalltalk
Object-oriented programming
ParcPlae Systems, Inc.
999 E. Arques Ave.
Sunnyvale, CA 94086
800-759-7272

Occam Explorer
Compiler and interpreter
Pacific Parallel Research, Inc.
922 Grange Hall Rd.
Cardiff by the Sea, CA 92007
619-436-1455

On-Line Help Construction Kit
Help system
DataPak Software
9317 NE Hwy. 99, Ste. G
Vancouver, WA 98665
206-573-9155

On Location
Find and view files
ON Technology, Inc.
One Cambridge Center
Cambridge, MA 02142
800-548-8871

Orphan Finder
Manages orphan files
Tuesday Software
215 Via Sevilla

Santa Barbara, CA 93109
800-945-7889

OSF/Motif
Environment
Integrated Computer
Solutions, Inc.
201 Broadway
Cambridge, MA 02139
617-621-0060

PHIGURE
Graphics library
G5G
Parc D'Activities Chateau
Rouquey
PO Box 168
Merignac Cedex, France
33708
33-566-34-82-48

PICT Detective
QuickDraw descriptions
Palomar Software, Inc.
PO Box 120
Oceanside, CA 92049
619-721-7000

PictureCDEF
Button look to applications
Paradigm Software, Inc.
PO Box 2995
Cambridge, MA 02238
617-576-7675

Professional IDL
For C programmers
Persistent Data Systems, Inc.
PO Box 38415
Pittsburg, PA 15238
412-963-1843

Programmer's "Bag Of Tricks"
Programming routines
DataPak Software
9317 NE Hwy. 99, Ste. G
Vancouver, WA 98665
206-573-9155

Prograph
Visual programming
Prograph International Inc.
2745 Dutch Village Rd., Ste. 200

Halifax, Nova Scotia, Canada
B3L 4G7
800-565-1978

QTBackup
Backup software
Tecmar, Inc.
6225 Cochran Rd.
Solon, OH 44139
800-624-8560

Qued/M
Quality editors with macros
Nisus Software, Inc.
PO Box 1300
107 S. Cedros Ave.
Solana Beach, CA 92075
800-922-2993

QuickControl
Animation control for ViewIt
FaceWare
1310 N. Broadway
Urbana, IL 61801
217-328-5842

RapidTrak
Disk management
Insignia Solutions, Inc.
1300 Charleston Rd.
Mountain View, CA 94043
800-848-7677

Redux
Backup utility
Inline Design
308 Main St.
Lakeville, CT 06039
800-453-7671

ReferenceSet
CD-ROM development tools
Dataware Technologies, Inc.
222 Third St.
Cambridge, MA 02142
617-621-0820

Remus
RAID disk array software
Trillium Research
220 Locust St., PO Box 845
Hudson, WI 54016
715-381-1900

ResEdit
Graphical resource editor
APDA- Apple Computer, Inc.
PO Box 319
Buffalo, NY 14207
800-282-2732

Resorcerer
Resource editor
Mathemaesthetics, Inc.
PO Box 67-156
Chestnut Hill, MA 02167
617-738-8803

Retrieve It!
File finding and opening
Claris Clear Choice
5201 Patrick Henry Dr.
PO Box 58168
Santa Clara, CA 95052
800-325-2747

Retrospect, Retrospect A/UX,
and Retrospect Remote
Powerful backup software
Dantz Development Corp.
4 Orinda Way, Bldg. C
Orinda, CA 94563
510-253-3000

Rio Command Package
*Productivity tools and system
utilities for A/UX and other
platforms*
Ganusa
34532 Northstar Ter.
Fremont, CA 94555
510-790-2254

Rulers
Object code module
DataPak Software
9317 NE Hwy. 99,
Ste. G
Vancouver, WA 98665
206-573-9155

SADE
Debugging environment
APDA- Apple Computer, Inc.
PO Box 319
Buffalo, NY 14207
800-282-2732

SafeDeposit
Real-time backup program
Dayna Communications
Sorenson Research Park
849 W. Levoy Dr.
Salt Lake City, UT 84123
801-269-7200

SafeDeposit Server
Real-time backup program
Dantz Development Corp.
4 Orinda Way, Bldg. C
Orinda, CA 94563
510-253-3000

Script-Ease
Utility for editing scripts
Glen Canyon Software
3921 Shasta View
Eugene, OR 97405
800-477-6947

ScriptGen Pro
Interface for generating scripts
StepUp Software
7110 Glendora Ave.
Dallas, TX 75230
214-360-9301

ScriptIt
AppleScript manager
FaceWare
1310 N. Broadway
Urbana, IL 61801
217-328-5842

SCSI Tool/SCSI View
SCSI hardware and software
Arborworks, Inc.
431 Virginia Ave.
Ann Arbor, MI 48103
800-346-6980

ShuttlePilot
File synchronizer
Xanatech, Inc.
61 Oriole Crescent, Ste. 1
Singapore 1128
65-2244073

Silverrun-Application
Development Environment
Distributed applications

Computer Systems
Advisers, Inc.
50 Tice Blvd.
Woodcliff Lake, NJ 07675
800-537-4262

Smalltalk Agents
*Object-oriented
development tool*
Quasar Knowledge Systems,
Inc. (QKS)
9818 Parkwood Dr.
Bethesda, MD 20814
800-296-1339

Smalltalk for Macintosh
Smalltalk programming
Digitalk, Inc.
5 Hutton Centre Dr.
Santa Ana, CA 92707
800-922-8255

SnapBack
Workgroup backup
Golden Triangle
Computers, Inc.
11175 Flintkote Ave.
San Diego, CA 92121
619-587-0110

SoftPolish
Quality assurance tool
Language Systems Corp.
441 Carlisle Dr.
Herndon, VA 22070
800-252-6479

SoftQuad ApplicationBuilder
Development environment
SoftQuad Inc.
56 Averfoyle Crescent, Ste. 810
Toronto, Ontario, Canada
M8X 2W4
416-239-4801

Source Code Tutorial For
Macintosh
Sample application
Bear River Associates, Inc.
PO Box 1900
Berkeley, CA 94701
510-644-9400

SourceBug
Debugging environment
APDA- Apple Computer, Inc.
PO Box 319
Buffalo, NY 14207
800-282-2732

SourceSafe
Version control system
One Tree Software
PO Box 11639
Raleigh, NC 27604
800-397-2323

Spinnaker PLUS
Hypermedia tool
Spinnaker Software Corp.
201 Broadway, 6th floor
Cambridge, MA 02139
800-323-8088

Spot CD
CD driver
MacPEAK
PO Box 163104
Austin, TX 78716
512-327-3211

Spot On
Caching software
MacPEAK
PO Box 163104
Austin, TX 78716
512-327-3211

Stacker For Macintosh
Doubles hard disk capacity
Stac Electronics
5993 Avenida Encinas
Carlsbad, CA 92008
800-522-7822

Stonehand Composition
Toolbox
Text formatting engine
Stonehead, Inc.
118 Magazine St.
Cambridge, MA 02139
617-864-5524

StuffIt Action Atoms and
InstallerMaker
StuffIt compression

Aladdin Systems, Inc.
165 Westridge Dr.
Watsonville, CA 95076
408-761-6200

SuperDisk!
Hard disk enhancement
Alysis Software Corp.
1331 Columbus Ave., 3rd Fl.
San Francisco, CA 94133
800-825-9747

SuperSpot
Caching software
MacPEAK
PO Box 163104
Austin, TX 78716
512-327-3211

SurfGuard
Archival utility
Surf City Software
1095 N. Main St. #M1
Orange, CA 92667
714-289-8543

TAOS
BBx developer's workbench
Basis International, Ltd.
5901 Jefferson St. NE
Albuquerque, NM 87109
505-345-5232

Think Reference
Online reference
Symantec Corp.
10201 Torre Ave.
Cupertino, CA 95014
800-3441-7234

TimesTwo
Increases disk storage
Golden Triangle
Computers, Inc.
11175 Flintkote Ave.
San Diego, CA 92121
619-587-0110

TwinIt
Personal continuous backup
Golden Triangle
Computers, Inc.
11175 Flintkote Ave.

San Diego, CA 92121
619-587-0110

Uniface
Client-server application
Uniface
1320 Harbor Bay Pkwy.,
Ste. 100
Alameda, CA 94502
800-365-3608

UserLand Frontier
Development platform
UserLand Software, Inc.
400 Seaport Ct.
Redwood City, CA 94063
415-369-6600

Verbum Development System
*Arabic object-oriented pro-
gramming language*
Paradigm Software, Inc.
PO Box 2995
Cambridge, MA 02238
617-576-7675

ViewIt
Advance window designer
FaceWare
1310 N. Broadway
Urbana, IL 61801
217-328-5842

Virtual Memory
Disk cashing module
DataPak Software
9317 NE Hwy. 99, Ste. G
Vancouver, WA 98665
206-573-9155

Virtual User
Automated testing system
APDA- Apple Computer, Inc.
PO Box 319
Buffalo, NY 14207
800-282-2732

VisionSoft
Software analyzer
MetaLINK Corp
1999 S. Bascom Ave., Ste. 700
Campbell, CA 95008
408-879-2672

VisualWorks
Programming tool
ParcPlace Systems, Inc.
999 E. Arques Ave.
Sunnyvale, CA 94086
800-759-7272

Word Solution Engine
Programmers tool
DataPak Software
9317 NE Hwy. 99, Ste. G
Vancouver, WA 98665
206-573-9155

Word Solutions Engine
Add-Ons
Programming tools
DataPak Software
9317 NE Hwy. 99, Ste. G
Vancouver, WA 98665
206-573-9155

XMWS
ATS compliant server
Integrated Solutions, Inc.
1020 8th Ave.
King of Prussia, PA 19406
215-660-0781

3DO: CD-ROM development system that is independent of computer systems. 3DO players are connected to television sets in the same way that video game systems are connected.

8mm: A video tape format that is also used in tape backup systems.

32-Bit Addressing: An expansion of the Macintosh computers system software that allows the central processing unit to process 32 bits of data per cycle.

680x0: The Model number of the Macintosh central processing unit. The *x* represents the digit that distinguishes the model types such as 68000 in early model Macintosh computers and 68040 in Quadras.

Accelerator Cards: NuBus expansion cards that enhance the processing power of the central processing unit.

Access Time: The period of time that it takes for data to be retrieved from a storage device such as a CD-ROM, hard drive, or RAM.

Actual Resolution: The resolution of images scanned by a scanner without additional enlargement.

ADB Devices: Input devices that are connected to the Macintosh computer via the Apple desktop bus.

Add Depth (Ray Dream): A three-dimensional graphics program that is designed to work specifically with lines and shapes imported from two-dimensional graphics programs.

AIFF: (Audio Interchange File Format): The most common sound file format for Macintosh software.

Aliasing: The jaggy effect that is noticeable when viewing bitmapped images.

Ambient Light: Stray light that reflects off surfaces illuminating them with no apparent direct source. Three-dimensional graphics programs simulate ambient light to add to an image's realism.

Analog: The waveform state of audio and video data.

Animation: The rapid presentation of graphic images that produces the illusion of motion in the images.

Anti-aliasing: The technique used to reduce the jaggy effect that is present in bitmapped graphics.

Apple Desktop Bus (ADB): An extension to the Macintosh computers motherboard that allows the keyboard, mouse, and other input devices such as digitizer tablets to be connected to the computer through the ADB port in the back of the computer.

Apple: The computer company that manufactures the Macintosh computer.

AT&T: (American Telephone and Telegraph): A large communications company that has recently entered a joint venture with Panasonic to develop a system CD-ROM entertainment that can be played on a television set.

Audio Bits: The number of bits of storage that are used by each sample of digitized audio.

Audio CD: Compact disks that are encoded with audio data only and that require only conventional CD players to operate.

Authorware Professional (Macromedia): An interactive authoring program whose emphasis is interactive training materials (courseware).

Avid (Avid Technologies): A desktop video system that is based upon the Macintosh computer.

Bar Code Reader: An alternative input device that allows the Macintosh computer to decode bar codes such as those found on food packages.

Bat Keyboard: An alternative keyboard that uses key combinations similar to chords in music to produce letters, numbers, symbols, and punctuation.

Bernoulli (Iomega): Removable media storage device that uses disks encased in cartridges.

Binary Code: The digital code that is the most fundamental computer language. It is composed of 0s and 1s, which are combined into patterns that produce software programs.

Bit: The smallest measure of computer data. A bit consists of one 0 or 1.

Bitmapped Graphics: Computer graphics that are composed of individually colored pixels. Similarly colored pixels are grouped together to form shapes and designs.

Block Size: The amount of data that a storage drive or CD-ROM passes into its cache before transfer to the computer memory.

Branching: A method of presentation in which the presentation proceeds to different areas depending upon the selections made by a viewer or scripting code written by the author. For example, pressing the **Checking** button in an automated teller machine will cause the program to branch to the checking portion of the program.

Built-in Audio: The built-in audio capabilities of the Macintosh computer in both playback and recording. All Macintosh computers have the capability of playing audio at 22 kHz; the Quadra AV and Power Macintosh computer can play audio at 44 kHz, which is CD audio quality. All the Macintosh computers released after the IIci, with the exception of the PowerBook 100, have the capability of recording audio directly to the hard drive. Macintosh computers that do not have built-in audio recording can be given this capability with audio capture cards and peripherals such as the MacRecorder.

Built-in Video: The built-in monitor display capability of Macintosh computers. Apple monitors and some third-party monitors can be connected to the built-in video port of the computer. The AV and Power Macintosh computers have the built-in capability of displaying to a television monitor.

Built-in Video Capture: The ability of some Macintosh computers to record video directly to the hard drive. The Quadra AV computers and Power Macintosh computers have built-in video capture capability.

Bus: A conduit of wires that runs through the computer's motherboard. The bus serves as the main data pathway of the computer.

Byte: A small unit of computer data. One byte consists of 8 bits.

C++: An object-oriented programming language.

Cache: A holding area for data that allows information to be read quickly from a hard drive to RAM.

Camcorder: A video camera that has a VCR built-in to it.

Camera: A video device that converts images from light information into electrical and magnetic signals recorded on video tape.

Cartridge Drives: Removable hard drives in which both the hard disk and the read/write mechanism are in the same cartridge and are installed in a docking mechanism connected to the computer.

Cast (Macromedia Director): The storage area of Macromedia Director in which video, audio, graphics, animation, other Director movies, QuickTime movies, and scripts are stored before they are incorporated in a Director presentation.

Cathode Ray Gun: The light source that fires electrons against the back of a television's or computer monitor's screen. The electrons illuminate a phosphor coating on the back of the screen and produce the image.

CCD (Charge-Coupled Device) Chip: The device in video cameras that converts light into electrical charges that are later converted to magnetic information and stored onto video tape.

CD-I (Compact Disc-Interactive): Users can interact with software that plays on a CD-I unit through the use of an infrared remote control.

CD-ROM (Compact Disk–Read Only Memory): Storage disks for digital data that are encoded with a laser and a magnetic read/write head. They can be encoded only once but can be read numerous times.

CD-ROM Burner: The device used to encode CD-ROM disks the one and only time that they can be encoded.

Central Processing Unit (CPU): The computer calculation device that is responsible for the orchestration of all the computer's functions.

Centris: A line of Macintosh computers that has been discontinued as a separate series and renamed as the lower-end Quadra computers.

Chroma-Keying: The process of overlaying a live video image on existing video or computer graphics. Chroma-Keying is used to superimpose weather forecasters over satellite images and graphics.

Clipboard: A portion of the Macintosh computer system software where graphics, text, audio, and other computer data are temporarily stored through the use of the **Cut** or **Copy** commands from the Edit menu. The data remains on the Clipboard until other data are cut or the **Copy** command is used again. Data on the Clipboard can be placed in other software programs with the **Paste** command.

Clipmedia: Collections of video, sound, animation, and graphics that are usually distributed on CD-ROM and can be incorporated in multimedia projects—usually royalty-free.

CMYK: A color combination scheme used in graphics software to produce the different colors in an image. The color combinations consist of varying concentrations of cyan, magenta, yellow, and black.

Color Depth (Bit Depth): The number of colors displayed by a computer monitor and capable of being scanned by a scanner. Color depth is measured in bits, such as 8 bits and 24 bits. The number of actual colors that are visible is calculated by raising 2 to the power of the bit value. For example, 8 bits are calculated as 2 to the eighth power, or 256 colors.

Color Palette: The group of colors displayed through the Macintosh computer system. The colors are taken from the unlimited number of available colors. Color palettes can be edited in some programs, such as Macromedia Director.

Color Scale: The number of colors that a scanner can produce in a scanned image or that a monitor can display. Color scale is represented in bit depth, such as 8 bits or 24 bits.

Composite Video: The connection between video devices that separates the video and audio channels through separate cables. All video peripherals are capable of transferring video through composite video channels.

Compression Rates: The ratio at which file sizes are reduced by compression software such as StuffIt Deluxe. Some compression rates are not measured as ratios such as 2:1 but as percentages of the original file size.

Computer Peripherals: Devices that are connected to a computer and that add functionality to the computer system, such as monitors, hard drives, and input devices.

Daisy Chain: The process of connecting SCSI or ADB devices to each other to form a chain that leads to the computer. The processes of the devices farther along the chain pass through the devices closer to the computer.

Default Shapes: The shapes that can be created automatically with graphics programs, such as the Oval and Rectangle tools in drawing programs.

Desktop Publishing: The digital composition of print media such as magazines and newspapers.

Desktop Video: The use of computers for the composition and editing of video while it is in a digital form.

Digital: Computer data. Information stored as binary code on computer peripheral storage devices or transferred through a computer.

Digital Audio Capture Card: The computer function expansion device that allows audio to be recorded directly to the hard drive.

Digital Audio Editing: The digital manipulation and alteration of audio data in a computer while the audio is in a digital form.

Digital Audio File Formats: The computer files for audio that allow audio files to be transferred from one program into another. AIFF is the most common digital audio file format.

Digital Audio Tape (DAT): High-quality audio tape that is used as the storage media in some tape backup systems.

Digital Still Photography: Digital cameras that combine the function of conventional photography with the technology of video to create electronic still images that can be imported easily into a computer.

Digital Video File Formats: The form that video takes when captured to a hard drive and converted into a file that can be used in multimedia software. The most common digital video format is QuickTime.

Digitizer Tablet: A pressure-sensitive plastic panel that is used as an alternative input device for computers. The operator runs a device similar to a pen or pencil along the surface of the panel. The movements of the pen against the surface are registered by the computer and are reflected in the movements of the pointer on the screen.

Dimensions (Adobe): A three-dimensional graphics program designed to convert two-dimensional PostScript artwork, such as that created by Adobe Illustrator, into three-dimensional images. Dimensions also simulates lighting effects such as shading and supports texture mapping for realistic three-dimensional images.

Direct Selection Tool: A tool in Macintosh and Windows software that allows objects to be clicked and selected with the mouse. When something is selected, it can be moved or becomes the subject of any property changes that you assign to it while it is selected, leaving the remainder of the image unchanged.

Directional Light: The lighting effect in three-dimensional graphics programs that simulates parallel rays of light from a distant source, such as the light of the sun.

Director (Macromedia): An interactive multimedia authoring and composition program for the Macintosh computer and Windows.

Disk Array: A hard disk drive construction that incorporates multiple storage disks and multiple read/write heads. All data encoding and retrieving is done to the multiple disks simultaneously so that all tasks of the drive are shared. This disbursement of tasks makes this type of drive faster than single-storage disk drives and excellent for multimedia production, especially video capture.

Display Area: The area of a monitor screen that actually displays an image. The display area is smaller than the screen size because there is usually an area of black along the edges of the screen that does not display anything.

Dots Per Inch (DPI): The numbers of pixels on-screen within an inch (monitors). The maximum size ratio that a graphic can be enlarged to and still retain its intended clarity (graphics). The number of dots in a row that are printed on paper to create an image (printing). Dots per inch is also called *Resolution.*

Drawing Software: Graphics software that allows for the creation of very precise lines and shapes that can be edited multiple times. This type of software is designed to simulate the art tools and environment of graphic artists and industrial designers, such as architects. The interface is based around a drawing board with pens, straightedges, and the ability to create very calculated curves such as those created with a compass.

DyCam: A digital photography camera manufacturer.

Edit Controller: The device used to edit video tape. It controls at least two VCRs and is used to determine what portions of existing video will be incorporated into the final edited tape.

Encapsulated PostScript: A file encoded in the PostScript programming language that contains additional information that allows it to be opened and edited in programs designed to work specifically with EPS documents. Adobe Illustrator produces EPS files.

Export: The process involved in saving a software file created in a program and transferring it out of the program as a file that can be opened in other software programs.

External Drives: Computer data storage drives that are contained in their own casing and attached to the Macintosh computer via the SCSI port.

Extrusion: The process of giving a two-dimensional graphic depth by "pulling" it into the third dimension. Extrusion is a function of three-dimensional graphics programs.

Fields: The division of individual video frames into two alternately displayed screens of even and odd screen lines. There are three fields displayed for each frame of video; there are 60 frames per second displayed for video in the United States standard of NTSC.

File Allocation Table (FAT): The area of a computer storage media in which an inventory of the contents of the media is recorded.

File Format Save Options: The selection of computer file formats that are available for the storage of a software program's files. For example, a file created in Adobe Photoshop can be saved as a PICT file, a TIFF, or a Photoshop file, among others.

Fill: The property of graphics programs that determines the appearance of the area within a shape. For example, a circle can be filled with a pattern, a gradient, or a solid color.

Film: A motion picture recording media that uses celluloid coated with a chemical solution to take pictures rapidly in a method similar to conventional photography. Film has a frame rate of 24 frames per second.

Filmstrip File: This file allows an animation produced with Adobe Premiere to be opened in Adobe Photoshop with all the frames visible simultaneously. Each frame can be graphically treated separately. Filmstrip files can be reopened in Premiere where they can be exported as animation file formats that can be opened in other programs.

Filters: Tools in graphics programs that are used to apply a uniform visual effect or alteration to all or part of an image.

Fixed Drive: A hard disk drive in which the disk cannot be removed from the drive.

Flatbed Scanner: A computer peripheral that replicates images in photographs and other hard copy media and converts them into digital information that can be used in graphics software.

Flat Shading: A three-dimensional graphics images rendering method in which edges are faceted and fine detail is not revealed. Flat shading is a fast rendering method that is used to preview the composition of a three-dimensional graphics scene.

Floppy Disk: A small-capacity storage media that is used with the Macintosh computer floppy disk drive.

Floptical Drives: A data storage media that combines laser technology with the compact disk size of floppy disks. The result is diskettes that can currently store 21M each. Floptical disks look like floppy disks but can be used only with floptical drives.

Fly-By Animation: An animation produced with three-dimensional graphics programs that simulate moving through the space surrounding an object or a scene, like a plane flying between the buildings of a city.

Font: The software used to produce the different text family styles. Helvetica is an example of a font.

Frame Accurate Recording: The process of recording a computer animation to video tape with one frame of the animation corresponding to exactly one frame of video.

Frame Rate: The number of frames per second that a motion media displays to produce the illusion of movement in the images. For example, the frame rate for video is 30 frames per second.

Freehand (Aldus): An object-oriented drawing program.

Freehand Tool: A tool in drawing programs that produces free form lines that correspond with the movements of the mouse.

Function Keys: Keys that are typically located along the top of a keyboard. Function keys can be programmed by the user to perform any function or group of functions the user chooses.

Gouraud Shading: A preview method of three-dimensional rendering that reveals highlights and renders smooth edges but does not reveal fine details in surfaces and shading.

Graphical User Interface (GUI): A computer operating environment that uses images to present information about the activity within a computer. The Macintosh computer and Microsoft Windows operating environments both use a graphical user interface.

Grayscale: A color scheme that uses multiple intensities of gray to produce images.

Hand-held Scanner: A compact scanning mechanism that is moved by hand along the surface of the area being scanned.

Hard Disk Drive: A data storage media that encodes computer information magnetically onto an aluminum or glass disk that is coated with a magnetically sensitive material.

Hard Drive Capacity: The amount of computer data that a hard drive can store.

Helical Scan tape Drives: Tape backup storage drives that use a circular read/write head, or drum, that contains two read and two write heads. The tape is stretched along the surface of the drum, and the drum rotates as the tape passes quickly reading and writing data with each pass.

Hi8mm: A video tape format that is compact. A Hi8mm cassette is about one-forth the size of a conventional VHS tape.

Hidden Line Removed: A preview rendering method in three-dimensional graphics programs that renders the scene as a wireframe, but does not include the parts of the wireframe that would not be visible if the images in the scene were opaque.

HyperCard: An early authoring program for the Macintosh that uses the analogy of a stack of index cards in conjunction with an included scripting language to produce animation and other multimedia productions.

HyperTalk: The scripting language that is part of HyperCard.

IIci and the II Series Computers: A line of Macintosh computers that were built in the late 1980s to early 1990s. They were the first to introduce color to the Macintosh computer large-screen monitors, the Motorola 68030 processor, and the NuBus expansion system.

Illustrator (Adobe): An object-oriented graphics program that creates only PostScript files.

Image Enhancement Software: The family of graphics software that is used to edit existing images by applying effects, removing portions of an image, or combining images. Image-editing software also includes graphics creation tools that are like those found in a paint program.

Import: The process of transporting a computer file into a software program. For example, graphics, animation, video, and sound files are imported into multimedia composition software where they are edited into a multimedia project.

In-Betweening: The process of creating an animation in a software program. Moments of pivotal change in an animation are first created; then the program automatically generates the intermittent frames of the animation. For example, an animation of a ball moving across a room is generated by creating the ball in the first position and then in the last position: these become the keyframes. The user then determines the length of time that it should take for the ball to complete the animation, and the program generates all the intermittent frames.

Independent Object Animation: Animation of any object within a three-dimensional scene.

Infrared Remote Mouse: A mouse input device that is linked to the computer by infrared pulses, eliminating the need for a mouse cable.

Input Devices: Devices connected to a computer to control the activity in software. The mouse and the keyboard are examples of input devices.

Interactive Authoring: The process of multimedia composition that includes elements that allow the viewer to control the presentation playback.

Interactive Interface Design: The part of an interactive application's design that the viewer interacts with. For example, the interface design of an Automated Teller Machine is menu-based. The viewer is initially presented with a selection menu, and the presentation advances to other menus based upon the viewer's selections. Another example is a data input interface in which the presentation advances based upon the information the user types into text fields.

Interactive Multimedia: Multimedia projects that allow the viewer to control the presentation. CD-ROM games and demonstration kiosks are examples of interactive multimedia projects.

Internal Drives: Hard disk drives that are installed within the computer.

Interpolated Resolution: The enhancement of the actual scanning resolution of a scanner through the use of a magnifying lens.

Keyboard: A computer input device that is similar to a typewriter in design.

Key Combinations: Shortcuts for accomplishing computer functions and commands by pressing combinations of keys on the keyboard. For example, pressing the **Command** key and S simultaneously is a key combination shortcut for saving a computer file. Other key combinations can involve the **Control** or **Option** keys as well.

Keyframe: The moments of pivotal change in an animation that are the basis for in-betweening. The designer of the animation arranges keyframes, and the software automatically generates the intermittent images that complete the animation.

Kilobyte: A small measure of computer data capacity. A kilobyte equals 1024 bytes.

Kodak Photo CD: A type of CD that photographs are stored on. Kodak manufactures Photo CD players that can be connected to a television set and that allow the contents of a photo CD to be viewed. Photo CDs can be viewed through computer CD players with the use of a software extension that is installed in image enhancement software.

Lathing: A three-dimensional graphics modeling technique in which a two-dimensional shape is rotated into a three-dimensional shape. Also called *Rotating*.

Lighting Gels: A three-dimensional graphics lighting special effect that simulates a filter placed over a projecting light.

Linear Scan Tape Drives: Computer tape storage drives in which the magnetic tape is pulled by reels across a single read/write head.

Linear Video Editing: Video editing accomplished with conventional, video-dedicated equipment.

Lingo: Macromedia Director's scripting language.

Lofting: A three-dimensional graphics modeling technique in which two-dimensional cross-sections are connected to form a three-dimensional shape. Also called *Skinning*.

Logic Flowchart: A drawn plan of an interactive application that takes the form of a flowchart.

Looping: An animation technique in which the end of the animation returns to the beginning.

Lossless Compression: Type of compression that reduces the size of a file while preserving all of its information.

Lossy Compression: Type of compression that loses some less-important information in order to create very small files.

Macintosh Computer: An easy to learn computer manufactured by Apple Computer. The Macintosh computer is noted for its graphical user interface that operates with a mouse.

MacRecorder Sound Digitizer (Macromedia): A sound input device that is connected to a Macintosh computer via the serial ports. The MacRecorder can be used to give sound-recording capability to Macintosh computers that do not have built-in audio input.

Macromind 3D (Macromedia): A three-dimensional rendering and animation program with limited modeling capability.

Megabyte: A measure of computer data storage. One megabyte is equal to 1024 kilobytes. The megabyte is the common convention for rating a storage drive's capacity.

Megahertz (MHz): A measure of electrical current that is used to rate the processing performance of a computer's central processing unit.

MIDI (Musical Instrument Digital Interface): A programming code that allows instruments that are equipped with a MIDI interface to be controlled by other MIDI instruments or by a computer.

Modeling: The process of creating three-dimensional geometry in a three-dimensional graphics program.

Monitor (Computer): A device that is similar in appearance to a television set but is connected to a computer and is used to observe the activity of software within the computer.

Monitor (Video): Devices that can receive an analog video signal and display it on a screen. Video monitors are capable of field interlace scanning, which allows them to display the separate field frames of video data. Some video monitors have only the capability of displaying an image from a video device that is connected directly to it, while others, such as a television set, have a receiver that allows them to receive video through airwaves.

Motherboard: A plastic panel within a computer that contains all the circuitry that permits one aspect of the computer to communicate with another. The motherboard contains the bus and the CPU.

Mouse: A computer input device that is used to move the cursor on-screen and control the operation of software. A small ball installed in the underside of the mouse moves when the mouse is dragged along a flat surface. The movement of the ball rotates rollers within the mouse and moves the cursor on-screen.

Movies: Documents created in conjunction with Apple's QuickTime software. A movie can contain any type of data, but usually contains digitized video or animation.

Multimedia: A form of creative media development in which video, animation, sound, and graphics are combined and manipulated within a computer.

Multimedia Composition: The process of combining video, graphics, animation, and sound into a single project within a computer.

Multimedia Peripherals: Devices that can be connected to a computer and that allow the computer to control video or audio devices, allow video or audio information to be transferred from video or audio tape into the computer by digitizing it, or allow digital information to be output to video or audio tape by converting it into an analog signal.

Multiple Track Audio: Audio data in which audio from multiple sources play simultaneously.

Narration: Voice recordings that are incorporated within a video or multimedia composition to provide information about the composition's contents.

Nonlinear Video Editing: The editing of video in its digital form within a computer. Nonlinear video editing is also characterized by the ability to access randomly and edit any portion of digital video footage without the need of rewinding or fast-forwarding.

Norton's Utilities: A software program that provides utilities for the repair of software, hard drive, and computer system failure.

NTSC: The American national standard for the recording and playback of video tape by the National Television and Standards Committee. The NTSC standard allows video equipment produced by different manufacturers to be compatible with each other and capable of receiving American broadcast video signals.

NuBus Cards: Devices that are installed within the computer via the NuBus slots. NuBus cards are used to enhance the performance of the computer or provide the computer with a new feature. For example, accelerator NuBus cards enhance the processing speed of a computer, and analog–digital transfer NuBus cards allow the computer to record or output information to and from video and sound equipment.

NuBus: A Macintosh feature that allows devices called NuBus cards to be installed within the computer through ports called NuBus slots. NuBus cards are used to expand the capability of a computer allowing it to be upgraded as technology improves.

NuBus Devices: Computer peripherals, such as scanners, which are connected to the computer via the NuBus slots.

NuBus Monitors: Monitors that are connected to the computer via the NuBus slots as opposed to the built-in video port.

Numeric Keypad: A small computer input keyboard that has a layout similar to a calculator.

Object-Oriented Graphics Software: Software that can create very precise lines and shapes that can be edited multiple times. Drawing programs are object-oriented.

Optical Drives: Storage devices that use a technology similar to CD-ROM technology to read and write information to a disc with a laser.

Paint Software: Software designed to simulate images created with natural media such as paint brushes and paint cans. Paint programs are also called bit-mapped software.

Painter (Fractal Design): A paint program that is capable of producing extremely realistic natural media effects such as oil paint and water color images.

PAL (Phase Alternating Line): A national video standard used primarily in Europe. Video recorded in PAL requires PAL standard equipment to be displayed.

Panasonic: A large electronics manufacturer that is in a joint venture with AT&T in the development of a television-based CD-ROM convention called 3D0.

Pascal: A programming language used to write software applications.

Pen Tool: A graphics tool in drawing programs that is used to create very precise lines and curves called Bezier curves.

Performa: A consumer-level line of Macintosh computers that is available in retail outlets, such as stationery stores.

Persistence of Vision: An effect of visual perception that leaves an afterimage on the retina. Animation exploits persistence of vision by displaying images quickly enough to have new images presented to the eye while the afterimage of the previous image is still present. The combination of the rapidity of image display and persistence of vision create the illusion of movement within the images.

Philips: A large manufacturer of electronic equipment that produces a television based CD-ROM player called CD-I.

Philips CD-I: A television-based CD-ROM convention developed by Philips Electronics.

Phong Shading: A method for rendering three-dimensional images that produces fine detail in surfaces and edges.

Photo-Realistic: The quality of a three-dimensional graphic that makes it appear similar to real-world objects in a photograph.

Photoshop (Adobe): A high-quality image-editing, enhancement, and paint program.

PICS: A Macintosh computer digital standard for storing animation. PICS files contain multiple, sequential images in a single file. When a PICS image is used in a multimedia composition program, all the individual images that it contains become available.

PICT: A Macintosh digital standard for storing individual graphics.

Pixel Count: The number of pixels that are capable of displaying an image on a computer monitor's screen.

Point Light: A lighting effect in three-dimensional graphics programs that simulates a multidirectional light, the intensity of which diminishes with distance. A point light can be used to simulate the effect of a light bulb in a room.

Point Size: The convention used to measure the size of a type font on-screen and on paper.

PostScript: A programming language developed by Adobe that is used to create object-oriented graphics.

Power Macintosh: A line of Macintosh computers released in early 1994 that is capable of running both IBM and Macintosh software. The Power Macintosh processor is also capable of running "native" software which is software designed specifically for the Power Macintosh CPU and system.

PowerBook: Portable, laptop Macintosh computers.

Prediction Update: A feature built into computer storage drives that automatically periodically scans the recordable area of the storage media for anything that may potentially lead to failure in the media. If the prediction update detects an area that it suspects will fail, then it transfers the data that is stored there elsewhere on the media, and records the new location in the file allocation table (FAT).

Premiere (Adobe): A multimedia composition software program that is used to combine different media elements into the same file. Adobe Premiere can be used to produce and edit QuickTime movies.

Previewing: The process of reviewing a project in a software program before exporting it as an independent file format.

Print-to-Tape: A command in multimedia programs such as Adobe Premiere that will output a project to a video device connected to the computer.

Programming Languages: Typewritten code that is used to create software programs.

Projector: A file format that Macromedia Director can output that converts a Macromedia Director file into an application that can be used independent of Director.

Proprietary Shading Techniques: A system for rendering three-dimensional surfaces that is available only from select manufacturers of plug-in software.

Pull-Down Menus: A part of the Macintosh GUI interface that allows commands to be selected and executed from window-shade style menus. These menus are drawn from the top of the screen with the mouse.

Quadra 840 AV and the AV line: A line of Macintosh computers that was manufactured with built-in multimedia capability such as the ability to record video directly to the hard drive.

Quadra Computers: A line of fast-processing Macintosh computers that introduced the Motorola 68040 CPU.

Quick Shading: A preview method of rendering three-dimensional graphics. Quick shading results in images with low surface definition and is used primarily to check quickly the geometry and placement of objects in a three-dimensional scene.

QuickTime: A system extension and file format for the Macintosh platform that combines animation, video, and audio in the same file. QuickTime files can be exported and imported in many multimedia software programs.

QWERTY: The key arrangement of typewriters and common computer keyboards. QWERTY represents the first six alphabetic keys on the top left corner of the arrangement.

Random Access Memory (RAM): The portion of a computer's memory storage capacity that is used to hold software data that is actively being used by the computer.

Raw Audio: Sound files that have been recorded to the hard drive but that have not been converted into a file format that can be used in software programs other than a sound-editing utility.

Ray Tracing: A three-dimensional graphics rendering technique that yields highly realistic results, such as reflective and transparent surfaces.

Read Only Memory (ROM): Data stored on a computer device that can not be changed. For example, CD-ROM is a CD that has computer data stored on it, but it cannot have information recorded on it a second time.

Real-Time Video Capture: The process of recording video directly to a hard drive at the video's actual frame rate. For example, NTSC video would record to the hard drive at 30 frame per second, just as if it were being recorded from one VCR to another.

Read/Write Head: The device that reads and writes information to and from a computer data storage media such as a hard drive.

Reflective Scanner: Scanners that capture an image by bouncing light off the image and into a lens. This type of scanner is used to digitize images such as photographs in magazines.

Removable Media Storage Drives: Data storage drives in which the actual media that the computer data are written to is enclosed in a cassette or cartridge and can be removed form the drive. Removable media cartridges and cassettes can then be inserted and used in other drives that are compatible.

Rendering: The process of creating an image in a three-dimensional graphics program.

RenderMan: A proprietary rendering convention developed by Pixar that generates highly realistic three-dimensional images. The RenderMan software engine is required in order to use the RenderMan convention. ShowPlace and Typestry have a graphic interface to the RenderMan engine and include it with their purchase. Some three-dimensional programs, such as Macromedia MacroModel, are compatible with RenderMan.

Resolution (Scanner and Monitor): The number of pixels per inch used on a monitor's screen to display an image; the number of pixels per inch that a scanner is capable of digitizing.

RGB (Red, Green, Blue): The colors of the three separate cathode rays that are fired against the back of the computer monitor's screen. Varying intensities and combinations of the three colors result in all the colors visible on-screen.

Rotating: A three-dimensional modeling technique that rotates a two-dimensional shape around one of its axes and produces a three-dimensional shape.

Rotoscoping: A method of manipulating computer animation and video files by treating the individual frames with the tools in an image enhancement program.

S-Video: A method for transferring video information between video devices that uses a single input and output port for both video and audio. S-Video is an optional feature of video equipment; not all video equipment has it.

Sampling Rate: The amount of computer data that is reserved for each sample of a sound that is recorded to a hard drive. Examples of current sampling rates for the Macintosh computer are 8 bit and 16 bit.

Scan Area: The dimensions of the area of a scanner where an image can actually be scanned.

Scanner: A computer peripheral that digitizes photographs and other flat images into the computer where the images can be altered or incorporated in multimedia projects.

Score (Macromedia Director): The software interface for Macromedia Director where graphics, sound, transitions, scripts, tempo settings, and color palettes are arranged into a multimedia project.

Scrapbook: Part of the Macintosh computer system software that allows for the storage of graphics, sound, animation, video, text, and anything else in the computer that can be cut, copied, and pasted.

Screen Savers: Software used to keep the pixels active on the screen during idle moments. Screen savers help prevent screen burn-in, which results in an afterimage being displayed on-screen even when the computer is shut down. Screen burn-in is caused when the phosphor on the opposite side of the screen is maintained in one active state for a prolonged period.

Screen Size: The distance from one corner of the screen to the opposite diagonal corner.

Scripting Languages: The programming languages that are used in authoring software. Lingo is the scripting language in Macromedia Director.

Scripting: The process of writing programs in an authoring program using a scripting language.

SECAM (Sequential Color and Modulation): A national video standard used primarily in Europe. Video recorded in SECAM requires SECAM standard equipment to be displayed.

Sequential PICT and TIFF: An image file output alternative in many programs that is used to create animation. Sequential PICT and TIFF files keep the animation as separate, automatically numbered, graphic files that can be opened individually.

Service Bureau: A business that is designed to support computer-based projects. For example, a service bureau may have high-quality digital-to-analog transfer equipment that would be too expensive for small multimedia developers to own on their own.

ShowPlace (Pixar): A three-dimensional rendering program that uses the RenderMan rendering engine to create highly realistic images.

Signal Control Devices: Video dedicated equipment that is used to monitor and modify video signals while they are being recorded or edited.

Silicon Graphics Workstation: A fast computer system that is based upon the UNIX operating system and is used to create high-quality graphics quickly.

Skinning: A three-dimensional modeling procedure that stretches a surface across two-dimensional cross-sections, like tent fabric pulled over the tent frame.

Slide Scanner: A transmissive scanner that is designed to work with the small images of slides.

Small Computer System Interface (SCSI): An extension of the Macintosh hardware architecture that allows computer peripherals, such as external hard drives, to be connected to the computer via a port located in the back.

Sound Effect: A sound that is used to add realism to a scene or to attract attention to information. Any sound other than music or a voice recording can be used as a sound effect.

Sound Loop: A sound that has been edited so that it automatically returns to its beginning once it has reached its end. Sound loops are useful for creating sounds that last for extended periods of time in a presentation but that require little storage space.

Spigot and Sound Pro (SuperMac): A video and sound capture card for the Macintosh computer.

Spot light: A lighting effect in three-dimensional animations that simulates a concentrated beam of light, like a stage spotlight.

Storyboard: A series of drawings that represents the scenes of a multimedia, film, or video project. The storyboard is intended to serve as a visual plan of the project.

Strata StudioPro: A three-dimensional modeling, rendering, and animation program.

Stroke: The thickness applied to lines and the outlines of shapes in graphics programs.

Style (Fonts): A software manipulation of fonts that alters their appearance on-screen and in printing. Changing the style of a font does not change the font that is installed in the system.

SuperMac: A manufacturer of Macintosh computer video peripherals and monitors.

SVHS-C: A video tape format that uses the same technology and has the same resolution as SVHS but that uses compact cassettes similar in size to 8mm cassettes.

SVHS: A video-recording format that uses tapes that are similar to VHS cassettes, but with a higher resolution image. SVHS equipment and tapes can record and play regular VHS signals, although regular VHS equipment and tapes are not compatible with the SVHS signal and cassettes. As a result, a tape recorded in the SVHS format must be played on an SVHS player in order to be viewed.

System 7: The current version of system software for the Macintosh computer. The most recent versions include update numbers that are expressed as decimal figures, such as version 7.1.1.

SyQuest: The manufacturer of the most common removable storage drive mechanism for the Macintosh computer.

System Software: The software that manages the operation of the computer and allows different parts of the computer to communicate with each other, with computer peripherals, and with other software.

Template: An image used as a guide for creating reproductions of that image in a graphics program. Photographs are frequently used as templates to replicate real-world objects using graphics tools.

Texture: The images that are applied to the surfaces of objects in three-dimensional graphics programs to give them a realistic appearance.

Texture Mapping (Surfacing): The process of generating the image on the surface of objects in a three-dimensional graphics scene. For example, you would apply a "wood" texture map to an object that you want to appear to be made of wood, such as a floor. You can apply any PICT file as a texture map, so that you could scan a photograph of the Mona Lisa and apply it to the area within a frame on a wall in your three-dimensional scene.

Third-Party Manufacturers and Products: Any product or software that you use with your computer that was manufactured by a company other than the computer's manufacturer.

Three-Dimensional Rendering and Animation Software: Software used to generate graphics that simulate three-dimensional scenes. Three-dimensional rendering and animation software can be used to create highly realistic graphics and to create highly dynamic animation.

Touch Screen: A computer input device that is integrated into, or placed over the monitor screen. The screen registers touches to the screen made by the user as input. The computer responds as if the user had used a mouse or any other input device.

Trackball: A computer input device that uses an exposed ball that the user rotates within a socket to move the cursor on-screen. The concept is similar to a mouse except that the device remains stationary while the user manipulates the ball directly.

Transfer Rate: The speed at which information is passed to the computer from a computer component such as a hard drive or CD-ROM drive. Transfer rate is "measured" in kilobytes per second.

Transition Effects: Visual effects in film, video, and animation that are used to make a change from one portion of the film, video, or animation to another more interesting. Fade, wipe, and dissolve are examples of transition effects.

Transmissive Scanner: Scanners that digitize images by passing light through the image into a lens. Transmissive scanners are used to scan images like transparencies and slides.

Tweening: Synonym for *In-Betweening*.

Typestry: A three-dimensional text graphics program that uses the RenderMan interface to generate highly realistic images with type fonts.

Upgrade Path: The options available for a specific computer to modularly improve the computer's performance and maintain state-of-the-art technology in older machines.

VCR: (Video Cassette Recorder): The device used to record images onto video tape and to display images on video tape to a monitor.

VDig: Video Digitizer component. Software that controls a video digitizer board

VHS: The most common video tape format. VHS cassettes use 0.5-in. tape and can be used in most home component video players.

VHS-C: A video tape format that uses the same technology and has the same resolution as VHS but that uses compact cassettes similar in size to 8mm cassettes.

Video: The technology and equipment that is used to record images electronically onto magnetic tape.

Video Broadcast Standards: The government-established standards for video transmission that allows video recorded with devices made by different manufacturers to be transmitted along the same airwaves and to be displayed on the same television equipment at the receiving end of the transmission. NTSC is an example of a video broadcast standard.

Video Capture: The process of recording video to a computer's hard drive.

Video Equipment (Dedicated Video): Equipment that is designed to work specifically in the analog video environment.

Video RAM (VRAM): RAM in Macintosh computers that is reserved for the sole purpose of calculating and storing the images presented on the monitor.

Video Special Effects Equipment: Visual effects equipment that is designed to operate specifically with video equipment. This type of equipment is used to generate effects such as transitions and titles.

Video Tape: Magnetic tape, and the cartridge that contains it, that is used to record images through video cameras and video cassette recorders.

Video Tape Formats: The various types of video tape that are designed to operate with a specific type of video equipment. VHS and Hi8mm are examples of video tape formats.

Virtual Memory: A portion of the Macintosh computer system software that allows storage space on the hard drive to be used as RAM. The entire available capacity of the hard drive can be used as virtual memory, but it will still operate at the slower access times of a hard drive.

Voice-Over: Voice recordings that are used in video, film, and multimedia. The speaker is not visible during a voice-over.

Walk-Through Animation: Three-dimensional animation that simulates passing through an enclosed area, like walking through a room.

Windows (Microsoft): A software program for IBM computers that simulates a graphical user interface. Programs that are Windows compatible must run simultaneously with Windows; they will not operate on the IBM without Windows operating as well. Programs running on an IBM through Windows have a mouse-driven point-and-click interface that is similar to Macintosh computers.

Wireframe: The three-dimensional program modeling mode that presents the objects in the scene as wire meshes with no surface. Most of the work done in arranging a three-dimensional composition is done in wireframe.

WORM (Write Once Read Many) Drive: The drive used to create test prints of CD-ROMs before a master is made for mass production. WORM drives are also used to create CD-ROM projects that do not need to be mass produced, such as databases.

XCMD (External Command): Software modules used to control HyperCard functions and HyperTalk scripts from another program such as Macromedia Director.

XObject (External Objects): Software programs used to add new functions to authoring programs. For example, Macromedia Director can control laser disc players with an XObject. XObjects can also be used to link programs with each other, such as allowing Director to pass information into a database program.

Index

About the CD-ROM

This book includes a CD-ROM that will help you learn more about multimedia software. The following is a description of its contents with instructions on how to use it.

What's On the CD-ROM

The CD includes save-disabled versions of Adobe Illustrator, Photoshop, and Premiere, as well as Strata StudioPro, Fractal Design Painter, and Macromedia Director. These Programs have all of the functionality of the completed versions of the software, but you will not be able to save your work into a file outside of the program. The CD gives you the opportunity to experiment with some of the most powerful software for Macintosh multimedia before investing any money.

The CD also includes an interactive tour of the interfaces of the above software. The interactive tour was made with Macromedia Director and will guide you through the interfaces with animated portions that illustrate the functions of the tools and windows in each program. The interactive tutorials are designed to provide a general overview of the software interfaces and tools.

What You Need to Use the CD-ROM

The graphics, animation, transitions, and sounds used on the CD were selected and designed to work on any Macintosh with a CD-ROM player, 5 MB RAM, QuickTime, and System 7.0 or later. It will even operate on Macs with 9 inch black and white screens like the Classic. I recommend that you run the program with a maximum monitor setting of 256 colors (8 Bit), this will be sufficient for viewing everything including transition effects and the colors in the QuickTime movies.

WARNING
The entire contents of the CD-ROM must remain in one folder in order for the application to operate properly. If you want to move any of it to your hard disk for better play-back, you will need to copy the entire CD-ROM and not change any of the file names as they are linked through the software. You can, however, copy the save disabled-software to your hard drive without a problem and it will run.

Running the Save-Disabled Software

Some of the save-disabled versions have RAM allocations (set in the Get Info dialog box in the File menu) below the minimum recommended so that they can run simultaneously with the rest of the CD-ROM program. In order to run the save-disabled programs to their complete ability you need to copy them to the hard drive and allocate more RAM to them. You can do this by highlighting the program's icon on your hard drive while the program is not running. Then select **Get Info** from the File menu and type a larger number in the box labeled "Current Size".

WARNING
If you launch any of the save-disabled programs from within the "Welcome To Macintosh Multimedia" program, you will still be able to see the "Welcome To Macintosh Multimedia" interface menus. You must first quit out of the sub-launched program before making another selection from the menu or the "Welcome To Macintosh Multimedia" program will attempt to open two programs simultaneously, and you will likely have RAM problems as a result.

How to Use the Program

The program is designed to run directly from the CD-ROM. After mounting and double-clicking on the CD-ROM you will see a Macromedia Director Projector icon called "Welcome To Macintosh Multimedia". Double-Click on this icon and you will launch the program. You will then see a brief introduction to the CD that will lead you to the option to go to the save-disabled software and the interactive tutorial.

The program is menu based. Clicking the mouse on a button graphic will allow you to select that graphic. Throughout the program you will have the option to return to the previous menu (via the "Return" button). As you move through the selections in the interactive interface tutorials you will eventually reach text descriptions of the program tools and functions that will lead to QuickTime animations of how particular tools or windows are used. At the end of the animation session you will have three options: to replay the animation from the point of the description of the tool or window, to replay only the animated example, or to return to the main selection window and choose another selection.

Some of the interface tutorials have tool palettes wherein the buttons in the palette can be selected for information about each tool. You will also see text windows identifying these palettes. If you select a tool in the palette, it will branch off into a description and animation of that tool—just as the graphic buttons do.

The save-disabled software can be launched from the Save-Disabled Software menu. You can launch a program while the "Welcome to Macintosh Multimedia" program is still running. This is called a sub-launch. You can then work with the software, just as if you had clicked on that program's icon directly. When you quit out of the program you will automatically be returned to the "Save-Disabled Software" selection window.

Throughout the interactive interfaces, there are small buttons that will bring you to key areas of the program at any point. One is called the "Return to Main Window" button at the bottom left-hand corner of each program's interactive interface main window. Another is the "Return to Main Movie" button at the top right-hand corner of each program's interactive interface main window. This button will return you to the main selection menu. The last button is the Quit Button which is located in the main window of each interactive interface and throughout the main movie program. This button allows you to exit the program. With these buttons, you will achieve rapid navigation throughout the interface.

Difficulty Launching the Save-Disabled Software?

If you have trouble launching a save-disabled program from the "Welcome To Macintosh Multimedia" program, you probably have insufficient RAM. You can get around this by directly launching the save-disabled software on the CD. There are folders for each program. Quit out of the CD-ROM program and open the save-disabled program from its folder. The only other solution is to install more RAM.

Using Plug-ins

Photoshop, Illustrator, and Premiere all include plug-in folders that give the programs added functionality. You will need to install these plug-ins before you can apply their effects to images. See chapter 14 for more information about software plug-ins.

To install the plug-in folders, select the **Plug-In** option in the File menu. Then select the **Plug-Ins** folder from within the program folder on the CD-ROM. Then quit out of the program and restart it in order to initiate the plug-in.

A Look at How the CD-ROM is Constructed

The interactive interfaces in the CD-ROM were created with Macromedia Director, and can be opened with the save-disabled version of Macromedia Director. You can also import any of the graphics or QuickTime movies used in the CD-ROM into any of the graphics programs. You can find the Director movies and other files by selecting **Open** or **Import** from the File menu of the program and selecting the desired target CD-ROM folder through the Finder window.

How to Get the Complete Versions of the Software

Most mail order houses and hardware resellers that sell software will carry the complete versions of the software included on the CD-ROM. You can contact the software developers directly for information about a local distributor.